PowerXL Air Fryer Pro Cookbook

PowerXL Air Fryer Pro Cookbook

1000 Easy and Quick Air Fryer Recipes for Your PowerXL Air Fryer Pro to Air Fry, Bake, Dehydrate, and Rotisserie

Kenneth B. James

CONTENT

Introduction

The PowerXL Air Fryer Pro makes healthy cooking easy for you and your family. It can cook the perfect meal for any time of day.

The PowerXL Air Fryer Pro is an oven that uses air and convection to cook your food. Unlike traditional ovens, which rely on heat from the outside in, a convection oven circulates hot air around the food you are cooking from all sides, giving it a crispy crust on all sides as well as inside the food. This means you won't need to turn your food over and risk overcooking it while waiting for it to brown on one side.

This cookbook is full of recipes that have been tested in the PowerXL Air Fryer Pro. All the recipes use easy-to-find ingredients that can be purchased at any supermarket or grocery store. Each recipe indicates how long it will take to prep and cook the dish. You can prepare these recipes in large batches so they are ready to serve when you need them, and they are just as good, warm or cold, making them great for serving at parties.

The PowerXL Air Fryer Pro is great for any time of day. You can use it to prepare breakfast, lunch or dinner as well as snacks and desserts. The ovens come in different sizes of 6 Qt, 8 Qt, 10 Qt and 12 Qt. The different sizes make it suitable for different family sizes. If your family is big, you can choose the largest one.

The PowerXL Air Fryer Pro is a really smart oven that will make your life easier and you will love cooking with it.

Happy cooking!

What Is PowerXL Air Fryer Pro?

The PowerXL Air Fryer Pro is one of the multifunctional cooking appliances equipped with advanced technology. It makes your daily cooking process easy, fast and gives you healthy cooking results. It offers a set of different cooking functions for various cooking requirements. Moreover, the machine is designed with safety in mind, which makes its operation easy and safe.

The PowerXL Air Fryer Pro is a multifunctional machine that offers up to five settings for different types of cooking, including air frying/roasting, baking/grilling, and pan-frying. It's large enough to cook up to 20 pounds of French fries or potatoes in one batch with adjustable convection heating. It has a built-in lid that seals the food and lock in moisture.

The PowerXL Air Fryer Pro features an adjustable temperature and timer settings for cooking for up to 30 minutes. The device features a programmable up to 30 minutes timer function that cooks food automatically once the time is up.

The PowerXL Air Fryer Pro comes with several accessories, and you don't need to purchase them differently. The price is inclusive of all the accessories inside. The accessories are as follows:

- 3 Air Flow Racks
- Oil Drip Tray
- Rotating Rotisserie Spit
- 8 Stainless Skewers
- 3 Recipe Books
- Rotating Mesh Basket

Benefits of the PowerXL Air Fryer Pro

Multipurpose: The PowerXL Air Fryer Pro is designed with different smart cooking features.

These cooking functions are preprogrammed and you just cook with a touch of a button.

Fast Cooking: It greatly decreases typically long cooking times for all dishes. Cooking time can be reduced 60% to 80% (depending on the ingredient). Faster cooking times mean you can cook real foods from scratch in the time it takes for pizza delivery or to prepare a frozen dinner.

Safe and User-Friendly: PowerXL Air Fryer Pro is pre-programmed, and therefore, all you have to do is to press the correct cooking button.

Capacious: With PowerXL Air Fryer Pro, you can cook large serving sizes because it is big and capacious. You can cook a whole duck or chicken by putting on the rotisserie rod.

Save Energy: It cooks food faster, thus reducing cooking significantly. Reduced cooking time translates to energy saving. It can be the only appliance you use therefore making it economical.

Maintain Nutritional Value: As opposed to most of the existing cooking methods which drain or destroy food's nutrition, the PowerXL Air Fryer Pro preserves the nutritional value of the foods being cooked.

Convenient: No longer do you have to bother about the size of your kitchen or where you will store the multitude of kitchen appliances needed to concoct one single home-cooked meals. Simply place all of your ingredients in your PowerXL Air Fryer Pro and allow it to do its thing automatically.

Buttons of the PowerXL Air Fryer Pro

Power Button

This function is used to start and stop the cooking process. When the power supply is on, then the power button will light up and pressing the power button once the digital display of the oven will illuminate. If you press the power button, the second time it will start the cooking cycle at default temperature 370°F for default time 15 minutes. If you press the power button during the cooking cycle, it will shut down the oven. The oven fan will run for 20 seconds to reduce the oven temperature.

Light Button

This function is used to illuminate the oven internal light, which helps to check your current cooking progress. If you open the oven door during the cooking process, it will pause the cooking cycle and the internal oven light illuminates automatically until the door is open.

Rotation Button

This function is used when you are using a rotisserie cooking mode. You can use this function with a combination of any preset functions. While using this function, the rotation button icon will blink continuously.

Temperature Buttons

This up and down arrow buttons are used to increase or decrease the temperature settings at the interval of 5°F manually as per your recipe requirements. You can set the temperature settings between 140°F to 400°F except for dehydration. While using dehydration function, you can set the temperature between 90°F to 170°F as per recipe requirements.

Time Buttons

These up and down arrow buttons are used to increase or decrease the time settings as per your recipe requirements. You can set the time settings into minutes in between 1 minute to 60 minutes. While using dehydrating function, operating time will be set in between 2 to 24 hours.

Running Lights

While cooking process these lights blink continuously and after finishing the cooking process the lights blink for 20 seconds.

Cooking Functions

French Fries

Using this preset function, you can air fry your favorite fast food within very less oil compare to the deep-frying method. The default temperature at these settings is set at 400°F for 15 minutes.

Steak/Chops

These settings are ideal for making your favorite steak and chop dishes the default temperature at these settings is set at 370°F for 25 minutes.

Fish

Using this function, you can cook your favorite fish and the default temperature at these settings is set at 390°F for 15 minutes.

Shrimp

Using this function, you can cook your favorite shrimp dishes and the default temperature at these settings is set at 320°F for 12 minutes.

Chicken

This function is ideal for making your favorite chicken dishes, and the default temperature at these settings is set at 370ºF for 40 minutes.

Baking

This function is used for baking your favorite cake, cookies, and more. The default temperature at these settings is set at 350ºF for 30 minutes.

Rotisserie

It is also known as split roasting. Using these settings, you can roast your favorite meat. The default temperature at these settings is set at 400ºF for 30 minutes.

Dehydrator

Using these functions, you can dehydrate your favorite vegetables, meat and fruit slices. The default temperature at these settings is set at 90ºF for 4 hours.

Cleaning and Maintenance

Cleaning your appliances is one of the essential tasks regularly done after each use.

1. Before starting the cleaning process, remove the power cord from the power socket and let cool down your PowerXL air fryer oven at room temperature.

2. Pull your oven door at 45° upward for cleaning. Use soapy water with the help of damp cloth for cleaning the door. Do not wash the door into the dishwasher or submerge oven door into water.

3. Then remove all the accessories like rotating mesh basket, airflow rack, drip tray and more. These accessories are made up of stainless steel material and dishwasher safe you can easily clean all these accessories into the dishwasher.

4. Clean the inside of the oven with the help of mild detergent, hot water and a non-abrasive sponge.

5. Clean the outer body of the air fryer oven with the help of arm moist cloth. If you find any residue on upper side screen, then use a cleaning brush to clean it properly.

6. Before placing all the accessories at its original position, make sure they are dry completely. Then fix all the accessories and oven door at its original position.

Chapter 1 Breakfast

Baked Eggs in Avocado

Prep time: 5 minutes | Cook time: 9 minutes | Serves 2

1 large avocado, halved and pitted
2 large eggs
2 tomato slices, divided
½ cup nonfat Cottage cheese, divided
½ teaspoon fresh cilantro, for garnish

1. Line the sheet pan with the aluminium foil.
2. Slice a thin piece from the bottom of each avocado half so they sit flat. Remove a small amount from each avocado half to make a bigger hole to hold the egg.
3. Arrange the avocado halves on the pan, hollow-side up. Break 1 egg into each half. Top each half with 1 tomato slice and ¼ cup of the Cottage cheese.
4. Slide the pan into the air fryer oven. Press the Power Button and cook at 425ºF (220ºC) for 9 minutes.
5. When cooking is complete, remove from the air fryer oven. Garnish with the fresh cilantro and serve.

Banana Carrot Muffins

Prep time: 10 minutes | Cook time: 20 minutes | Serves 12

1½ cups whole-wheat flour
1 cup grated carrot
1 cup mashed banana
½ cup bran
½ cup low-fat buttermilk
2 tablespoons agave nectar
2 teaspoons baking powder
1 teaspoon vanilla
1 teaspoon baking soda
½ teaspoon nutmeg
Pinch cloves
2 egg whites

1. Line a muffin pan with 12 paper liners.
2. In a large bowl, stir together all the ingredients. Mix well, but do not over beat.
3. Scoop the mixture into the muffin cups.
4. Slide the pan into the air fryer oven. Press the Power Button and cook at 400ºF (205ºC) for 20 minutes.
5. When cooking is complete, remove the pan and let rest for 5 minutes.
6. Serve warm or at room temperature.

Maple Bacon Knots

Prep time: 5 minutes | Cook time: 7 to 8 minutes | Serves 6

1 pound (454 g) maple smoked center-cut bacon
¼ cup maple syrup
¼ cup brown sugar
Coarsely cracked black peppercorns, to taste

1. On a clean work surface, tie each bacon strip in a loose knot.
2. Stir together the maple syrup and brown sugar in a bowl. Generously brush this mixture over the bacon knots.
3. Place the bacon knots on the air flow racks and sprinkle with the coarsely cracked black peppercorns.
4. Slide the racks into the air fryer oven. Press the Power Button and cook at 390ºF (199ºC) for 8 minutes.
5. After 5 minutes, remove the racks from the air fryer oven and flip the bacon knots. Return the racks to the air fryer oven and continue cooking for 2 to 3 minutes more.
6. When cooking is complete, the bacon should be crisp. Remove from the air fryer oven to a paper towel-lined plate. Let the bacon knots cool for a few minutes and serve warm.

Cinnamon Sweet Potato Chips

Prep time: 5 minutes | Cook time: 8 minutes | Makes 6 to 8 slices

1 small sweet potato, cut into ⅜ inch-thick slices
2 tablespoons olive oil
1 to 2 teaspoon ground cinnamon

1. Add the sweet potato slices and olive oil in a bowl and toss to coat. Fold in the cinnamon and stir to combine.
2. Lay the sweet potato slices in a single layer on the air flow racks.
3. Slide the racks into the air fryer oven. Press the Power Button and cook at 390ºF (199ºC) for 8 minutes.
4. Stir the potato slices halfway through the cooking time.
5. When cooking is complete, the chips should be crisp. Remove the racks from the air fryer oven. Allow to cool for 5 minutes before serving.

Bacon Breakfast Sandwiches

Prep time: 5 minutes | Cook time: 8 minutes | Serves 4

4 English muffins, split
8 slices Canadian bacon

4 slices Parmesan cheese
Cooking spray

1. Make the sandwiches: Top each of 4 muffin halves with 2 slices of Canadian bacon, 1 slice of cheese, and finish with the remaining muffin half.
2. Place the sandwiches on the air flow racks and spritz the tops with cooking spray.
3. Slide the racks into the air fryer oven. Press the Power Button and cook at 370ºF (188ºC) for 8 minutes.
4. Flip the sandwiches halfway through the cooking time.
5. When cooking is complete, remove the racks from the air fryer oven. Divide the sandwiches among four plates and serve warm.

Banana Oat Bread Pudding

Prep time: 10 minutes | Cook time: 18 minutes | Serves 4

2 medium ripe bananas, mashed
½ cup low-fat milk
2 tablespoons maple syrup
2 tablespoons peanut butter
1 teaspoon vanilla

extract
1 teaspoon ground cinnamon
2 slices whole-grain bread, torn into bite-sized pieces
¼ cup quick oats
Cooking spray

1. Spritz the sheet pan with cooking spray.
2. In a large bowl, combine the bananas, milk, maple syrup, peanut butter, vanilla extract and cinnamon. Use an immersion blender to mix until well combined.
3. Stir in the bread pieces to coat well. Add the oats and stir until everything is combined.
4. Transfer the mixture to the sheet pan. Cover with the aluminum foil.
5. Slide the pan into the air fryer oven. Press the Power Button and cook at 375ºF (190ºC) for 18 minutes.
6. After 10 minutes, remove the foil and continue to cook for 8 minutes.
7. Serve immediately.

Cashew Cranberry Granola

Prep time: 5 minutes | Cook time: 12 minutes | Serves 6

3 cups old-fashioned rolled oats
2 cups raw cashews
1 cup unsweetened coconut chips
½ cup honey
¼ cup vegetable oil

$^1/_3$ cup packed light brown sugar
¼ teaspoon kosher salt
1 cup dried cranberries

1. In a large bowl, stir together all the ingredients, except for the cranberries. Spread the mixture on a sheet pan.
2. Slide the pan into the air fryer oven. Press the Power Button and cook at 325ºF (163ºC) for 12 minutes.
3. After 5 to 6 minutes, remove the pan and stir the granola. Return to the air fryer oven and continue cooking.
4. When cooking is complete, remove the pan. Let the granola cool to room temperature. Stir in the cranberries before serving.

Cheese and Tomato Sandwiches

Prep time: 5 minutes | Cook time: 8 minutes | Serves 2

1 teaspoon butter, softened
4 slices bread
4 slices smoked

country ham
4 slices Cheddar cheese
4 thick slices tomato

1. Spoon ½ teaspoon of butter onto one side of 2 slices of bread and spread it all over.
2. Assemble the sandwiches: Top each of 2 slices of unbuttered bread with 2 slices of ham, 2 slices of cheese, and 2 slices of tomato. Put the remaining 2 slices of bread on top, butter-side up.
3. Lay the sandwiches on the air flow racks, buttered side down.
4. Slide the racks into the air fryer oven. Press the Power Button and cook at 370ºF (188ºC) for 8 minutes.
5. Flip the sandwiches halfway through the cooking time.
6. When cooking is complete, the sandwiches should be golden brown on both sides and the cheese should be melted. Remove from the air fryer oven. Allow to cool for 5 minutes before slicing to serve.

Eggs in Pepper Rings

Prep time: 5 minutes | Cook time: 7 minutes | Serves 4

1 large red, yellow, or orange bell pepper, cut into four ¾-inch rings
4 eggs
Salt and freshly ground black pepper, to taste
2 teaspoons salsa
Cooking spray

1. Coat a baking pan lightly with cooking spray.
2. Put 4 bell pepper rings in the prepared baking pan. Crack one egg into each bell pepper ring and sprinkle with salt and pepper. Top each egg with ½ teaspoon of salsa.
3. Put the pan into the air fryer oven. Press the Power Button and cook at 350°F (180°C) for 7 minutes.
4. When done, the eggs should be cooked to your desired doneness.
5. Remove the rings from the pan to a plate and serve warm.

French Toast Casserole

Prep time: 5 minutes | Cook time: 12 minutes | Serves 6

3 large eggs, beaten
1 cup whole milk
1 tablespoon pure maple syrup
1 teaspoon vanilla extract
¼ teaspoon cinnamon
¼ teaspoon kosher salt
3 cups stale bread cubes
1 tablespoon unsalted butter, at room temperature

1. In a medium bowl, whisk together the eggs, milk, maple syrup, vanilla extract, cinnamon and salt. Stir in the bread cubes to coat well.
2. Grease the bottom of a sheet pan with the butter. Spread the bread mixture into the pan in an even layer.
3. Slide the pan into the air fryer oven. Press the Power Button and cook at 350°F (180°C) for 12 minutes.
4. After about 10 minutes, remove the pan and check the casserole. The top should be browned and the middle of the casserole just set. If more time is needed, return the pan to the air fryer oven and continue cooking.
5. When cooking is complete, serve warm.

Maple Oat Granola

Prep time: 5 minutes | Cook time: 40 minutes | Serves 4

1 cup rolled oats
3 tablespoons maple syrup
1 tablespoon sunflower oil
1 tablespoon coconut sugar
¼ teaspoon vanilla
¼ teaspoon cinnamon
¼ teaspoon sea salt

1. Mix the oats, maple syrup, sunflower oil, coconut sugar, vanilla, cinnamon, and sea salt in a medium bowl and stir to combine. Transfer the mixture to a baking pan.
2. Slide the pan into the air fryer oven. Press the Power Button and cook at 248°F (120°C) for 40 minutes.
3. Stir the granola four times during cooking.
4. When cooking is complete, the granola will be mostly dry and lightly browned.
5. Let the granola stand for 5 to 10 minutes before serving.

Mini Brown Rice and Veg Quiches

Prep time: 10 minutes | Cook time: 14 minutes | Serves 6

4 ounces (113 g) diced green chilies
3 cups cooked brown rice
1 cup shredded reduced-fat Cheddar cheese, divided
½ cup egg whites
⅓ cup fat-free milk
¼ cup diced pimiento
½ teaspoon cumin
1 small eggplant, cubed
1 bunch fresh cilantro, finely chopped
Cooking spray

1. Spritz a 12-cup muffin pan with cooking spray.
2. In a large bowl, stir together all the ingredients, except for ½ cup of the cheese.
3. Scoop the mixture evenly into the muffin cups and sprinkle the remaining ½ cup of the cheese on top.
4. Slide the pan into the air fryer oven. Press the Power Button and cook at 400°F (205°C) for 14 minutes.
5. When cooking is complete, remove the pan and check the quiches. They should be set.
6. Carefully transfer the quiches to a platter and serve immediately.

Mixed Berry Pancake

Prep time: 10 minutes | Cook time: 14 minutes | Serves 4

1 tablespoon unsalted butter, at room temperature	1 teaspoon pure vanilla extract
1 egg	1 cup sliced fresh strawberries
2 egg whites	½ cup fresh raspberries
½ cup 2% milk	½ cup fresh blueberries
½ cup whole-wheat pastry flour	

1. Grease a baking pan with the butter.
2. Using a hand mixer, beat together the egg, egg whites, milk, pastry flour, and vanilla in a medium mixing bowl until well incorporated.
3. Pour the batter into the pan.
4. Slide the pan into the air fryer oven. Press the Power Button and cook at 330ºF (166ºC) for 14 minutes.
5. When cooked, the pancake should puff up in the center and the edges should be golden brown
6. Allow the pancake to cool for 5 minutes and serve topped with the berries.

Monkey Bread

Prep time: 5 minutes | Cook time: 8 minutes | Serves 4

1 (8-ounce / 227-g) can refrigerated biscuits	¼ cup white sugar
3 tablespoons melted unsalted butter	3 tablespoons brown sugar
	½ teaspoon cinnamon
	⅛ teaspoon nutmeg

1. On a clean work surface, cut each biscuit into 4 pieces.
2. In a shallow bowl, place the melted butter. In another shallow bowl, stir together the white sugar, brown sugar, cinnamon, and nutmeg until combined.
3. Dredge the biscuits, one at a time, in the melted butter, then roll them in the sugar mixture to coat well. Spread the biscuits evenly in a baking pan.
4. Slide the baking pan into the air fryer oven. Press the Power Button and cook at 350ºF (180ºC) for 8 minutes.
5. When cooked, the biscuits should be golden brown.
6. Cool for 5 minutes before serving.

Whole-Wheat Blueberry Muffins

Prep time: 5 minutes | Cook time: 25 minutes | Makes 8 muffins

½ cup unsweetened applesauce	2 cups whole-wheat flour
½ cup plant-based milk	½ teaspoon baking soda
½ cup maple syrup	1 cup blueberries
1 teaspoon vanilla extract	Cooking spray

1. Spritz a 8-cup muffin pan with cooking spray.
2. In a large bowl, stir together the applesauce, milk, maple syrup and vanilla extract. Whisk in the flour and baking soda until no dry flour is left and the batter is smooth. Gently mix in the blueberries until they are evenly distributed throughout the batter.
3. Spoon the batter into the muffin cups, three-quarters full.
4. Slide the pan into the air fryer oven. Press the Power Button and cook at 375ºF (190ºC) for 25 minutes.
5. When cooking is complete, remove the pan and check the muffins. You can stick a knife into the center of a muffin and it should come out clean.
6. Let rest for 5 minutes before serving.

Strawberry Toast

Prep time: 5 minutes | Cook time: 8 minutes | Makes 4 toasts

4 slices bread, ½-inch thick	strawberries
1 cup sliced	1 teaspoon sugar
	Cooking spray

1. On a clean work surface, lay the bread slices and spritz one side of each slice of bread with cooking spray.
2. Place the bread slices on the air flow racks, sprayed side down. Top with the strawberries and a sprinkle of sugar.
3. Slide the racks into the air fryer oven. Press the Power Button and cook at 375ºF (190ºC) for 8 minutes.
4. When cooking is complete, the toast should be well browned on each side. Remove from the air fryer oven to a plate and serve.

Blueberry Quesadillas

Prep time: 5 minutes | Cook time: 4 minutes | Serves 2

¼ cup nonfat Ricotta cheese
¼ cup plain nonfat Greek yogurt
2 tablespoons finely ground flaxseeds
1 tablespoon granulated stevia
½ teaspoon cinnamon
¼ teaspoon vanilla extract
2 (8-inch) low-carb whole-wheat tortillas
½ cup fresh blueberries, divided

1. Line the sheet pan with the aluminum foil.
2. In a small bowl, whisk together the Ricotta cheese, yogurt, flaxseeds, stevia, cinnamon and vanilla.
3. Put the tortillas on the sheet pan. Spread half of the yogurt mixture on each tortilla, almost to the edges. Top each tortilla with ¼ cup of blueberries. Fold the tortillas in half.
4. Slide the pan into the air fryer oven. Press the Power Button and cook at 400ºF (205ºC) for 4 minutes.
5. When cooking is complete, remove from the air fryer oven. Serve immediately.

Hash Brown Cups

Prep time: 10 minutes | Cook time: 9 minutes | Serves 6

4 eggs, beaten
2¼ cups frozen hash browns, thawed
1 cup diced ham
½ cup shredded
Cheddar cheese
½ teaspoon Cajun seasoning
Cooking spray

1. Lightly spritz a 12-cup muffin tin with cooking spray.
2. Combine the beaten eggs, hash browns, diced ham, cheese, and Cajun seasoning in a medium bowl and stir until well blended.
3. Spoon a heaping 1½ tablespoons of egg mixture into each muffin cup.
4. Put the muffin tin into the air fryer oven. Press the Power Button and cook at 350ºF (180ºC) for 9 minutes.
5. When cooked, the muffins will be golden brown.
6. Allow to cool for 5 to 10 minutes on a wire rack and serve warm.

Cheddar Egg Bake

Prep time: 5 minutes | Cook time: 6 to 7 minutes | Serves 2

2 large eggs
2 tablespoons half-and-half
2 teaspoons shredded Cheddar cheese
Salt and freshly ground black pepper, to taste
Cooking spray

1. Spritz 2 ramekins lightly with cooking spray. Crack an egg into each ramekin.
2. Top each egg with 1 tablespoon of half-and-half and 1 teaspoon of Cheddar cheese. Sprinkle with salt and black pepper. Stir the egg mixture with a fork until well combined.
3. Put the ramekins in the air fryer oven. Press the Power Button and cook at 330ºF (166ºC) for 6 minutes.
4. When cooking is complete, the eggs should be set. Check for doneness and continue cooking for 1 minute more as needed. Allow to cool for 5 minutes before removing and serving.

Egg in a Hole

Prep time: 5 minutes | Cook time: 5 minutes | Serves 1

1 slice bread
1 teaspoon butter, softened
1 egg
Salt and pepper, to taste
1 tablespoon shredded Cheddar cheese
2 teaspoons diced ham

1. On a flat work surface, cut a hole in the center of the bread slice with a 2½-inch-diameter biscuit cutter.
2. Spread the butter evenly on each side of the bread slice and transfer to a baking dish.
3. Crack the egg into the hole and season as desired with salt and pepper. Scatter the shredded cheese and diced ham on top.
4. Put the baking dish in the air fryer oven. Press the Power Button and cook at 330ºF (166ºC) for 5 minutes.
5. When cooking is complete, the bread should be lightly browned and the egg should be set. Remove from the air fryer oven and serve hot.

Sausage and Cheddar Quiche

Prep time: 5 minutes | Cook time: 25 minutes | Serves 4

12 large eggs	breakfast sausage
1 cup heavy cream	2 cups shredded
Salt and black pepper,	Cheddar cheese
to taste	Cooking spray
12 ounces (340 g)	

1. Coat a casserole dish with cooking spray.
2. Beat together the eggs, heavy cream, salt and pepper in a large bowl until creamy. Stir in the breakfast sausage and Cheddar cheese.
3. Pour the sausage mixture into the prepared casserole dish.
4. Slide the dish into the air fryer oven. Press the Power Button and cook at 375°F (190°C) for 25 minutes.
5. When done, the top of the quiche should be golden brown and the eggs will be set.
6. Remove from the air fryer oven and let sit for 5 to 10 minutes before serving.

Fried Cheesy Grits

Prep time: 10 minutes | Cook time: 11 minutes | Serves 4

²/₃ cup instant grits	room temperature
1 teaspoon salt	1 large egg, beaten
1 teaspoon freshly	1 tablespoon butter,
ground black pepper	melted
¾ cup whole or 2%	1 cup shredded mild
milk	Cheddar cheese
3 ounces (85 g)	Cooking spray
cream cheese, at	

1. Mix the grits, salt, and black pepper in a large bowl. Add the milk, cream cheese, beaten egg, and melted butter and whisk to combine. Fold in the Cheddar cheese and stir well.
2. Spray a baking pan with cooking spray. Spread the grits mixture into the baking pan.
3. Put the pan into the air fryer oven. Press the Power Button and cook at 400°F (205°C) for 11 minutes.
4. Stir the mixture halfway through the cooking time.
5. When done, a knife inserted in the center should come out clean.
6. Rest for 5 minutes and serve warm.

Shrimp and Spinach Frittata

Prep time: 15 minutes | Cook time: 16 minutes | Serves 4

4 eggs	½ cup baby spinach
Pinch salt	½ cup grated
½ cup cooked rice	Monterey Jack cheese
½ cup chopped	Nonstick cooking
cooked shrimp	spray

1. Spritz a baking pan with nonstick cooking spray.
2. Whisk the eggs and salt in a small bowl until frothy.
3. Put the cooked rice, shrimp, and baby spinach in the baking pan. Pour in the whisked eggs and scatter the cheese on top.
4. Slide the pan into the air fryer oven. Press the Power Button and cook at 320°F (160°C) for 16 minutes.
5. When cooking is complete, the frittata should be golden and puffy.
6. Let the frittata cool for 5 minutes before slicing to serve.

Creamy Hash Brown Casserole

Prep time: 15 minutes | Cook time: 30 minutes | Serves 4

3½ cups frozen hash	g) can cream of
browns, thawed	chicken soup
1 teaspoon salt	½ cup sour cream
1 teaspoon freshly	1 cup minced onion
ground black pepper	½ cup shredded
3 tablespoons butter,	sharp Cheddar cheese
melted	Cooking spray
1 (10.5-ounce / 298-	

1. Put the hash browns in a large bowl and season with salt and black pepper. Add the melted butter, cream of chicken soup, and sour cream and stir until well incorporated. Mix in the minced onion and cheese and stir well.
2. Spray a baking pan with cooking spray.
3. Spread the hash brown mixture evenly into the baking pan.
4. Put the pan into the air fryer oven. Press the Power Button and cook at 325°F (163°C) for 30 minutes.
5. When cooked, the hash brown mixture will be browned.
6. Cool for 5 minutes before serving.

Maple Blueberry Cobbler

Prep time: 5 minutes | Cook time: 15 minutes | Serves 4

¾ teaspoon baking powder
1/3 cup whole-wheat pastry flour
Dash sea salt
1/3 cup unsweetened nondairy milk
2 tablespoons maple syrup
½ teaspoon vanilla
Cooking spray
½ cup blueberries
¼ cup granola
Nondairy yogurt, for topping (optional)

1. Spritz a baking pan with cooking spray.
2. Mix the baking powder, flour, and salt in a medium bowl. Add the milk, maple syrup, and vanilla and whisk to combine.
3. Scrape the mixture into the prepared pan. Scatter the blueberries and granola on top.
4. Slide the pan into the air fryer oven. Press the Power Button and cook at 347ºF (175ºC) for 15 minutes.
5. When done, the top should be browned and a knife inserted in the center should come out clean.
6. Let the cobbler cool for 5 minutes and serve with a drizzle of nondairy yogurt.

Chocolate Banana Bread

Prep time: 10 minutes | Cook time: 30 minutes | Serves 4

¼ cup cocoa powder
6 tablespoons plus 2 teaspoons all-purpose flour, divided
½ teaspoon kosher salt
¼ teaspoon baking soda
1½ ripe bananas
1 large egg, whisked
¼ cup vegetable oil
½ cup sugar
3 tablespoons buttermilk or plain yogurt (not Greek)
½ teaspoon vanilla extract
6 tablespoons chopped white chocolate
6 tablespoons chopped walnuts

1. Mix the cocoa powder, 6 tablespoons of the flour, salt, and baking soda in a medium bowl.
2. Mash the bananas with a fork in another medium bowl until smooth. Fold in the egg, oil, sugar, buttermilk, and vanilla, and whisk until thoroughly combined. Add the wet mixture to the dry mixture and stir until well incorporated.

3. Combine the white chocolate, walnuts, and the remaining 2 tablespoons of flour in a third bowl and toss to coat. Add this mixture to the batter and stir until well incorporated. Pour the batter into a baking pan and smooth the top with a spatula.
4. Slide the pan into the air fryer oven. Press the Power Button and cook at 310ºF (154ºC) for 30 minutes.
5. When done, a toothpick inserted into the center of the bread should come out clean.
6. Remove from the air fryer oven and allow to cool on a wire rack for 10 minutes before serving.

Asparagus Cheese Strata

Prep time: 10 minutes | Cook time: 17 minutes | Serves 4

6 asparagus spears, cut into 2-inch pieces
1 tablespoon water
2 slices whole-wheat bread, cut into ½-inch cubes
4 eggs
3 tablespoons whole milk
2 tablespoons chopped flat-leaf parsley
½ cup grated Havarti or Swiss cheese
Pinch salt
Freshly ground black pepper, to taste
Cooking spray

1. Add the asparagus spears and 1 tablespoon of water in a baking pan.
2. Slide the pan into the air fryer oven. Press the Power Button and cook at 330ºF (166ºC) for 4 minutes.
3. When cooking is complete, the asparagus spears will be crisp-tender.
4. Remove the asparagus from the pan and drain on paper towels.
5. Spritz the pan with cooking spray. Put the bread and asparagus in the pan.
6. Whisk together the eggs and milk in a medium mixing bowl until creamy. Fold in the parsley, cheese, salt, and pepper and stir to combine. Pour this mixture into the baking pan.
7. Put the racks back into the air fryer oven. Cook for 13 minutes. When done, the eggs will be set and the top will be lightly browned.
8. Let cool for 5 minutes before slicing and serving.

Corned Beef and Potato Hash

Prep time: 10 minutes | Cook time: 25 minutes | Serves 4

2 medium Yukon Gold potatoes, peeled and cut into ¼-inch cubes
1 medium onion, chopped
¹/₃ cup diced red bell pepper
3 tablespoons vegetable oil
½ teaspoon dried thyme
½ teaspoon kosher salt, divided
½ teaspoon freshly ground black pepper, divided
¾ pound (340 g) corned beef, cut into ¼-inch pieces
4 large eggs

1. In a large bowl, stir together the potatoes, onion, red pepper, vegetable oil, thyme, ¼ teaspoon of the salt and ¼ teaspoon of the pepper. Spread the vegetable mixture on the sheet pan in an even layer.
2. Slide the pan into the air fryer oven. Press the Power Button and cook at 375ºF (190ºC) for 25 minutes.
3. After 15 minutes, remove from the air fryer oven and add the corned beef. Stir the mixture to incorporate the corned beef. Return to the air fryer oven and continue cooking.
4. After 5 minutes, remove from the air fryer oven. Using a large spoon, create 4 circles in the hash to hold the eggs. Gently crack an egg into each circle. Season the eggs with the remaining ¼ teaspoon of the salt and ¼ teaspoon of the pepper. Return the pan to the air fryer oven. Continue cooking for 3 to 5 minutes, depending on how you like your eggs.
5. When cooking is complete, remove from the air fryer oven. Serve immediately.

Pumpkin Muffins

Prep time: 10 minutes | Cook time: 25 minutes | Serves 2

2 tablespoons powdered peanut butter
2 tablespoons finely ground flaxseeds
2 tablespoons coconut flour
1 tablespoon dried cranberries
1 teaspoon pumpkin pie spice
½ teaspoon baking powder
½ cup water
1 cup canned pumpkin
2 large eggs
½ teaspoon vanilla extract
Cooking spray

1. In a bowl, stir together the powdered peanut butter, flaxseeds, coconut flour, dried cranberries, pumpkin pie spice, baking powder and water.
2. In another bowl, stir together the pumpkin and eggs until smooth.
3. Add the pumpkin mixture to the peanut butter mixture. Stir to combine. Add the vanilla extract to the bowl. Mix well.
4. Spritz 2 ramekins with cooking spray. Spoon half of the batter into each ramekin. Put the ramekins on a sheet pan.
5. Slide the pan into the air fryer oven. Press the Power Button and cook at 350ºF (180ºC) for 25 minutes.
6. When cooking is complete, a toothpick inserted in the center should come out clean. Serve immediately.

Cornmeal Pancake

Prep time: 10 minutes | Cook time: 6 minutes | Serves 4

1½ cups yellow cornmeal
½ cup all-purpose flour
2 tablespoons sugar
1 teaspoon salt
1 teaspoon baking powder
1 cup whole or 2% milk
1 large egg, lightly beaten
1 tablespoon butter, melted
Cooking spray

1. Line the air flow racks with parchment paper.
2. Stir together the cornmeal, flour, sugar, salt, and baking powder in a large bowl. Mix in the milk, egg, and melted butter and whisk to combine.
3. Drop tablespoonfuls of the batter onto the parchment paper for each pancake. Spray the pancakes with cooking spray. Arrange the pancakes on the air flow racks.
4. Slide the racks into the air fryer oven. Press the Power Button and cook at 350ºF (180ºC) for 6 minutes.
5. Flip the pancakes and spray with cooking spray again halfway through the cooking time.
6. When cooking is complete, remove the pancakes from the air fryer oven to a plate.
7. Cool for 5 minutes and serve immediately.

Kale and Pecorino Baked Eggs

Prep time: 5 minutes | Cook time: 11 minutes | Serves 2

1 cup roughly chopped kale leaves, stems and center ribs removed
¼ cup grated pecorino cheese
¼ cup olive oil
1 garlic clove, peeled
3 tablespoons whole almonds

Kosher salt and freshly ground black pepper, to taste
4 large eggs
2 tablespoons heavy cream
3 tablespoons chopped pitted mixed olives

1. Put the kale, pecorino, olive oil, garlic, almonds, salt, and pepper in a small blender and blitz until well incorporated.
2. One at a time, crack the eggs in a baking pan. Drizzle the kale pesto on top of the egg whites. Top the yolks with the cream and swirl together the yolks and the pesto.
3. Slide the pan into the air fryer oven. Press the Power Button and cook at 300ºF (150ºC) for 11 minutes.
4. When cooked, the top should be browned and the eggs should be set.
5. Allow the eggs to cool for 5 minutes. Scatter the olives on top and serve warm.

Blueberry Cake

Prep time: 5 minutes | Cook time: 10 minutes | Serves 8

1½ cups Bisquick
¼ cup granulated sugar
2 large eggs, beaten
¾ cup whole milk
1 teaspoon vanilla

extract
½ teaspoon lemon zest
Cooking spray
2 cups blueberries

1. Stir together the Bisquick and sugar in a medium bowl. Stir together the eggs, milk, vanilla and lemon zest. Add the wet ingredients to the dry ingredients and stir until well combined.
2. Spritz the sheet pan with cooking spray and line with the parchment paper, pressing it into place. Spray the parchment paper with cooking spray. Pour the batter on the pan and spread it out evenly. Sprinkle the blueberries evenly over the top.

3. Slide the pan into the air fryer oven. Press the Power Button and cook at 375ºF (190ºC) for 10 minutes.
4. When cooking is complete, the cake should be pulled away from the edges of the pan and the top should be just starting to turn golden brown.
5. Let the cake rest for a minute before cutting into 16 squares. Serve immediately.

French Toast Sticks with Strawberry Sauce

Prep time: 5 minutes | Cook time: 12 minutes | Serves 4

3 slices low-sodium whole-wheat bread, each cut into 4 strips
1 tablespoon unsalted butter, melted
1 tablespoon 2 percent milk

1 tablespoon sugar
1 egg, beaten
1 egg white
1 cup sliced fresh strawberries
1 tablespoon freshly squeezed lemon juice

1. Arrange the bread strips on a plate and drizzle with the melted butter.
2. In a bowl, whisk together the milk, sugar, egg and egg white.
3. Dredge the bread strips into the egg mixture and place on a wire rack to let the batter drip off. Arrange half the coated bread strips on the sheet pan.
4. Slide the pan into the air fryer oven. Press the Power Button and cook at 380ºF (193ºC) for 6 minutes.
5. After 3 minutes, remove from the air fryer oven. Use a tong to turn the strips over. Rotate the pan and return the pan to the air fryer oven to continue cooking.
6. When cooking is complete, the strips should be golden brown. Repeat with the remaining strips.
7. In a small bowl, mash the strawberries with a fork and stir in the lemon juice. Serve the French toast sticks with the strawberry sauce.

Super Vegetable Frittata

Prep time: 10 minutes | Cook time: 22 minutes | Serves 2

4 large eggs
4 ounces (113 g) baby bella mushrooms, chopped
1 cup (1 ounce / 28-g) baby spinach, chopped
½ cup (2 ounces / 57-g) shredded Cheddar cheese
⅓ cup (from 1 large) chopped leek, white part only
¼ cup halved grape tomatoes
1 tablespoon 2% milk
¼ teaspoon dried oregano
¼ teaspoon garlic powder
½ teaspoon kosher salt
Freshly ground black pepper, to taste
Cooking spray

1. Lightly spritz a baking dish with cooking spray.
2. Whisk the eggs in a large bowl until frothy. Add the mushrooms, baby spinach, cheese, leek, tomatoes, milk, oregano, garlic powder, salt, and pepper and stir until well blended. Pour the mixture into the prepared baking dish.
3. Slide the baking dish into the air fryer oven. Press the Power Button and cook at 300ºF (150ºC) for 22 minutes.
4. When cooked, the center will be puffed up and the top will be golden brown.
5. Let the frittata cool for 5 minutes before slicing to serve.

Turkey and Apple Patties

Prep time: 5 minutes | Cook time: 10 minutes | Serves 4

1 tablespoon chopped fresh thyme
1 tablespoon chopped fresh sage
1¼ teaspoons kosher salt
1 teaspoon chopped fennel seeds
¾ teaspoon smoked paprika
½ teaspoon onion powder
½ teaspoon garlic powder
⅛ teaspoon crushed red pepper flakes
⅛ teaspoon freshly ground black pepper
1 pound (454 g) 93% lean ground turkey
½ cup finely minced sweet apple (peeled)

1. Thoroughly combine the thyme, sage, salt, fennel seeds, paprika, onion powder, garlic powder, red pepper flakes, and black pepper in a medium bowl.
2. Add the ground turkey and apple and stir until well incorporated. Divide the mixture into 8 equal portions and shape into patties with your hands, each about ¼ inch thick and 3 inches in diameter.
3. Put the patties on the air flow racks.
4. Slide the racks into the air fryer oven. Press the Power Button and cook at 400ºF (205ºC) for 10 minutes.
5. Flip the patties halfway through the cooking time.
6. When cooking is complete, the patties should be nicely browned and cooked through. Remove from the air fryer oven to a plate and serve warm.

Cheddar Ham Toast

Prep time: 5 minutes | Cook time: 6 minutes | Serves: 1

1 slice bread
1 teaspoon butter, at room temperature
1 egg
Salt and freshly ground black pepper,
to taste
2 teaspoons diced ham
1 tablespoon grated Cheddar cheese

1. On a clean work surface, use a 2½-inch biscuit cutter to make a hole in the center of the bread slice with about ½-inch of bread remaining.
2. Spread the butter on both sides of the bread slice. Crack the egg into the hole and season with salt and pepper to taste. Transfer the bread to the air flow racks.
3. Slide the racks into the air fryer oven. Press the Power Button and cook at 325ºF (163ºC) for 6 minutes.
4. After 5 minutes, remove from the air fryer oven. Scatter the cheese and diced ham on top and continue cooking for an additional 1 minute.
5. When cooking is complete, the egg should be set and the cheese should be melted. Remove the toast from the air fryer oven to a plate and let cool for 5 minutes before serving.

Simple Buttermilk Biscuits

Prep time: 5 minutes | Cook time: 18 minutes | Makes 16 biscuits

2½ cups all-purpose flour
1 tablespoon baking powder
1 teaspoon kosher salt
1 teaspoon sugar
½ teaspoon baking soda
8 tablespoons (1 stick) unsalted butter, at room temperature
1 cup buttermilk, chilled

1. Stir together the flour, baking powder, salt, sugar, and baking powder in a large bowl.
2. Add the butter and stir to mix well. Pour in the buttermilk and stir with a rubber spatula just until incorporated.
3. Put the dough onto a lightly floured surface and roll the dough out to a disk, ½ inch thick. Cut out the biscuits with a 2-inch round cutter and re-roll any scraps until you have 16 biscuits.
4. Arrange the biscuits on the air flow racks.
5. Slide the racks into the air fryer oven. Press the Power Button and cook at 325ºF (163ºC) for 18 minutes.
6. When cooked, the biscuits will be golden brown.
7. Remove from the air fryer oven to a plate and serve hot.

Bourbon Vanilla French Toast

Prep time: 15 minutes | Cook time: 6 minutes | Serves 4

2 large eggs
2 tablespoons water
2/3 cup whole or 2% milk
1 tablespoon butter, melted
2 tablespoons
bourbon
1 teaspoon vanilla extract
8 (1-inch-thick) French bread slices
Cooking spray

1. Line the air flow racks with parchment paper and spray it with cooking spray.
2. Beat the eggs with the water in a shallow bowl until combined. Add the milk, melted butter, bourbon, and vanilla and stir to mix well.
3. Dredge 4 slices of bread in the batter, turning to coat both sides evenly. Transfer the bread slices onto the parchment paper.

4. Slide the racks into the air fryer oven. Press the Power Button and cook at 320ºF (160ºC) for 6 minutes.
5. Flip the slices halfway through the cooking time.
6. When cooking is complete, the bread slices should be nicely browned.
7. Remove from the air fryer oven to a plate and serve warm.

Coconut Brown Rice and Date Porridge

Prep time: 5 minutes | Cook time: 23 minutes | Serves 1 or 2

½ cup cooked brown rice
1 cup canned coconut milk
¼ cup unsweetened shredded coconut
¼ cup packed dark brown sugar
4 large Medjool dates,
pitted and roughly chopped
½ teaspoon kosher salt
¼ teaspoon ground cardamom
Heavy cream, for serving (optional)

1. Put all the ingredients except the heavy cream in a baking pan and stir until blended.
2. Slide the pan into the air fryer oven. Press the Power Button and cook at 375ºF (190ºC) for 23 minutes.
3. Stir the porridge halfway through the cooking time.
4. When cooked, the porridge will be thick and creamy.
5. Remove from the air fryer oven and ladle the porridge into bowls.
6. Serve hot with a drizzle of the cream, if desired.

Walnut Pancake

Prep time: 10 minutes | Cook time: 20 minutes | Serves 4

3 tablespoons melted butter, divided
1 cup flour
2 tablespoons sugar
1½ teaspoons baking powder
¼ teaspoon salt
1 egg, beaten

¾ cup milk
1 teaspoon pure vanilla extract
½ cup roughly chopped walnuts
Maple syrup or fresh sliced fruit, for serving

1. Grease a baking pan with 1 tablespoon of melted butter.
2. Mix the flour, sugar, baking powder, and salt in a medium bowl. Add the beaten egg, milk, the remaining 2 tablespoons of melted butter, and vanilla and stir until the batter is sticky but slightly lumpy.
3. Slowly pour the batter into the greased baking pan and scatter with the walnuts.
4. Put the pan into the air fryer oven. Press the Power Button and cook at 330°F (166°C) for 20 minutes.
5. When cooked, the pancake should be golden brown and cooked through.
6. Let the pancake rest for 5 minutes and serve topped with the maple syrup or fresh fruit, if desired.

Broccoli and Fontina Quiche

Prep time: 5 minutes | Cook time: 10 minutes | Serves 4

1 cup broccoli florets
¾ cup chopped roasted red peppers
1¼ cups grated Fontina cheese
6 eggs

¾ cup heavy cream
½ teaspoon salt
Freshly ground black pepper, to taste
Cooking spray

1. Spritz a baking pan with cooking spray
2. Add the broccoli florets and roasted red peppers to the pan and scatter the grated Fontina cheese on top.
3. In a bowl, beat together the eggs and heavy cream. Sprinkle with salt and pepper. Pour the egg mixture over the top of the cheese. Wrap the pan in foil.
4. Slide the pan into the air fryer oven. Press the Power Button and cook at 325°F (163°C) for 10 minutes.
5. After 8 minutes, remove from the air fryer oven. Remove the foil. Return to the air fryer oven and continue to cook another 2 minutes.
6. When cooked, the quiche should be golden brown.
7. Rest for 5 minutes before cutting into wedges and serve warm.

Fried Potatoes and Bell Peppers

Prep time: 10 minutes | Cook time: 35 minutes | Serves 4

1 pound (454 g) red potatoes, cut into ½-inch dices
1 large red bell pepper, cut into ½-inch dices
1 large green bell pepper, cut into ½-inch dices
1 medium onion, cut into ½-inch dices

1½ tablespoons extra-virgin olive oil
1¼ teaspoons kosher salt
¾ teaspoon sweet paprika
¾ teaspoon garlic powder
Freshly ground black pepper, to taste

1. Mix the potatoes, bell peppers, onion, oil, salt, paprika, garlic powder, and black pepper in a large mixing and toss to coat.
2. Transfer the potato mixture to the air flow racks.
3. Slide the racks into the air fryer oven. Press the Power Button and cook at 350°F (180°C) for 35 minutes.
4. Stir the potato mixture three times during cooking.
5. When done, the potatoes should be nicely browned.
6. Remove from the air fryer oven to a plate and serve warm.

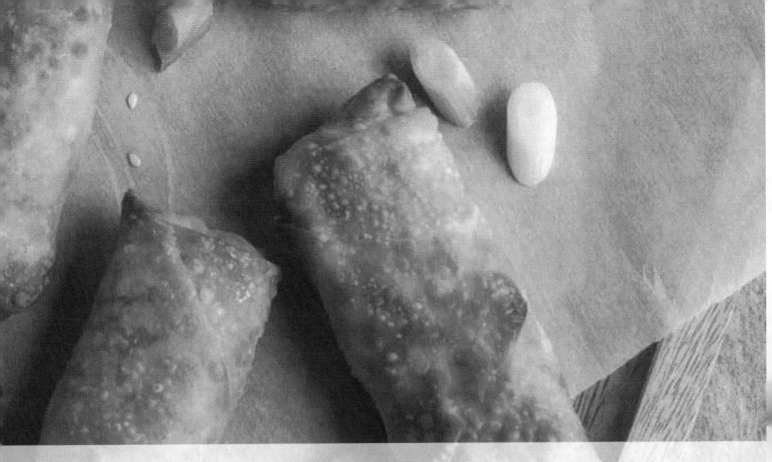

Chapter 2 Appetizers and Snacks

Cinnamon Apple Chips

Prep time: 10 minutes | Cook time: 10 minutes | Serves 4

2 apples, cored and cut into thin slices
2 heaped teaspoons

ground cinnamon
Cooking spray

1. Spritz the air flow racks with cooking spray.
2. In a medium bowl, sprinkle the apple slices with the cinnamon. Toss until evenly coated. Spread the coated apple slices on the racks.
3. Slide the racks into the air fryer oven. Press the Power Button and cook at 350ºF (180ºC) for 10 minutes.
4. After 5 minutes, remove from the air fryer oven. Stir the apple slices and return the racks to the air fryer oven to continue cooking.
5. When cooking is complete, the slices should be until crispy Remove the racks from the air fryer oven and let rest for 5 minutes before serving.

Caramelized Peaches

Prep time: 10 minutes | Cook time: 10 to 13 minutes | Serves 4

2 tablespoons sugar
¼ teaspoon ground cinnamon

4 peaches, cut into wedges
Cooking spray

1. Toss the peaches with the sugar and cinnamon in a medium bowl until evenly coated.
2. Lightly spray the air flow racks with cooking spray. Place the peaches on the air flow racks. Lightly mist the peaches with cooking spray.
3. Slide the racks into the air fryer oven. Press the Power Button and cook at 350ºF (180ºC) for 10 minutes.
4. After 5 minutes, remove from the air fryer oven and flip the peaches. Return to the air fryer oven and continue cooking for 5 minutes.
5. When cooking is complete, the peaches should be caramelized. If necessary, continue cooking for 3 minutes. Remove from the air fryer oven. Let the peaches cool for 5 minutes and serve warm.

Crab Toasts

Prep time: 10 minutes | Cook time: 5 minutes | Makes 15 to 18 toasts

1 (6-ounce / 170-g) can flaked crab meat, well drained
3 tablespoons light mayonnaise
¼ cup shredded Parmesan cheese
¼ cup shredded Cheddar cheese

1 teaspoon Worcestershire sauce
½ teaspoon lemon juice
1 loaf artisan bread, French bread, or baguette, cut into ⅜-inch-thick slices

1. In a large bowl, stir together all the ingredients except the bread slices.
2. On a clean work surface, lay the bread slices. Spread ½ tablespoon of crab mixture onto each slice of bread.
3. Arrange the bread slices on the air flow racks.
4. Slide the racks into the air fryer oven. Press the Power Button and cook at 360ºF (182ºC) for 5 minutes.
5. When cooking is complete, the tops should be lightly browned. Remove from the air fryer oven. Serve warm.

Prosciutto-Wrapped Anjou Pears

Prep time: 12 minutes | Cook time: 6 minutes | Serves 8

2 large, ripe Anjou pears
4 thin slices Parma

prosciutto
2 teaspoons aged balsamic vinegar

1. Peel the pears. Slice into 8 wedges and cut out the core from each wedge.
2. Cut the prosciutto into 8 long strips. Wrap each pear wedge with a strip of prosciutto. Put the wrapped pears in a sheet pan.
3. Slide the pan into the air fryer oven. Press the Power Button and cook at 350ºF (180ºC) for 6 minutes.
4. After 2 or 3 minutes, check the pears. The pears should be turned over if the prosciutto is beginning to crisp up and brown. Return to the air fryer oven and continue cooking.
5. When cooking is complete, remove from the air fryer oven. Drizzle the pears with the balsamic vinegar and serve warm.

Browned Ricotta with Capers

Prep time: 10 minutes | Cook time: 8 minutes | Serves 4 to 6

1½ cups whole milk ricotta cheese
2 tablespoons extra-virgin olive oil
2 tablespoons capers, rinsed
Zest of 1 lemon, plus more for garnish
1 teaspoon finely

chopped fresh rosemary
Pinch crushed red pepper flakes
Salt and freshly ground black pepper, to taste
1 tablespoon grated Parmesan cheese

1. In a mixing bowl, stir together the ricotta cheese, olive oil, capers, lemon zest, rosemary, red pepper flakes, salt, and pepper until well combined.
2. Spread the mixture evenly in a baking dish.
3. Slide the baking dish into the air fryer oven. Press the Power Button and cook at 380ºF (193ºC) for 8 minutes.
4. When cooking is complete, the top should be nicely browned. Remove from the air fryer oven and top with Parmesan cheese. Garnish with the lemon zest and serve warm.

Roasted Yogurt Grapes

Prep time: 5 minutes | Cook time: 10 minutes | Serves 6

2 cups seedless red grapes, rinsed and patted dry
1 tablespoon apple cider vinegar
1 tablespoon honey

1 cup low-fat Greek yogurt
2 tablespoons 2 percent milk
2 tablespoons minced fresh basil

1. Spread the red grapes on the air flow racks and drizzle with the cider vinegar and honey. Lightly toss to coat.
2. Slide the racks into the air fryer oven. Press the Power Button and cook at 380ºF (193ºC) for 10 minutes.
3. When cooking is complete, the grapes will be wilted but still soft. Remove from the air fryer oven.
4. In a medium bowl, whisk together the yogurt and milk. Gently fold in the grapes and basil.
5. Serve immediately.

Sesame Kale Chips

Prep time: 15 minutes | Cook time: 8 minutes | Serves 5

8 cups deribbed kale leaves, torn into 2-inch pieces
1½ tablespoons olive oil
¾ teaspoon chili

powder
¼ teaspoon garlic powder
½ teaspoon paprika
2 teaspoons sesame seeds

1. In a large bowl, toss the kale with the olive oil, chili powder, garlic powder, paprika, and sesame seeds until well coated.
2. Transfer the kale to the air flow racks.
3. Slide the racks into the air fryer oven. Press the Power Button and cook at 350ºF (180ºC) for 8 minutes.
4. Flip the kale twice during cooking.
5. When cooking is complete, the kale should be crispy. Remove from the air fryer oven and serve warm.

Cuban Flavor Sandwiches

Prep time: 20 minutes | Cook time: 8 minutes | Makes 4 sandwiches

8 slices ciabatta bread, about ¼-inch thick
Cooking spray
1 tablespoon brown mustard
Toppings:
6 to 8 ounces (170 to 227 g) thinly sliced leftover roast pork
4 ounces (113 g) thinly sliced deli turkey

⅓ cup bread and butter pickle slices
2 to 3 ounces (57 to 85 g) Pepper Jack cheese slices

1. On a clean work surface, spray one side of each slice of bread with cooking spray. Spread the other side of each slice of bread evenly with brown mustard.
2. Top 4 of the bread slices with the roast pork, turkey, pickle slices, cheese, and finish with remaining bread slices. Transfer to the air flow racks.
3. Slide the racks into the air fryer oven. Press the Power Button and cook at 390ºF (199ºC) for 8 minutes.
4. When cooking is complete, remove from the air fryer oven. Cool for 5 minutes and serve warm.

Lemon Pepper Chicken Wings

Prep time: 5 minutes | Cook time: 24 minutes | Serves 10

2 pounds (907 g) chicken wings	1½ teaspoons baking powder
4½ teaspoons salt-free lemon pepper seasoning	1½ teaspoons kosher salt

1. In a large bowl, toss together all the ingredients until well coated. Put the wings on a sheet pan, making sure they don't crowd each other too much.
2. Slide the pan into the air fryer oven. Press the Power Button and cook at 375°F (190°C) for 24 minutes.
3. After 12 minutes, remove from the air fryer oven. Use a tong to turn the wings over. Return the pan to the air fryer oven to continue cooking.
4. When cooking is complete, the wings should be dark golden brown and charred. Remove the pan from the air fryer oven and let rest for 5 minutes before serving.

Chili Chickpeas

Prep time: 5 minutes | Cook time: 18 minutes | Serves 4

½ teaspoon chili powder	¼ teaspoon salt
½ teaspoon ground cumin	1 (19-ounce / 539-g) can chickpeas, drained and rinsed
¼ teaspoon cayenne pepper	Cooking spray

1. Line the air flow racks with parchment paper and lightly spritz with cooking spray.
2. Mix the chili powder, cumin, cayenne pepper, and salt in a small bowl.
3. Put the chickpeas in a medium bowl and lightly mist with cooking spray.
4. Add the spice mixture to the chickpeas and toss until evenly coated. Transfer the chickpeas to the parchment.
5. Slide the racks into the air fryer oven. Press the Power Button and cook at 390°F (199°C) for 18 minutes.
6. Stir the chickpeas twice during cooking.
7. When cooking is complete, the chickpeas should be crunchy. Remove from the air fryer oven. Let the chickpeas cool for 5 minutes before serving.

Dill Pickle Deviled Eggs

Prep time: 20 minutes | Cook time: 16 minutes | Serves 12

3 cups ice	2 teaspoons salt
12 large eggs	2 teaspoons yellow mustard
½ cup mayonnaise	
10 hamburger dill pickle chips, diced	1 teaspoon freshly ground black pepper
¼ cup diced onion	½ teaspoon paprika

1. Put the ice in a large bowl and set aside. Carefully place the eggs on the air flow racks.
2. Slide the racks into the air fryer oven. Press the Power Button and cook at 250°F (121°C) for 16 minutes.
3. When cooking is complete, transfer the eggs to the large bowl of ice to cool.
4. When cool enough to handle, peel the eggs. Slice them in half lengthwise and scoop out yolks into a small bowl. Stir in the mayonnaise, pickles, onion, salt, mustard, and pepper. Mash the mixture with a fork until well combined.
5. Fill each egg white half with 1 to 2 teaspoons of the egg yolk mixture.
6. Sprinkle the paprika on top and serve immediately.

Carrot Chips

Prep time: 15 minutes | Cook time: 10 minutes | Serves 4

4 to 5 medium carrots, trimmed and thinly sliced	oil, plus more for greasing
1 tablespoon olive	1 teaspoon seasoned salt

1. Toss the carrot slices with 1 tablespoon of olive oil and salt in a medium bowl until thoroughly coated.
2. Grease the air flow racks with the olive oil. Place the carrot slices on the greased racks.
3. Slide the racks into the air fryer oven. Press the Power Button and cook at 390°F (199°C) for 10 minutes.
4. Stir the carrot slices halfway through the cooking time.
5. When cooking is complete, the chips should be crisp-tender. Remove the racks from the air fryer oven and allow to cool for 5 minutes before serving.

Spicy and Sweet Nuts

Prep time: 5 minutes | Cook time: 15 minutes | Makes 4 cups

1 pound (454 g) walnut halves and pieces
½ cup granulated sugar
3 tablespoons vegetable oil
1 teaspoon cayenne pepper
½ teaspoon fine salt

1. Soak the walnuts in a large bowl with boiling water for a minute or two. Drain the walnuts. Stir in the sugar, oil and cayenne pepper to coat well. Spread the walnuts in a single layer on a sheet pan.
2. Slide the pan into the air fryer oven. Press the Power Button and cook at 325ºF (163ºC) for 15 minutes.
3. After 7 or 8 minutes, remove from the air fryer oven. Stir the nuts. Return to the air fryer oven and continue cooking, check frequently.
4. When cooking is complete, the walnuts should be dark golden brown. Remove from the air fryer oven. Sprinkle the nuts with the salt and let cool. Serve.

Fried Pickle Spears

Prep time: 5 minutes | Cook time: 15 minutes | Serves 6

2 jars sweet and sour pickle spears, patted dry
2 medium eggs
⅓ cup milk
1 teaspoon garlic powder
1 teaspoon sea salt
½ teaspoon shallot powder
⅓ teaspoon chili powder
⅓ cup all-purpose flour
Cooking spray

1. Spritz the air flow racks with cooking spray.
2. In a bowl, beat together the eggs with milk. In another bowl, combine garlic powder, sea salt, shallot powder, chili powder and all-purpose flour until well blended.
3. One by one, roll the pickle spears in the powder mixture, then dredge them in the egg mixture. Dip them in the powder mixture a second time for additional coating.
4. Place the coated pickles on the air flow racks.

5. Slide the racks into the air fryer oven. Press the Power Button and cook at 385ºF (196ºC) for 15 minutes.
6. Stir the pickles halfway through the cooking time.
7. When cooking is complete, they should be golden and crispy. Transfer to a plate and let cool for 5 minutes before serving.

Sausage Rolls

Prep time: 15 minutes | Cook time: 15 minutes | Serves 12

1 pound (454 g) bulk breakfast sausage
½ cup finely chopped onion
½ cup fresh bread crumbs
½ teaspoon dried mustard
½ teaspoon dried sage
¼ teaspoon cayenne pepper
1 large egg, beaten
1 garlic clove, minced
2 sheets (1 package) frozen puff pastry, thawed
All-purpose flour, for dusting

1. In a medium bowl, break up the sausage. Stir in the onion, bread crumbs, mustard, sage, cayenne pepper, egg and garlic. Divide the sausage mixture in half and tightly wrap each half in plastic wrap. Refrigerate for 5 to 10 minutes.
2. Lay the pastry sheets on a lightly floured work surface. Using a rolling pin, lightly roll out the pastry to smooth out the dough. Take out one of the sausage packages and form the sausage into a long roll. Remove the plastic wrap and place the sausage on top of the puff pastry about 1 inch from one of the long edges. Roll the pastry around the sausage and pinch the edges of the dough together to seal. Repeat with the other pastry sheet and sausage.
3. Slice the logs into lengths about 1½ inches long. Put the sausage rolls on a sheet pan, cut-side down.
4. Slide the pan into the air fryer oven. Press the Power Button and cook at 350ºF (180ºC) for 15 minutes.
5. After 7 or 8 minutes, rotate the pan and continue cooking.
6. When cooking is complete, the rolls will be golden brown and sizzling. Remove the pan from the air fryer oven and let cool for 5 minutes.

Artichoke Bites

Prep time: 10 minutes | Cook time: 8 minutes | Serves 4

14 whole artichoke hearts packed in water
½ cup all-purpose flour
1 egg
⅓ cup panko bread crumbs
1 teaspoon Italian seasoning
Cooking spray

1. Drain the artichoke hearts and dry thoroughly with paper towels.
2. Place the flour on a plate. Beat the egg in a shallow bowl until frothy. Thoroughly combine the bread crumbs and Italian seasoning in a separate shallow bowl.
3. Dredge the artichoke hearts in the flour, then in the beaten egg, and finally roll in the bread crumb mixture until evenly coated.
4. Place the artichoke hearts on the air flow racks and mist them with cooking spray.
5. Slide the racks into the air fryer oven. Press the Power Button and cook at 375ºF (190ºC) for 8 minutes.
6. Flip the artichoke hearts halfway through the cooking time.
7. When cooking is complete, the artichoke hearts should be browned and the edges should be crispy. Remove from the air fryer oven. Let the artichoke hearts sit for 5 minutes before serving.

Olive Muffuletta

Prep time: 10 minutes | Cook time: 6 minutes | Makes 8 sliders

¼ pound (113 g) thinly sliced deli ham
¼ pound (113 g) thinly sliced pastrami
4 ounces (113 g) low-fat Mozzarella cheese, grated
8 slider buns, split in half
Cooking spray
1 tablespoon sesame seeds

Olive Mix:

½ cup sliced green olives with pimentos
¼ cup sliced black olives
¼ cup chopped kalamata olives
1 teaspoon red wine vinegar
¼ teaspoon basil
⅛ teaspoon garlic powder

1. Combine all the ingredients for the olive mix in a small bowl and stir well.

2. Stir together the ham, pastrami, and cheese in a medium bowl and divide the mixture into 8 equal portions.
3. Assemble the sliders: Top each bottom bun with 1 portion of meat and cheese, 2 tablespoons of olive mix, finished by the remaining buns. Lightly spritz the tops with cooking spray. Scatter the sesame seeds on top.
4. Arrange the sliders on the air flow racks.
5. Slide the racks into the air fryer oven. Press the Power Button and cook at 360ºF (182ºC) for 6 minutes.
6. When cooking is complete, the cheese should be melted. Remove the racks from the air fryer oven and serve.

Paprika Corn Tortilla Chips

Prep time: 5 minutes | Cook time: 5 minutes | Serves 4

½ teaspoon ground cumin
½ teaspoon paprika
½ teaspoon chili powder
½ teaspoon salt
Pinch cayenne pepper
8 (6-inch) corn tortillas, each cut into 6 wedges
Cooking spray

1. Lightly spritz the air flow racks with cooking spray.
2. Stir together the cumin, paprika, chili powder, salt, and pepper in a small bowl.
3. Place the tortilla wedges on the air flow racks. Lightly mist them with cooking spray. Sprinkle the seasoning mixture on top of the tortilla wedges.
4. Slide the racks into the air fryer oven. Press the Power Button and cook at 375ºF (190ºC) for 5 minutes.
5. Stir the tortilla wedges halfway through the cooking time.
6. When cooking is complete, the chips should be lightly browned and crunchy. Remove from the air fryer oven. Let the tortilla chips cool for 5 minutes and serve.

Crispy Avocado Chips

Prep time: 15 minutes | Cook time: 10 minutes | Serves 4

1 egg
1 tablespoon lime juice
⅛ teaspoon hot sauce
2 tablespoons flour
¾ cup panko bread crumbs

¼ cup cornmeal
¼ teaspoon salt
1 large avocado, pitted, peeled, and cut into ½-inch slices
Cooking spray

1. Whisk together the egg, lime juice, and hot sauce in a small bowl.
2. On a sheet of wax paper, place the flour. In a separate sheet of wax paper, combine the bread crumbs, cornmeal, and salt.
3. Dredge the avocado slices one at a time in the flour, then in the egg mixture, finally roll them in the bread crumb mixture to coat well.
4. Place the breaded avocado slices on the air flow racks and mist them with cooking spray.
5. Slide the racks into the air fryer oven. Press the Power Button and cook at 390°F (199°C) for 10 minutes.
6. When cooking is complete, the slices should be nicely browned and crispy. Transfer the avocado slices to a plate and serve.

Pepperoni Pizza Bites

Prep time: 5 minutes | Cook time: 12 minutes | Serves 8

1 cup finely shredded Mozzarella cheese
½ cup chopped pepperoni
¼ cup Marinara sauce

1 (8-ounce / 227-g) can crescent roll dough
All-purpose flour, for dusting

1. In a small bowl, stir together the cheese, pepperoni and Marinara sauce.
2. Lay the dough on a lightly floured work surface. Separate it into 4 rectangles. Firmly pinch the perforations together and pat the dough pieces flat.
3. Divide the cheese mixture evenly between the rectangles and spread it out over the dough, leaving a ¼-inch border. Roll a rectangle up tightly, starting with the short end. Pinch the edge down to seal the roll. Repeat with the remaining rolls.

4. Slice the rolls into 4 or 5 even slices. Put the slices on a sheet pan, leaving a few inches between each slice.
5. Slide the pan into the air fryer oven. Press the Power Button and cook at 350°F (180°C) for 12 minutes.
6. After 6 minutes, rotate the pan and continue cooking.
7. When cooking is complete, the rolls will be golden brown with crisp edges. Remove from the air fryer oven. Serve hot.

Old Bay Wings

Prep time: 10 minutes | Cook time: 13 minutes | Serves 4

2 tablespoons Old Bay seasoning
2 teaspoons baking powder
2 teaspoons salt

2 pounds (907 g) chicken wings, patted dry
Cooking spray

1. Combine the Old Bay seasoning, baking powder, and salt in a large zip-top plastic bag. Add the chicken wings, seal, and shake until the wings are thoroughly coated in the seasoning mixture.
2. Lightly spray the air flow racks with cooking spray. Lay the chicken wings on the air flow racks and lightly mist them with cooking spray.
3. Slide the racks into the air fryer oven. Press the Power Button and cook at 400°F (205°C) for 13 minutes.
4. Flip the wings halfway through the cooking time.
5. When cooking is complete, the wings should reach an internal temperature of 165°F (74°C) on a meat thermometer. Remove from the air fryer oven to a plate and serve hot.

Garlic Edamame

Prep time: 5 minutes | Cook time: 9 minutes | Serves 4

1 (16-ounce / 454-g) bag frozen edamame in pods
2 tablespoon olive oil, divided
½ teaspoon garlic salt
½ teaspoon salt
¼ teaspoon freshly ground black pepper
½ teaspoon red pepper flakes (optional)

1. Put the edamame in a medium bowl and drizzle with 1 tablespoon of olive oil. Toss to coat well.
2. Stir together the garlic salt, salt, pepper, and red pepper flakes (if desired) in a small bowl. Pour the mixture into the bowl of edamame and toss until the edamame is fully coated.
3. Grease the air flow racks with the remaining 1 tablespoon of olive oil.
4. Place the edamame on the greased air flow racks.
5. Slide the racks into the air fryer oven. Press the Power Button and cook at 375°F (190°C) for 9 minutes.
6. Stir the edamame once halfway through the cooking time.
7. When cooking is complete, the edamame should be crisp. Remove from the air fryer oven to a plate and serve warm.

Polenta Fries with Chili-Lemon Mayo

Prep time: 10 minutes | Cook time: 28 minutes | Serves 4

Polenta Fries:
2 teaspoons vegetable or olive oil
¼ teaspoon paprika
1 pound (454 g) prepared polenta, cut
into 3-inch × ½-inch strips
Salt and freshly ground black pepper, to taste

Chili-Lemon Mayo:
½ cup mayonnaise
1 teaspoon chili powder
1 teaspoon chopped fresh cilantro
¼ teaspoon ground
cumin
Juice of ½ lemon
Salt and freshly ground black pepper, to taste

1. Mix the oil and paprika in a bowl. Add the polenta strips and toss until evenly coated. Transfer the polenta strips to the air flow racks.

2. Slide the racks into the air fryer oven. Press the Power Button and cook at 400°F (205°C) for 28 minutes.
3. Stir the polenta strips halfway through the cooking time.
4. Meanwhile, whisk together all the ingredients for the chili-lemon mayo in a small bowl.
5. When cooking is complete, remove the polenta fries from the air fryer oven to a plate. Season as desired with salt and pepper. Serve alongside the chili-lemon mayo as a dipping sauce.

Jalapeño Cheese Poppers with Bacon

Prep time: 10 minutes | Cook time: 15 minutes | Serves 8

6 ounces (170 g) cream cheese, at room temperature
4 ounces (113 g) shredded Cheddar cheese
1 teaspoon chili powder
12 large jalapeño
peppers, deseeded and sliced in half lengthwise
2 slices cooked bacon, chopped
¼ cup panko bread crumbs
1 tablespoon butter, melted

1. In a medium bowl, whisk together the cream cheese, Cheddar cheese and chili powder. Spoon the cheese mixture into the jalapeño halves and arrange them on a sheet pan.
2. In a small bowl, stir together the bacon, bread crumbs and butter. Sprinkle the mixture over the jalapeño halves.
3. Slide the pan into the air fryer oven. Press the Power Button and cook at 375°F (190°C) for 15 minutes.
4. After 7 or 8 minutes, rotate the pan and continue cooking until the peppers are softened, the filling is bubbling and the bread crumbs are browned.
5. When cooking is complete, remove from the air fryer oven. Let the poppers cool for 5 minutes before serving.

Tomato Sardines

Prep time: 10 minutes | Cook time: 20 minutes | Serves 4

2 pounds (907 g) fresh sardines
3 tablespoons olive oil, divided
4 Roma tomatoes, peeled and chopped
1 small onion, sliced thinly

Zest of 1 orange
Sea salt and freshly ground pepper, to taste
2 tablespoons whole-wheat bread crumbs
½ cup white wine

1. Brush a sheet pan with a little olive oil. Set aside.
2. Rinse the sardines under running water. Slit the belly, remove the spine and butterfly the fish. Set aside.
3. Heat the remaining olive oil in a large skillet. Add the tomatoes, onion, orange zest, salt and pepper to the skillet and simmer for 20 minutes, or until the mixture thickens and softens.
4. Put half the sauce in the bottom of the sheet pan. Arrange the sardines on top and spread the remaining half the sauce over the fish. Sprinkle with the bread crumbs and drizzle with the white wine.
5. Slide the pan into the air fryer oven. Press the Power Button and cook at 425ºF (220ºC) for 20 minutes.
6. When cooking is complete, remove from the air fryer oven. Serve immediately.

Sweet Snack Mix

Prep time: 5 minutes | Cook time: 10 minutes | Makes about 10 cups

3 tablespoons butter, melted
½ cup honey
1 teaspoon salt
2 cups granola
2 cups sesame sticks
2 cups crispy corn

puff cereal
2 cups mini pretzel crisps
1 cup cashews
1 cup pepitas
1 cup dried cherries

1. In a small mixing bowl, mix the butter, honey, and salt until well incorporated.
2. In a large bowl, combine the granola, sesame sticks, corn puff cereal and pretzel crisps, cashews, and pepitas. Drizzle with the butter mixture and toss until evenly coated. Transfer the snack mix to a sheet pan.
3. Slide the pan into the air fryer oven. Press the Power Button and cook at 370ºF (188ºC) for 10 minutes.
4. Stir the snack mix halfway through the cooking time.
5. When cooking is complete, they should be lightly toasted. Remove from the air fryer oven and allow to cool completely. Scatter with the dried cherries and mix well. Serve immediately.

Sausage and Cheese Balls

Prep time: 10 minutes | Cook time: 10 minutes | Serves 8

12 ounces (340 g) mild ground sausage
1½ cups baking mix
1 cup shredded mild Cheddar cheese

3 ounces (85 g) cream cheese, at room temperature
1 to 2 tablespoons olive oil

1. Line the air flow racks with parchment paper. Set aside.
2. Mix the ground sausage, baking mix, Cheddar cheese, and cream cheese in a large bowl and stir to incorporate.
3. Divide the sausage mixture into 16 equal portions and roll them into 1-inch balls with your hands. Arrange the sausage balls on the parchment, leaving space between each ball. Brush the sausage balls with the olive oil.
4. Slide the racks into the air fryer oven. Press the Power Button and cook at 325ºF (163ºC) for 10 minutes.
5. Flip the balls halfway through the cooking time.
6. When cooking is complete, the balls should be firm and lightly browned on both sides. Remove from the air fryer oven to a plate and serve warm.

Zucchini Tots

Prep time: 15 minutes | Cook time: 6 minutes | Serves 8

2 medium zucchini (about 12 ounces / 340 g), shredded
1 large egg, whisked
½ cup grated pecorino romano cheese
½ cup panko bread crumbs
¼ teaspoon black pepper
1 clove garlic, minced
Cooking spray

1. Using your hands, squeeze out as much liquid from the zucchini as possible. In a large bowl, mix the zucchini with the remaining ingredients except the oil until well incorporated.
2. Make the zucchini tots: Use a spoon or cookie scoop to place tablespoonfuls of the zucchini mixture onto a lightly floured cutting board and form into 1-inch logs.
3. Spritz the air flow racks with cooking spray. Place the zucchini tots on the racks.
4. Slide the racks into the air fryer oven. Press the Power Button and cook at 375ºF (190ºC) for 6 minutes.
5. When cooking is complete, the tots should be golden brown. Remove from the air fryer oven to a serving plate and serve warm.

Green Chile Nachos

Prep time: 10 minutes | Cook time: 10 minutes | Serves 6

8 ounces (227 g) tortilla chips
3 cups shredded Monterey Jack cheese, divided
2 (7-ounce / 198-g) cans chopped green chiles, drained
1 (8-ounce / 227-g)
can tomato sauce
¼ teaspoon dried oregano
¼ teaspoon granulated garlic
¼ teaspoon freshly ground black pepper
Pinch cinnamon
Pinch cayenne pepper

1. Arrange the tortilla chips close together in a single layer on a sheet pan. Sprinkle 1½ cups of the cheese over the chips. Arrange the green chiles over the cheese as evenly as possible. Top with the remaining 1½ cups of the cheese.
2. Slide the pan into the air fryer oven. Press the Power Button and cook at 375ºF (190ºC) for 10 minutes.

3. After 5 minutes, rotate the pan and continue cooking.
4. Meanwhile, stir together the remaining ingredients in a bowl.
5. When cooking is complete, the cheese will be melted and starting to crisp around the edges of the pan. Remove from the air fryer oven. Drizzle the sauce over the nachos and serve warm.

Potato Chips

Prep time: 5 minutes | Cook time: 22 minutes | Serves 3

2 medium potatoes, preferably Yukon Gold, scrubbed
Cooking spray
2 teaspoons olive oil
½ teaspoon garlic granules
¼ teaspoon paprika
¼ teaspoon plus ⅛ teaspoon sea salt
¼ teaspoon freshly ground black pepper
Ketchup or hot sauce, for serving

1. Spritz the air flow racks with cooking spray.
2. On a flat work surface, cut the potatoes into ¼-inch-thick slices. Transfer the potato slices to a medium bowl, along with the olive oil, garlic granules, paprika, salt, and pepper and toss to coat well. Transfer the potato slices to the air flow racks.
3. Slide the racks into the air fryer oven. Press the Power Button and cook at 392ºF (200ºC) for 22 minutes.
4. Stir the potato slices twice during the cooking process.
5. When cooking is complete, the potato chips should be tender and nicely browned. Remove from the air fryer oven and serve alongside the ketchup for dipping.

Roasted Cauliflower with Parmesan Cheese

Prep time: 15 minutes | Cook time: 15 minutes | Makes 5 cups

8 cups small cauliflower florets (about 1¼ pounds / 567 g)
3 tablespoons olive oil
1 teaspoon garlic powder
½ teaspoon salt
½ teaspoon turmeric
¼ cup shredded Parmesan cheese

1. In a bowl, combine the cauliflower florets, olive oil, garlic powder, salt, and turmeric and toss to coat. Transfer to the air flow racks.
2. Slide the racks into the air fryer oven. Press the Power Button and cook at 390ºF (199ºC) for 15 minutes.
3. After 5 minutes, remove from the air fryer oven and stir the cauliflower florets. Return to the air fryer oven and continue cooking.
4. After 6 minutes, remove from the air fryer oven and stir the cauliflower. Return to the air fryer oven and continue cooking for 4 minutes. The cauliflower florets should be crisp-tender.
5. When cooking is complete, remove from the air fryer oven to a plate. Sprinkle with the shredded Parmesan cheese and toss well. Serve warm.

Tomato Bruschetta

Prep time: 5 minutes | Cook time: 3 minutes | Serves 6

4 tomatoes, diced
1/3 cup shredded fresh basil
¼ cup shredded Parmesan cheese
1 tablespoon balsamic vinegar
1 tablespoon minced garlic
1 teaspoon olive oil
1 teaspoon salt
1 teaspoon freshly ground black pepper
1 loaf French bread, cut into 1-inch-thick slices
Cooking spray

1. Mix the tomatoes and basil in a medium bowl. Add the cheese, vinegar, garlic, olive oil, salt, and pepper and stir until well incorporated. Set aside.
2. Spritz the air flow racks with cooking spray and lay the bread slices on the racks. Spray with cooking spray.

3. Slide the racks into the air fryer oven. Press the Power Button and cook at 250ºF (121ºC) for 3 minutes.
4. When cooking is complete, remove from the air fryer oven to a plate. Top each slice with a generous spoonful of the tomato mixture and serve.

Garlicky Roasted Mushrooms

Prep time: 5 minutes | Cook time: 27 minutes | Serves 4

16 garlic cloves, peeled
2 teaspoons olive oil, divided
16 button mushrooms
½ teaspoon dried marjoram
1/8 teaspoon freshly ground black pepper
1 tablespoon white wine

1. Put the garlic cloves on a sheet pan and drizzle with 1 teaspoon of the olive oil. Toss to coat well.
2. Slide the pan into the air fryer oven. Press the Power Button and cook at 350ºF (180ºC) for 12 minutes.
3. When cooking is complete, remove from the air fryer oven. Stir in the mushrooms, marjoram and pepper. Drizzle with the remaining 1 teaspoon of the olive oil and the white wine. Toss to coat well. Return the pan to the air fryer oven.
4. Press the Power Button and cook at 350ºF (180ºC) for 15 minutes.
5. Once done, the mushrooms and garlic cloves will be softened. Remove from the air fryer oven.
6. Serve warm.

Tuna Melts

Prep time: 10 minutes | Cook time: 6 minutes | Serves 6

2 (5- to 6-ounce / 142- to 170-g) cans oil-packed tuna, drained
1 large scallion, chopped
1 small stalk celery, chopped
1/3 cup mayonnaise
1 tablespoon chopped fresh dill
1 tablespoon capers, drained
¼ teaspoon celery salt
12 slices cocktail rye bread
2 tablespoons butter, melted
6 slices sharp Cheddar cheese

1. In a medium bowl, stir together the tuna, scallion, celery, mayonnaise, dill, capers and celery salt.
2. Brush one side of the bread slices with the butter. Arrange the bread slices on a sheet pan, buttered-side down. Scoop a heaping tablespoon of the tuna mixture on each slice of bread, spreading it out even to the edges.
3. Cut the cheese slices to fit the dimensions of the bread and place a cheese slice on each piece.
4. Slide the pan into the air fryer oven. Press the Power Button and cook at 375ºF (190ºC) for 6 minutes.
5. After 4 minutes, remove from the air fryer oven and check the tuna melts. The tuna melts are done when the cheese has melted and the tuna is heated through. If needed, continue cooking.
6. When cooking is complete, remove from the air fryer oven. Use a spatula to transfer the tuna melts to a clean work surface and slice each one in half diagonally. Serve warm.

Mushroom and Sausage Empanadas

Prep time: 5 minutes | Cook time: 12 minutes | Serves 4

½ pound (227 g) Kielbasa smoked sausage, chopped
4 chopped canned mushrooms
2 tablespoons chopped onion
½ teaspoon ground cumin
¼ teaspoon paprika
Salt and black pepper, to taste
½ package puff pastry dough, at room temperature
1 egg, beaten
Cooking spray

1. Combine the sausage, mushrooms, onion, cumin, paprika, salt, and pepper in a bowl and stir to mix well.
2. Make the empanadas: Put the puff pastry dough on a lightly floured surface. Cut circles into the dough with a glass. Put 1 tablespoon of the sausage mixture into the center of each pastry circle. Fold each in half and pinch the edges to seal. Using a fork, crimp the edges. Brush them with the beaten egg and mist with cooking spray.
3. Spritz the air flow racks with cooking spray. Place the empanadas on the air flow racks.
4. Slide the racks into the air fryer oven. Press the Power Button and cook at 360ºF (182ºC) for 12 minutes.
5. Flip the empanadas halfway through the cooking time.
6. When cooking is complete, the empanadas should be golden brown. Remove from the air fryer oven. Allow them to cool for 5 minutes and serve hot.

Chapter 3 Casseroles, Frittata, and Quiche

Herbed Cheddar Frittata

Prep time: 10 minutes | Cook time: 20 minutes | Serves 4

½ cup shredded Cheddar cheese
½ cup half-and-half
4 large eggs
2 tablespoons chopped scallion greens

2 tablespoons chopped fresh parsley
½ teaspoon kosher salt
½ teaspoon ground black pepper
Cooking spray

1. Spritz a baking pan with cooking spray.
2. Whisk together all the ingredients in a large bowl, then pour the mixture into the prepared baking pan.
3. Slide the pan into the air fryer oven. Press the Power Button and cook at 300°F (150°C) for 20 minutes.
4. Stir the mixture halfway through.
5. When cooking is complete, the eggs should be set.
6. Serve immediately.

Mediterranean Crustless Quiche

Prep time: 10 minutes | Cook time: 30 minutes | Serves 4

4 eggs
¼ cup chopped Kalamata olives
½ cup chopped tomatoes
¼ cup chopped onion
½ cup milk
1 cup crumbled feta

cheese
½ tablespoon chopped oregano
½ tablespoon chopped basil
Salt and ground black pepper, to taste
Cooking spray

1. Spritz a baking pan with cooking spray.
2. Whisk the eggs with remaining ingredients in a large bowl. Stir to mix well.
3. Pour the mixture into the prepared baking pan.
4. Slide the pan into the air fryer oven. Press the Power Button and cook at 340°F (171°C) for 30 minutes.
5. When cooking is complete, the eggs should be set and a toothpick inserted in the center should come out clean.
6. Serve immediately.

Green Bean Casserole

Prep time: 4 minutes | Cook time: 6 minutes | Serves 4

1 tablespoon melted butter
1 cup green beans
6 ounces (170 g) Cheddar cheese, shredded

7 ounces (198 g) Parmesan cheese, shredded
¼ cup heavy cream
Sea salt, to taste

1. Grease a baking pan with the melted butter.
2. Add the green beans, Cheddar, salt, and black pepper to the prepared baking pan. Stir to mix well, then spread the Parmesan and cream on top.
3. Slide the pan into the air fryer oven. Press the Power Button and cook at 400°F (205°C) for 6 minutes.
4. When cooking is complete, the beans should be tender and the cheese should be melted.
5. Serve immediately.

Chorizo and Potato Frittata

Prep time: 8 minutes | Cook time: 12 minutes | Serves 4

2 tablespoons olive oil
1 chorizo, sliced
4 eggs
½ cup corn
1 large potato, boiled and cubed

1 tablespoon chopped parsley
½ cup feta cheese, crumbled
Salt and ground black pepper, to taste

1. Heat the olive oil in a nonstick skillet over medium heat until shimmering.
2. Add the chorizo and cook for 4 minutes or until golden brown.
3. Whisk the eggs in a bowl, then sprinkle with salt and ground black pepper.
4. Mix the remaining ingredients in the egg mixture, then pour the chorizo and its fat into a baking pan. Pour in the egg mixture.
5. Slide the pan into the air fryer oven. Press the Power Button and cook at 330°F (166°C) for 8 minutes.
6. Stir the mixture halfway through.
7. When cooking is complete, the eggs should be set.
8. Serve immediately.

Ranch Broccoli and Cheese Casserole

Prep time: 5 minutes | Cook time: 30 minutes | Serves 6

4 cups broccoli florets
¼ cup heavy whipping cream
½ cup sharp Cheddar cheese, shredded
¼ cup ranch dressing
Kosher salt and ground black pepper, to taste

1. Combine all the ingredients in a large bowl. Toss to coat well broccoli well.
2. Pour the mixture into a baking pan.
3. Slide the pan into the air fryer oven. Press the Power Button and cook at 375ºF (190ºC) for 30 minutes.
4. When cooking is complete, the broccoli should be tender.
5. Remove the baking pan from the air fryer oven and serve immediately.

Smoked Trout Frittata with Crème Fraiche

Prep time: 8 minutes | Cook time: 17 minutes | Serves 4

2 tablespoons olive oil
1 onion, sliced
1 egg, beaten
½ tablespoon horseradish sauce
6 tablespoons crème
fraiche
1 cup diced smoked trout
2 tablespoons chopped fresh dill
Cooking spray

1. Spritz a baking pan with cooking spray.
2. Heat the olive oil in a nonstick skillet over medium heat until shimmering.
3. Add the onion and sauté for 3 minutes or until translucent.
4. Combine the egg, horseradish sauce, and crème fraiche in a large bowl. Stir to mix well, then mix in the sautéed onion, smoked trout, and dill.
5. Pour the mixture in the prepared baking pan.
6. Slide the pan into the air fryer oven. Press the Power Button and cook at 350ºF (180ºC) for 14 minutes.
7. Stir the mixture halfway through.
8. When cooking is complete, the egg should be set and the edges should be lightly browned.
9. Serve immediately.

Spinach Mushroom Frittata

Prep time: 7 minutes | Cook time: 8 minutes | Serves 2

1 cup chopped mushrooms
2 cups spinach, chopped
4 eggs, lightly beaten
3 ounces (85 g) feta cheese, crumbled
2 tablespoons heavy cream
A handful of fresh parsley, chopped
Salt and ground black pepper, to taste
Cooking spray

1. Spritz a baking pan with cooking spray.
2. Whisk together all the ingredients in a large bowl. Stir to mix well.
3. Pour the mixture in the prepared baking pan.
4. Slide the pan into the air fryer oven. Press the Power Button and cook at 350ºF (180ºC) for 8 minutes.
5. Stir the mixture halfway through.
6. When cooking is complete, the eggs should be set.
7. Serve immediately.

Cauliflower and Okra Casserole

Prep time: 8 minutes | Cook time: 12 minutes | Serves 4

1 head cauliflower, cut into florets
1 cup okra, chopped
1 yellow bell pepper, chopped
2 eggs, beaten
½ cup chopped onion
1 tablespoon soy sauce
2 tablespoons olive oil
Salt and ground black pepper, to taste

1. Spritz a baking pan with cooking spray.
2. Put the cauliflower in a food processor and pulse to rice the cauliflower.
3. Pour the cauliflower rice in the baking pan and add the remaining ingredients. Stir to mix well.
4. Slide the pan into the air fryer oven. Press the Power Button and cook at 380ºF (193ºC) for 12 minutes.
5. When cooking is complete, the eggs should be set.
6. Remove the baking pan from the air fryer oven and serve immediately.

Hearty Veggie Frittata

Prep time: 15 minutes | Cook time: 20 minutes | Serves 2

4 eggs
1/3 cup milk
2 teaspoons olive oil
1 large zucchini, sliced
2 asparagus, sliced thinly
1/3 cup sliced mushrooms
1 cup baby spinach
1 small red onion, sliced
1/3 cup crumbled feta cheese
1/3 cup grated Cheddar cheese
1/4 cup chopped chives
Salt and ground black pepper, to taste

1. Line a baking pan with parchment paper.
2. Whisk together the eggs, milk, salt, and ground black pepper in a large bowl. Set aside.
3. Heat the olive oil in a nonstick skillet over medium heat until shimmering.
4. Add the zucchini, asparagus, mushrooms, spinach, and onion to the skillet and sauté for 5 minutes or until tender.
5. Pour the sautéed vegetables into the prepared baking pan, then spread the egg mixture over and scatter with cheeses.
6. Slide the pan into the air fryer oven. Press the Power Button and cook at 380ºF (193ºC) for 15 minutes.
7. Stir the mixture halfway through.
8. When cooking is complete, the egg should be set and the edges should be lightly browned.
9. Remove the frittata from the air fryer oven and sprinkle with chives before serving.

Tilapia and Rockfish Casserole

Prep time: 8 minutes | Cook time: 22 minutes | Serves 2

1 tablespoon olive oil
1 small yellow onion, chopped
2 garlic cloves, minced
4 ounces (113 g) tilapia pieces
4 ounces (113 g) rockfish pieces
1/2 teaspoon dried basil
Salt and ground white pepper, to taste
4 eggs, lightly beaten
1 tablespoon dry sherry
4 tablespoons cheese, shredded

1. Heat the olive oil in a nonstick skillet over medium-high heat until shimmering.

2. Add the onion and garlic and sauté for 2 minutes or until fragrant.
3. Add the tilapia, rockfish, basil, salt, and white pepper to the skillet. Sauté to combine well and transfer them on a baking pan.
4. Combine the eggs, sherry and cheese in a large bowl. Stir to mix well. Pour the mixture in the baking pan over the fish mixture.
5. Slide the pan into the air fryer oven. Press the Power Button and cook at 360ºF (182ºC) for 20 minutes.
6. When cooking is complete, the eggs should be set and the casserole edges should be lightly browned.
7. Serve immediately.

Creamy Chickpea and Spinach Casserole

Prep time: 10 minutes | Cook time: 21 to 22 minutes | Serves 4

2 tablespoons olive oil
2 garlic cloves, minced
1 tablespoon ginger, minced
1 onion, chopped
1 chili pepper, minced
Salt and ground black pepper, to taste
1 pound (454 g) spinach
1 can coconut milk
1/2 cup dried tomatoes, chopped
1 (14-ounce / 397-g) can chickpeas, drained

1. Heat the olive oil in a saucepan over medium heat. Sauté the garlic and ginger in the olive oil for 1 minute, or until fragrant.
2. Add the onion, chili pepper, salt and pepper to the saucepan. Sauté for 3 minutes.
3. Mix in the spinach and sauté for 3 to 4 minutes or until the vegetables become soft. Remove from heat.
4. Pour the vegetable mixture into a baking pan. Stir in coconut milk, dried tomatoes and chickpeas until well blended.
5. Slide the pan into the air fryer oven. Press the Power Button and cook at 370ºF (188ºC) for 15 minutes.
6. When cooking is complete, transfer the casserole to a serving dish. Let cool for 5 minutes before serving.

Beef Burgundy Casserole

Prep time: 10 minutes | Cook time: 25 minutes | Serves 4

1½ pounds (680 g) beef steak	mushroom soup
1 ounce (28 g) dry onion soup mix	½ cup beef broth
2 cups sliced mushrooms	¼ cup red wine
1 (14.5-ounce / 411-g) can cream of	3 garlic cloves, minced
	1 whole onion, chopped

1. Put the beef steak in a large bowl, then sprinkle with dry onion soup mix. Toss to coat well.
2. Combine the mushrooms with mushroom soup, beef broth, red wine, garlic, and onion in a large bowl. Stir to mix well.
3. Transfer the beef steak in a baking pan, then pour in the mushroom mixture.
4. Slide the pan into the air fryer oven. Press the Power Button and cook at 360ºF (182ºC) for 25 minutes.
5. When cooking is complete, the mushrooms should be soft and the beef should be well browned.
6. Remove the baking pan from the air fryer oven and serve immediately.

Frittata with Shrimp and Spinach

Prep time: 6 minutes | Cook time: 14 minutes | Serves 4

4 whole eggs	½ cup rice, cooked
1 teaspoon dried basil	½ cup Monterey Jack cheese, grated
½ cup shrimp, cooked and chopped	Salt, to taste
½ cup baby spinach	Cooking spray

1. Spritz a baking pan with cooking spray.
2. Whisk the eggs with basil and salt in a large bowl until bubbly, then mix in the shrimp, spinach, rice, and cheese.
3. Pour the mixture into the baking pan.
4. Slide the pan into the air fryer oven. Press the Power Button and cook at 360ºF (182ºC) for 14 minutes.
5. Stir the mixture halfway through.
6. When cooking is complete, the eggs should be set and the frittata should be golden brown.
7. Slice to serve.

Pastrami Casserole

Prep time: 10 minutes | Cook time: 8 minutes | Serves 2

1 cup pastrami, sliced	cheese, grated
1 bell pepper, chopped	4 eggs
¼ cup Greek yogurt	¼ teaspoon ground black pepper
2 spring onions, chopped	Sea salt, to taste
½ cup Cheddar	Cooking spray

1. Spritz a baking pan with cooking spray.
2. Whisk together all the ingredients in a large bowl. Stir to mix well. Pour the mixture into the baking pan.
3. Slide the pan into the air fryer oven. Press the Power Button and cook at 330ºF (166ºC) for 8 minutes.
4. When cooking is complete, the eggs should be set and the casserole edges should be lightly browned.
5. Remove the baking pan from the air fryer oven and allow to cool for 10 minutes before serving.

Creamed Corn Casserole with Bell Pepper

Prep time: 10 minutes | Cook time: 20 minutes | Serves 4

1 cup corn kernels	powder
¼ cup bell pepper, finely chopped	2 tablespoons melted unsalted butter
½ cup low-fat milk	1 tablespoon granulated sugar
1 large egg, beaten	Pinch of cayenne pepper
½ cup yellow cornmeal	¼ teaspoon kosher salt
½ cup all-purpose flour	Cooking spray
½ teaspoon baking	

1. Spritz a baking pan with cooking spray.
2. Combine all the ingredients in a large bowl. Stir to mix well. Pour the mixture into the baking pan.
3. Slide the pan into the air fryer oven. Press the Power Button and cook at 330ºF (166ºC) for 20 minutes.
4. When cooking is complete, the casserole should be lightly browned and set.
5. Remove the baking pan from the air fryer oven and serve immediately.

Sausage and Triple Pepper Casserole

Prep time: 15 minutes | Cook time: 25 minutes | Serves 6

1 pound (454 g) minced breakfast sausage
1 yellow pepper, diced
1 red pepper, diced
1 green pepper, diced
1 sweet onion, diced
2 cups Cheddar cheese, shredded
6 eggs
Salt and freshly ground black pepper, to taste
Fresh parsley, for garnish

1. Cook the sausage in a nonstick skillet over medium heat for 10 minutes or until well browned. Stir constantly.
2. When the cooking is finished, transfer the cooked sausage to a baking pan and add the peppers and onion. Scatter with Cheddar cheese.
3. Whisk the eggs with salt and ground black pepper in a large bowl, then pour the mixture into the baking pan.
4. Slide the pan into the air fryer oven. Press the Power Button and cook at 360ºF (182ºC) for 15 minutes.
5. When cooking is complete, the egg should be set and the edges of the casserole should be lightly browned.
6. Remove the baking pan from the air fryer oven and top with fresh parsley before serving.

Ham Chicken Casserole

Prep time: 15 minutes | Cook time: 15 minutes | Serves 4 to 6

2 cups diced cooked chicken
1 cup diced ham
¼ teaspoon ground nutmeg
½ cup half-and-half
½ teaspoon ground black pepper
6 slices Swiss cheese
Cooking spray

1. Spritz a baking pan with cooking spray.
2. Combine the chicken, ham, nutmeg, half-and-half, and ground black pepper in a large bowl. Stir to mix well.
3. Pour half of the mixture into the baking pan, then top the mixture with 3 slices of Swiss cheese, then pour in the remaining mixture and top with remaining cheese slices.

4. Slide the pan into the air fryer oven. Press the Power Button and cook at 350ºF (180ºC) for 15 minutes.
5. When cooking is complete, the egg should be set and the cheese should be melted.
6. Serve immediately.

Broccoli Cheese Quiche

Prep time: 6 minutes | Cook time: 14 minutes | Serves 4

4 eggs
1 teaspoon dried thyme
1 cup whole milk
1 steamed carrots, diced
2 cups steamed broccoli florets
2 medium tomatoes, diced
¼ cup crumbled feta cheese
1 cup grated Cheddar cheese
1 teaspoon chopped parsley
Salt and ground black pepper, to taste
Cooking spray

1. Spritz a baking pan with cooking spray.
2. Whisk together the eggs, thyme, salt, and ground black pepper in a bowl and fold in the milk while mixing.
3. Put the carrots, broccoli, and tomatoes in the prepared baking pan, then spread with feta cheese and ½ cup Cheddar cheese. Pour the egg mixture over, then scatter with remaining Cheddar on top.
4. Slide the pan into the air fryer oven. Press the Power Button and cook at 350ºF (180ºC) for 14 minutes.
5. When cooking is complete, the egg should be set and the quiche should be puffed.
6. Remove the quiche from the air fryer oven and top with chopped parsley, then slice to serve.

Chapter 4 Fast and Easy Everyday Favorites

Cinnamon-Sugar Chickpeas

Prep time: 10 minutes | Cook time: 10 minutes | Serves 2

1 tablespoon cinnamon
1 tablespoon sugar
1 cup chickpeas, soaked in water overnight, rinsed and drained

1. Combine the cinnamon and sugar in a bowl. Stir to mix well.
2. Add the chickpeas to the bowl, then toss to coat well.
3. Pour the chickpeas on the air flow racks.
4. Slide the racks into the air fryer oven. Press the Power Button and cook at 390ºF (199ºC) for 10 minutes.
5. Stir the chickpeas three times during cooking.
6. When cooked, the chickpeas should be golden brown and crispy. Remove from the air fryer oven.
7. Serve immediately.

French Fries

Prep time: 5 minutes | Cook time: 25 minutes | Serves 2

2 russet potatoes, peeled and cut into ½-inch sticks
2 teaspoons olive oil
Salt, to taste
¼ cup ketchup, for serving

1. Bring a pot of salted water to a boil. Put the potato sticks into the pot and blanch for 4 minutes.
2. Rinse the potatoes under running cold water and pat dry with paper towels.
3. Put the potato sticks in a large bowl and drizzle with olive oil. Toss to coat well.
4. Transfer the potato sticks to the air flow racks.
5. Slide the racks into the air fryer oven. Press the Power Button and cook at 400ºF (205ºC) for 25 minutes.
6. Stir the potato sticks and sprinkle with salt halfway through.
7. When cooked, the potato sticks will be crispy and golden brown. Remove the French fries from the air fryer oven and serve with ketchup.

Soy Kale Chips

Prep time: 5 minutes | Cook time: 5 minutes | Serves 2

4 medium kale leaves, about 1 ounce (28 g) each, stems removed, tear the leaves in thirds
2 teaspoons soy sauce
2 teaspoons olive oil

1. Toss the kale leaves with soy sauce and olive oil in a large bowl to coat well. Put the leaves in a baking pan.
2. Slide the pan into the air fryer oven. Press the Power Button and cook at 400ºF (205ºC) for 5 minutes.
3. Flip the leaves with tongs gently halfway through.
4. When cooked, the kale leaves should be crispy. Remove from the air fryer oven.
5. Serve immediately.

Corn on the Cob

Prep time: 10 minutes | Cook time: 10 minutes | Serves 4

2 tablespoons mayonnaise
2 teaspoons minced garlic
½ teaspoon sea salt
1 cup panko bread crumbs
4 (4-inch length) ears corn on the cob, husk and silk removed
Cooking spray

1. Spritz the air flow racks with cooking spray.
2. Combine the mayonnaise, garlic, and salt in a bowl. Stir to mix well. Pour the panko on a plate.
3. Brush the corn on the cob with mayonnaise mixture, then roll the cob in the bread crumbs and press to coat well.
4. Transfer the corn on the cob on the air flow racks and spritz with cooking spray.
5. Slide the racks into the air fryer oven. Press the Power Button and cook at 400ºF (205ºC) for 10 minutes.
6. Flip the corn on the cob at least three times during the cooking.
7. When cooked, the corn kernels on the cob should be almost browned. Remove from the air fryer oven.
8. Serve immediately.

Lemon Brussels Sprouts

Prep time: 5 minutes | Cook time: 20 minutes | Serves 4

¼ teaspoon salt
⅛ teaspoon ground black pepper
1 tablespoon extra-virgin olive oil

1 pound (454 g) Brussels sprouts, trimmed and halved
Lemon wedges, for garnish

1. Combine the salt, black pepper, and olive oil in a large bowl. Stir to mix well.
2. Add the Brussels sprouts to the bowl of mixture and toss to coat well. Arrange the Brussels sprouts on the air flow racks.
3. Slide the racks into the air fryer oven. Press the Power Button and cook at 350ºF (180ºC) for 20 minutes.
4. Stir the Brussels sprouts two times during cooking.
5. When cooked, the Brussels sprouts will be lightly browned and wilted. Remove from the air fryer oven.
6. Transfer the cooked Brussels sprouts to a large plate and squeeze the lemon wedges on top to serve.

Hot Peanuts

Prep time: 5 minutes | Cook time: 5 minutes | Serves 9

3 cups shelled raw peanuts
1 tablespoon hot red pepper sauce

3 tablespoons granulated white sugar

1. Put the peanuts in a large bowl, then drizzle with hot red pepper sauce and sprinkle with sugar. Toss to coat well.
2. Pour the peanuts on the air flow racks.
3. Slide the racks into the air fryer oven. Press the Power Button and cook at 400ºF (205ºC) for 5 minutes.
4. Stir the peanuts halfway through the cooking time.
5. When cooking is complete, the peanuts will be crispy and browned. Remove from the air fryer oven.
6. Serve immediately.

Lemon Pepper Green Beans

Prep time: 5 minutes | Cook time: 10 minutes | Makes 2 cups

½ teaspoon lemon pepper
2 teaspoons granulated garlic
½ teaspoon salt

1 tablespoon olive oil
2 cups fresh green beans, trimmed and snapped in half

1. Combine the lemon pepper, garlic, salt, and olive oil in a bowl. Stir to mix well.
2. Add the green beans to the bowl of mixture and toss to coat well.
3. Arrange the green beans on the air flow racks.
4. Slide the racks into the air fryer oven. Press the Power Button and cook at 370ºF (188ºC) for 10 minutes.
5. Stir the green beans halfway through the cooking time.
6. When cooking is complete, the green beans will be tender and crispy. Remove from the air fryer oven.
7. Serve immediately.

Cinnamon Vanilla Toast

Prep time: 5 minutes | Cook time: 5 minutes | Serves 6

1½ teaspoons cinnamon
1½ teaspoons vanilla extract
½ cup sugar
2 teaspoons ground

black pepper
2 tablespoons melted coconut oil
12 slices whole wheat bread

1. Combine all the ingredients, except for the bread, in a large bowl. Stir to mix well.
2. Dunk the bread in the bowl of mixture gently to coat and infuse well. Shake the excess off. Arrange the bread slices on the air flow racks.
3. Slide the racks into the air fryer oven. Press the Power Button and cook at 400ºF (205ºC) for 5 minutes.
4. Flip the bread halfway through.
5. When cooking is complete, the bread should be golden brown.
6. Remove the bread slices from the air fryer oven and slice to serve.

Jalapeño Cheddar Cornbread

Prep time: 10 minutes | Cook time: 20 minutes | Serves 8

$^2/_3$ cup cornmeal
$^1/_3$ cup all-purpose flour
¾ teaspoon baking powder
2 tablespoons buttery spread, melted
½ teaspoon kosher salt
1 tablespoon granulated sugar
¾ cup whole milk
1 large egg, beaten
1 jalapeño pepper, thinly sliced
$^1/_3$ cup shredded sharp Cheddar cheese
Cooking spray

1. Spritz a baking pan with cooking spray.
2. Combine all the ingredients in a large bowl. Stir to mix well. Pour the mixture in the baking pan.
3. Slide the pan into the air fryer oven. Press the Power Button and cook at 300°F (150°C) for 20 minutes.
4. When the cooking is complete, a toothpick inserted in the center of the bread should come out clean.
5. Remove the baking pan from the air fryer oven and allow the bread to cool for 5 minutes before slicing to serve.

Potato Latkes

Prep time: 15 minutes | Cook time: 10 minutes | Makes 4 latkes

1 egg
2 tablespoons all-purpose flour
2 medium potatoes, peeled and shredded,
rinsed and drained
¼ teaspoon granulated garlic
½ teaspoon salt
Cooking spray

1. Spritz the air flow racks with cooking spray.
2. Whisk together the egg, flour, potatoes, garlic, and salt in a large bowl. Stir to mix well.
3. Divide the mixture into four parts, then flatten them into four circles. Arrange the circles into the air flow racks and spritz with cooking spray.
4. Slide the racks into the air fryer oven. Press the Power Button and cook at 380°F (193°C) for 10 minutes.
5. Flip the latkes halfway through.
6. When cooked, the latkes will be golden brown and crispy. Remove from the air fryer oven.
7. Serve immediately.

Manchego Cheese Wafer

Prep time: 5 minutes | Cook time: 5 minutes | Serves 2

1 cup shredded aged Manchego cheese
1 teaspoon all-purpose flour
½ teaspoon cumin seeds
¼ teaspoon cracked black pepper

1. Line the air flow racks with parchment paper.
2. Combine the cheese and flour in a bowl. Stir to mix well. Spread the mixture on the racks into a 4-inch round.
3. Combine the cumin and black pepper in a small bowl. Stir to mix well. Sprinkle the cumin mixture over the cheese round.
4. Slide the racks into the air fryer oven. Press the Power Button and cook at 375°F (190°C) for 5 minutes.
5. When cooked, the cheese will be lightly browned and frothy.
6. Use tongs to transfer the cheese wafer onto a plate and slice to serve.

Cayenne Shrimp

Prep time: 10 minutes | Cook time: 10 minutes | Makes 2 cups

½ teaspoon Old Bay seasoning
1 teaspoon ground cayenne pepper
½ teaspoon paprika
1 tablespoon olive oil
⅛ teaspoon salt
½ pound (227 g) shrimps, peeled and deveined
Juice of half a lemon

1. Combine the Old Bay seasoning, cayenne pepper, paprika, olive oil, and salt in a large bowl, then add the shrimps and toss to coat well.
2. Put the shrimps on the air flow racks.
3. Slide the racks into the air fryer oven. Press the Power Button and cook at 390°F (199°C) for 10 minutes.
4. Flip the shrimps halfway through the cooking time.
5. When cooking is complete, the shrimps should be opaque. Remove from the air fryer oven.
6. Serve the shrimps with lemon juice on top.

Parmesan Shrimp

Prep time: 10 minutes | Cook time: 8 minutes | Serves 4 to 6

²/₃ cup grated Parmesan cheese
4 minced garlic cloves
1 teaspoon onion powder
½ teaspoon oregano
1 teaspoon basil
1 teaspoon ground

black pepper
2 tablespoons olive oil
2 pounds (907 g) cooked large shrimps, peeled and deveined
Lemon wedges, for topping
Cooking spray

1. Spritz the air flow racks with cooking spray.
2. Combine all the ingredients, except for the shrimps, in a large bowl. Stir to mix well.
3. Dunk the shrimps in the mixture and toss to coat well. Shake the excess off. Arrange the shrimps on the air flow racks.
4. Slide the racks into the air fryer oven. Press the Power Button and cook at 350°F (180°C) for 8 minutes.
5. Flip the shrimps halfway through the cooking time.
6. When cooking is complete, the shrimps should be opaque. Remove from the air fryer oven.
7. Transfer the cooked shrimps on a large plate and squeeze the lemon wedges over before serving.

Okra Chips

Prep time: 5 minutes | Cook time: 16 minutes | Serves 6

2 pounds (907 g) fresh okra pods, cut into 1-inch pieces
2 tablespoons canola

oil
1 teaspoon coarse sea salt

1. Stir the oil and salt in a bowl to mix well. Add the okra and toss to coat well. Put the okra on the air flow racks.
2. Slide the racks into the air fryer oven. Press the Power Button and cook at 400°F (205°C) for 16 minutes.
3. Flip the okra at least three times during cooking.
4. When cooked, the okra should be lightly browned. Remove from the air fryer oven.
5. Serve immediately.

Spiced Pecans

Prep time: 5 minutes | Cook time: 10 minutes | Makes 4 cups

2 egg whites
1 tablespoon cumin
2 teaspoons smoked paprika
½ cup brown sugar

2 teaspoons kosher salt
1 pound (454 g) pecan halves
Cooking spray

1. Spritz the air flow racks with cooking spray.
2. Combine the egg whites, cumin, paprika, sugar, and salt in a large bowl. Stir to mix well. Add the pecans to the bowl and toss to coat well.
3. Transfer the pecans to the air flow racks.
4. Slide the racks into the air fryer oven. Press the Power Button and cook at 300°F (150°C) for 10 minutes.
5. Stir the pecans at least two times during the cooking.
6. When cooking is complete, the pecans should be lightly caramelized. Remove from the air fryer oven.
7. Serve immediately.

Spicy Chicken Wings

Prep time: 5 minutes | Cook time: 15 minutes | Makes 16 wings

16 chicken wings
3 tablespoons hot

sauce
Cooking spray

1. Spritz the air flow racks with cooking spray.
2. Arrange the chicken wings on the air flow racks.
3. Slide the racks into the air fryer oven. Press the Power Button and cook at 360°F (182°C) for 15 minutes.
4. Flip the wings at lease three times during cooking.
5. When cooking is complete, the chicken wings will be well browned. Remove from the air fryer oven.
6. Transfer the air fried wings to a plate and serve with hot sauce.

Super Easy Air Fried Edamame

Prep time: 5 minutes | Cook time: 7 minutes | Serves 6

1½ pounds (680 g) unshelled edamame	2 tablespoons olive oil
	1 teaspoon sea salt

1. Put the edamame in a large bowl, then drizzle with olive oil. Toss to coat well. Transfer the edamame to the air flow racks.
2. Slide the racks into the air fryer oven. Press the Power Button and cook at 400ºF (205ºC) for 7 minutes.
3. Stir the edamame at least three times during cooking.
4. When done, the edamame will be tender and warmed through.
5. Transfer the cooked edamame onto a plate and sprinkle with salt. Toss to combine well and set aside for 3 minutes to infuse before serving.

Tortilla Chips

Prep time: 5 minutes | Cook time: 10 minutes | Serves 4

4 six-inch corn tortillas, cut in half and slice into thirds	oil
	¼ teaspoon kosher salt
1 tablespoon canola	Cooking spray

1. Spritz the air flow racks with cooking spray.
2. On a clean work surface, brush the tortilla chips with canola oil, then transfer the chips to the air flow racks.
3. Slide the racks into the air fryer oven. Press the Power Button and cook at 360ºF (182ºC) for 10 minutes.
4. Flip the chips and sprinkle with salt halfway through the cooking time.
5. When cooked, the chips will be crunchy and lightly browned. Transfer the chips to a plate lined with paper towels. Serve immediately.

Air Fried Shishito Peppers

Prep time: 5 minutes | Cook time: 5 minutes | Serves 4

½ pound (227 g) shishito peppers (about 24)	taste
	Lemon wedges, for serving
1 tablespoon olive oil	Cooking spray
Coarse sea salt, to	

1. Spritz the air flow racks with cooking spray.
2. Toss the peppers with olive oil in a large bowl to coat well.
3. Arrange the peppers on the air flow racks.
4. Slide the racks into the air fryer oven. Press the Power Button and cook at 400ºF (205ºC) for 5 minutes.
5. Flip the peppers and sprinkle the peppers with salt halfway through the cooking time.
6. When cooked, the peppers should be blistered and lightly charred. Transfer the peppers onto a plate and squeeze the lemon wedges on top before serving.

Baked Cherry Tomatoes

Prep time: 5 minutes | Cook time: 5 minutes | Serves 2

2 cups cherry tomatoes	salt
1 clove garlic, thinly sliced	1 tablespoon freshly chopped basil, for topping
1 teaspoon olive oil	Cooking spray
⅛ teaspoon kosher	

1. Spritz a baking pan with cooking spray and set aside.
2. In a large bowl, toss together the cherry tomatoes, sliced garlic, olive oil, and kosher salt. Spread the mixture in an even layer in the prepared pan.
3. Slide the pan into the air fryer oven. Press the Power Button and cook at 360ºF (182ºC) for 5 minutes.
4. When cooking is complete, the tomatoes should be the soft and wilted.
5. Transfer to a bowl and rest for 5 minutes. Top with the chopped basil and serve warm.

Potato Chips

Prep time: 20 minutes | Cook time: 15 minutes | Serves 2 to 4

2 large russet potatoes, sliced into ⅛-inch slices, rinsed
Sea salt and freshly

ground black pepper, to taste
Cooking spray

Lemony Cream Dip:

½ cup sour cream
¼ teaspoon lemon juice
2 scallions, white part only, minced

1 tablespoon olive oil
¼ teaspoon salt
Freshly ground black pepper, to taste

1. Soak the potato slices in water for 10 minutes, then pat dry with paper towels.
2. Transfer the potato slices on the air flow racks. Spritz the slices with cooking spray.
3. Slide the racks into the air fryer oven. Press the Power Button and cook at 300ºF (150ºC) for 15 minutes.
4. Stir the potato slices three times during cooking. Sprinkle with salt and ground black pepper in the last minute.
5. Meanwhile, combine the ingredients for the dip in a small bowl. Stir to mix well.
6. When cooking is complete, the potato slices will be crispy and golden brown. Remove from the air fryer oven.
7. Serve the potato chips immediately with the dip.

Parsnip Fries

Prep time: 10 minutes | Cook time: 10 minutes | Serves 4

3 medium parsnips, peeled, cut into sticks
¼ teaspoon kosher salt

1 teaspoon olive oil
1 garlic clove, unpeeled
Cooking spray

Dip:

¼ cup plain Greek yogurt
⅛ teaspoon garlic powder
1 tablespoon sour

cream
¼ teaspoon kosher salt
Freshly ground black pepper, to taste

1. Spritz the air flow racks with cooking spray.
2. Put the parsnip sticks in a large bowl, then sprinkle with salt and drizzle with olive oil.

3. Transfer the parsnip into the air flow racks and add the garlic.
4. Slide the racks into the air fryer oven. Press the Power Button and cook at 360ºF (182ºC) for 10 minutes.
5. Stir the parsnip halfway through the cooking time.
6. Meanwhile, peel the garlic and crush it. Combine the crushed garlic with the ingredients for the dip. Stir to mix well.
7. When cooked, the parsnip sticks should be crisp. Remove the parsnip fries from the air fryer oven and serve with the dipping sauce.

Salmon Croquettes

Prep time: 15 minutes | Cook time: 10 minutes | Serves 6

2 egg whites
1 cup almond flour
1 cup panko bread crumbs
1 pound (454 g) chopped salmon fillet
⅔ cup grated carrots

2 tablespoons minced garlic cloves
½ cup chopped onion
2 tablespoons chopped chives
Cooking spray

1. Spritz the air flow racks with cooking spray.
2. Whisk the egg whites in a bowl. Put the flour in a second bowl. Pour the bread crumbs in a third bowl. Set aside.
3. Combine the salmon, carrots, garlic, onion, and chives in a large bowl. Stir to mix well.
4. Form the mixture into balls with your hands. Dredge the balls into the flour, then egg, and then bread crumbs to coat well.
5. Arrange the salmon balls on the air flow racks and spritz with cooking spray.
6. Slide the racks into the air fryer oven. Press the Power Button and cook at 350ºF (180ºC) for 10 minutes.
7. Flip the salmon balls halfway through cooking.
8. When cooking is complete, the salmon balls will be crispy and browned. Remove from the air fryer oven.
9. Serve immediately.

Lemon-Honey Pears

Prep time: 10 minutes | Cook time: 8 minutes | Serves 4

2 large Bartlett pears, peeled, cut in half, cored
3 tablespoons melted butter
½ teaspoon ground ginger
¼ teaspoon ground cardamom
3 tablespoons brown sugar
½ cup whole-milk ricotta cheese
1 teaspoon pure lemon extract
1 teaspoon pure almond extract
1 tablespoon honey, plus additional for drizzling

1. Toss the pears with butter, ginger, cardamom, and sugar in a large bowl. Toss to coat well. Arrange the pears in a baking pan, cut side down.
2. Slide the pan into the air fryer oven. Press the Power Button and cook at 375ºF (190ºC) for 8 minutes.
3. After 5 minutes, remove the pan and flip the pears. Return to the air fryer oven and continue cooking.
4. When cooking is complete, the pears should be soft and browned. Remove from the air fryer oven.
5. In the meantime, combine the remaining ingredients in a separate bowl. Whip for 1 minute with a hand mixer until the mixture is puffed.
6. Divide the mixture into four bowls, then put the pears over the mixture and drizzle with more honey to serve.

Southwest Roasted Corn

Prep time: 10 minutes | Cook time: 10 minutes | Serves 4

Corn:
1½ cups thawed frozen corn kernels
1 cup mixed diced bell peppers
1 jalapeño, diced
1 cup diced yellow onion
½ teaspoon ancho
chile powder
1 tablespoon fresh lemon juice
1 teaspoon ground cumin
½ teaspoon kosher salt
Cooking spray
For Serving:
¼ cup feta cheese
¼ cup chopped fresh cilantro
1 tablespoon fresh lemon juice

1. Spritz the air flow racks with cooking spray.
2. Combine the ingredients for the corn in a large bowl. Stir to mix well.
3. Pour the mixture into the air flow racks.
4. Slide the racks into the air fryer oven. Press the Power Button and cook at 375ºF (190ºC) for 10 minutes.
5. Stir the mixture halfway through the cooking time.
6. When done, the corn and bell peppers should be soft.
7. Transfer them onto a large plate, then spread with feta cheese and cilantro. Drizzle with lemon juice and serve.

Spiralized Squash

Prep time: 10 minutes | Cook time: 10 minutes | Serves 4

2 large zucchini, peeled and spiralized
2 large yellow summer squash, peeled and spiralized
1 tablespoon olive oil, divided
½ teaspoon kosher salt
1 garlic clove, whole
2 tablespoons fresh basil, chopped
Cooking spray

1. Spritz the air flow racks with cooking spray.
2. Combine the zucchini and summer squash with 1 teaspoon of the olive oil and salt in a large bowl. Toss to coat well.
3. Transfer the zucchini and summer squash to the air flow racks and add the garlic.
4. Slide the racks into the air fryer oven. Press the Power Button and cook at 360ºF (182ºC) for 10 minutes.
5. Stir the zucchini and summer squash halfway through the cooking time.
6. When cooked, the zucchini and summer squash will be tender and fragrant. Transfer the cooked zucchini and summer squash onto a plate and set aside.
7. Remove the garlic from the air fryer oven and allow to cool for 5 minutes. Mince the garlic and combine with remaining olive oil in a small bowl. Stir to mix well.
8. Drizzle the spiralized zucchini and summer squash with garlic oil and sprinkle with basil. Toss to serve.

Citrus Avocado Fries

Prep time: 10 minutes | Cook time: 8 minutes | Makes 12 fries

1 cup all-purpose flour
3 tablespoons lime juice
¾ cup orange juice
1¼ cups plain dried bread crumbs
1 cup yellow cornmeal
1½ tablespoons chile powder
2 large Hass avocados, peeled, pitted, and cut into wedges
Coarse sea salt, to taste
Cooking spray

1. Spritz the air flow racks with cooking spray.
2. Pour the flour in a bowl. Mix the lime juice with orange juice in a second bowl. Combine the bread crumbs, cornmeal, and chile powder in a third bowl.
3. Dip the avocado wedges in the bowl of flour to coat well, then dredge the wedges into the bowl of juice mixture, and then dunk the wedges in the bread crumbs mixture. Shake the excess off.
4. Arrange the coated avocado wedges in a single layer on the air flow racks. Spritz with cooking spray.
5. Slide the racks into the air fryer oven. Press the Power Button and cook at 400ºF (205ºC) for 8 minutes.
6. Stir the avocado wedges and sprinkle with salt halfway through the cooking time.
7. When cooking is complete, the avocado wedges should be tender and crispy.
8. Serve immediately.

Butternut Squash with Hazelnuts

Prep time: 10 minutes | Cook time: 23 minutes | Makes 3 cups

2 tablespoons whole hazelnuts
3 cups butternut squash, peeled, deseeded and cubed
¼ teaspoon kosher salt
¼ teaspoon freshly ground black pepper
2 teaspoons olive oil
Cooking spray

1. Spritz the air flow racks with cooking spray. Spread the hazelnuts on the racks.
2. Slide the racks into the air fryer oven. Press the Power Button and cook at 300ºF (150ºC) for 3 minutes.
3. When done, the hazelnuts should be soft. Remove from the air fryer oven. Chopped the hazelnuts roughly and transfer to a small bowl. Set aside.
4. Put the butternut squash in a large bowl, then sprinkle with salt and pepper and drizzle with olive oil. Toss to coat well. Transfer the squash to the lightly greased air flow racks.
5. Slide the racks into the air fryer oven. Press the Power Button and cook at 360ºF (182ºC) for 20 minutes.
6. Slide the racks into the air fryer oven. Flip the squash halfway through the cooking time.
7. When cooking is complete, the squash will be soft. Transfer the squash to a plate and sprinkle with the chopped hazelnuts before serving.

Gold Tomatoes Slices

Prep time: 10 minutes | Cook time: 8 minutes | Makes 12 slices

½ cup all-purpose flour
1 egg
½ cup buttermilk
1 cup cornmeal
1 cup panko bread crumbs
2 green tomatoes, cut into ¼-inch-thick slices, patted dry
½ teaspoon salt
½ teaspoon ground black pepper
Cooking spray

1. Spritz a baking sheet with cooking spray.
2. Pour the flour in a bowl. Whisk the egg and buttermilk in a second bowl. Combine the cornmeal and panko in a third bowl.
3. Dredge the tomato slices in the bowl of flour first, then into the egg mixture, and then dunk the slices into the cornmeal mixture. Shake the excess off.
4. Transfer the well-coated tomato slices in the baking sheet and sprinkle with salt and ground black pepper. Spritz the tomato slices with cooking spray.
5. Slide the baking sheet into the air fryer oven. Press the Power Button and cook at 400ºF (205ºC) for 8 minutes.
6. Flip the slices halfway through the cooking time.
7. When cooking is complete, the tomato slices should be crispy and lightly browned. Remove the baking sheet from the air fryer oven.
8. Serve immediately.

Chapter 5 Vegan and Vegetarian

Lemon Brussels Sprouts with Tomatoes

Prep time: 15 minutes | Cook time: 20 minutes | Serves 4

1 pound (454 g) Brussels sprouts, trimmed and halved
1 tablespoon extra-virgin olive oil
Sea Salt and freshly ground black pepper, to taste
½ cup sun-dried tomatoes, chopped
2 tablespoons freshly squeezed lemon juice
1 teaspoon lemon zest

1. Line a large baking sheet with aluminum foil.
2. Toss the Brussels sprouts with the olive oil in a large bowl. Sprinkle with salt and black pepper.
3. Spread the Brussels sprouts in a single layer on the baking sheet.
4. Slide the baking sheet into the air fryer oven. Press the Power Button and cook at 400ºF (205ºC) for 20 minutes.
5. When done, the Brussels sprouts should be caramelized. Remove from the air fryer oven to a serving bowl, along with the tomatoes, lemon juice, and lemon zest. Toss to combine. Serve immediately.

Lemon Wax Beans

Prep time: 5 minutes | Cook time: 12 minutes | Serves 4

2 pounds (907 g) wax beans
2 tablespoons extra-virgin olive oil
Salt and freshly ground black pepper, to taste
Juice of ½ lemon, for serving

1. Line a baking sheet with aluminum foil.
2. Toss the wax beans with the olive oil in a large bowl. Lightly season with salt and pepper.
3. Spread out the wax beans on the baking sheet.
4. Put the baking sheet into the air fryer oven. Press the Power Button and cook at 400ºF (205ºC) for 12 minutes.
5. When done, the beans will be caramelized and tender. Remove from the air fryer oven to a plate and serve sprinkled with the lemon juice.

Mediterranean Spinach Frittata

Prep time: 10 minutes | Cook time: 10 minutes | Serves 2

2 tablespoons olive oil
4 eggs, whisked
5 ounces (142 g) fresh spinach, chopped
1 medium tomato, chopped
1 teaspoon fresh
lemon juice
½ teaspoon ground black pepper
½ teaspoon coarse salt
½ cup roughly chopped fresh basil leaves, for garnish

1. Generously grease a baking pan with olive oil.
2. Stir together the remaining ingredients except the basil leaves in the greased baking pan until well incorporated.
3. Slide the baking pan in the air fryer oven. Press the Power Button and cook at 280ºF (137ºC) for 10 minutes.
4. When cooking is complete, the eggs should be completely set and the vegetables should be tender. Remove from the air fryer oven and serve garnished with the fresh basil leaves.

Mozzarella Cabbage Wedges

Prep time: 5 minutes | Cook time: 20 minutes | Serves 4

4 tablespoons melted butter
1 head cabbage, cut into wedges
1 cup shredded
Parmesan cheese
Salt and black pepper, to taste
½ cup shredded Mozzarella cheese

1. Brush the melted butter over the cut sides of cabbage wedges and sprinkle both sides with the Parmesan cheese. Season with salt and pepper to taste.
2. Put the cabbage wedges on the air flow racks.
3. Slide the racks into the air fryer oven. Press the Power Button and cook at 380ºF (193ºC) for 20 minutes.
4. Flip the cabbage halfway through the cooking time.
5. When cooking is complete, the cabbage wedges should be lightly browned. Transfer the cabbage wedges to a plate and serve with the Mozzarella cheese sprinkled on top.

Paprika Cauliflower Florets

Prep time: 10 minutes | Cook time: 20 minutes | Serves 4

1 large head cauliflower, broken into small florets
2 teaspoons smoked paprika
1 teaspoon garlic powder
Salt and freshly ground black pepper, to taste
Cooking spray

1. Spray the air flow racks with cooking spray.
2. In a medium bowl, toss the cauliflower florets with the smoked paprika and garlic powder until evenly coated. Sprinkle with salt and pepper.
3. Put the cauliflower florets on the air flow racks and lightly mist with cooking spray.
4. Slide the racks into the air fryer oven. Press the Power Button and cook at 400ºF (205ºC) for 20 minutes.
5. Stir the cauliflower four times during cooking.
6. Remove the cauliflower from the air fryer oven and serve hot.

Pecan Granola

Prep time: 5 minutes | Cook time: 20 minutes | Serves 4

1½ cups rolled oats
¼ cup maple syrup
¼ cup pecan pieces
1 teaspoon vanilla
extract
½ teaspoon ground cinnamon

1. Line a baking sheet with parchment paper.
2. Mix together the oats, maple syrup, pecan pieces, vanilla, and cinnamon in a large bowl and stir until the oats and pecan pieces are completely coated. Spread the mixture evenly on the baking sheet.
3. Slide the baking sheet into the air fryer oven. Press the Power Button and cook at 300ºF (150ºC) for 20 minutes.
4. Stir once halfway through the cooking time.
5. When done, remove from the air fryer oven and cool for 30 minutes before serving. The granola may still be a bit soft right after removing, but it will gradually firm up as it cools.

Garlic Stuffed Mushrooms

Prep time: 5 minutes | Cook time: 12 minutes | Serves 2

18 medium white mushrooms
1 small onion, peeled and chopped
4 garlic cloves, peeled and minced
2 tablespoons olive oil
2 teaspoons cumin powder
Pinch ground allspice
Fine sea salt and freshly ground black pepper, to taste

1. On a clean work surface, remove the mushroom stems. Using a spoon, scoop out the mushroom gills and discard.
2. Thoroughly combine the onion, garlic, olive oil, cumin powder, allspice, salt, and pepper in a mixing bowl. Stuff the mushrooms evenly with the mixture.
3. Put the stuffed mushrooms on the air flow racks.
4. Slide the racks into the air fryer oven. Press the Power Button and cook at 345ºF (174ºC) for 12 minutes.
5. When cooking is complete, the mushroom should be browned.
6. Cool for 5 minutes before serving.

Celery Roots with Butter and Cinnamon

Prep time: 10 minutes | Cook time: 20 minutes | Serves 4

2 celery roots, peeled and diced
1 teaspoon extra-virgin olive oil
1 teaspoon butter, melted
½ teaspoon ground cinnamon
Sea salt and freshly ground black pepper, to taste

1. Line a baking sheet with aluminum foil.
2. Toss the celery roots with the olive oil in a large bowl until well coated. Transfer them to the prepared baking sheet.
3. Slide the baking sheet into the air fryer oven. Press the Power Button and cook at 350ºF (180ºC) for 20 minutes.
4. When done, the celery roots should be tender. Remove from the air fryer oven to a serving bowl. Stir in the butter and cinnamon and mash them with a potato masher until fluffy.
5. Season with salt and pepper to taste. Serve immediately.

Air Fried Tofu

Prep time: 5 minutes | Cook time: 10 minutes | Serves 2

1 tablespoon soy sauce
1 tablespoon water
$\frac{1}{3}$ teaspoon garlic powder
$\frac{1}{3}$ teaspoon onion powder
$\frac{1}{3}$ teaspoon dried oregano
$\frac{1}{3}$ teaspoon dried basil
Black pepper, to taste
6 ounces (170 g) extra firm tofu, pressed and cubed

1. In a large mixing bowl, whisk together the soy sauce, water, garlic powder, onion powder, oregano, basil, and black pepper. Add the tofu cubes, stirring to coat, and let them marinate for 10 minutes.
2. Arrange the tofu on the air flow racks.
3. Slide the racks into the air fryer oven. Press the Power Button and cook at 390°F (199°C) for 10 minutes.
4. Flip the tofu halfway through the cooking time.
5. When cooking is complete, the tofu should be crisp.
6. Remove from the air fryer oven to a plate and serve.

Vegetable Mélange

Prep time: 10 minutes | Cook time: 16 minutes | Serves 4

1 (8-ounce / 227-g) package sliced mushrooms
1 yellow summer squash, sliced
1 red bell pepper, sliced
3 cloves garlic, sliced
1 tablespoon olive oil
½ teaspoon dried basil
½ teaspoon dried thyme
½ teaspoon dried tarragon

1. Toss the mushrooms, squash, and bell pepper with the garlic and olive oil in a large bowl until well coated. Mix in the basil, thyme, and tarragon and toss again.
2. Spread the vegetables evenly on the air flow racks.
3. Slide the racks into the air fryer oven. Press the Power Button and cook at 350°F (180°C) for 16 minutes.
4. When cooking is complete, the vegetables should be fork-tender. Remove from the air fryer oven. Cool for 5 minutes before serving.

Zucchini and Turnip Bake

Prep time: 5 minutes | Cook time: 18 minutes | Serves 4

3 turnips, sliced
1 large zucchini, sliced
1 large red onion, cut into rings
2 cloves garlic, crushed
1 tablespoon olive oil
Salt and black pepper, to taste

1. Put the turnips, zucchini, red onion, and garlic in a baking pan. Drizzle the olive oil over the top and sprinkle with the salt and pepper.
2. Slide the pan into the air fryer oven. Press the Power Button and cook at 330°F (166°C) for 18 minutes.
3. When cooking is complete, the vegetables should be tender. Remove from the air fryer oven and serve on a plate.

Rosemary Broccoli Florets

Prep time: 5 minutes | Cook time: 18 minutes | Serves 4

1 large-sized head broccoli, stemmed and cut into small florets
2½ tablespoons canola oil
2 teaspoons dried basil
2 teaspoons dried rosemary
Salt and ground black pepper, to taste
$\frac{1}{3}$ cup grated yellow cheese

1. Bring a pot of lightly salted water to a boil. Add the broccoli florets to the boiling water and let boil for about 3 minutes.
2. Drain the broccoli florets well and transfer to a large bowl. Add the canola oil, basil, rosemary, salt, and black pepper to the bowl and toss until the broccoli is fully coated. Put the broccoli on the air flow racks.
3. Slide the racks into the air fryer oven. Press the Power Button and cook at 390°F (199°C) for 15 minutes.
4. Stir the broccoli halfway through the cooking time.
5. When cooking is complete, the broccoli should be crisp. Remove from the air fryer oven. Serve the broccoli warm with grated cheese sprinkled on top.

Chili Okra

Prep time: 5 minutes | Cook time: 10 minutes | Serves 4

3 tablespoons sour cream
2 tablespoons flour
2 tablespoons semolina
½ teaspoon red chili powder
Salt and black pepper, to taste
1 pound (454 g) okra, halved
Cooking spray

1. Spray the air flow racks with cooking spray. Set aside.
2. In a shallow bowl, place the sour cream. In another shallow bowl, thoroughly combine the flour, semolina, red chili powder, salt, and pepper.
3. Dredge the okra in the sour cream, then roll in the flour mixture until evenly coated. Transfer the okra to the air flow racks.
4. Slide the racks into the air fryer oven. Press the Power Button and cook at 400ºF (205ºC) for 10 minutes.
5. Flip the okra halfway through the cooking time.
6. When cooking is complete, the okra should be golden brown and crispy. Remove from the air fryer oven. Cool for 5 minutes before serving.

Honey-Dill Carrots

Prep time: 5 minutes | Cook time: 12 minutes | Serves 4

1 pound (454 g) baby carrots
2 tablespoons olive oil
1 tablespoon honey
1 teaspoon dried dill
Salt and black pepper, to taste

1. Put the carrots in a large bowl. Add the olive oil, honey, dill, salt, and pepper and toss to coat well.
2. Transfer the carrots to the air flow racks.
3. Slide the racks into the air fryer oven. Press the Power Button and cook at 350ºF (180ºC) for 12 minutes.
4. Stir the carrots once during cooking.
5. When cooking is complete, the carrots should be crisp-tender. Remove from the air fryer oven and serve warm.

Parmesan Green Beans

Prep time: 5 minutes | Cook time: 15 minutes | Serves 4

½ cup flour
2 eggs
1 cup panko bread crumbs
½ cup grated Parmesan cheese
1 teaspoon cayenne pepper
Salt and black pepper, to taste
1½ pounds (680 g) green beans

1. In a bowl, place the flour. In a separate bowl, lightly beat the eggs. In a separate shallow bowl, thoroughly combine the bread crumbs, cheese, cayenne pepper, salt, and pepper.
2. Dip the green beans in the flour, then in the beaten eggs, finally in the bread crumb mixture to coat well. Transfer the green beans to the air flow racks.
3. Slide the racks into the air fryer oven. Press the Power Button and cook at 400ºF (205ºC) for 15 minutes.
4. Stir the green beans halfway through the cooking time.
5. When cooking is complete, remove from the air fryer oven to a bowl and serve.

Stuffed Peppers with Cream Cheese

Prep time: 5 minutes | Cook time: 15 minutes | Serves 2

2 bell peppers, tops and seeds removed
Salt and pepper, to taste
⅔ cup cream cheese
2 tablespoons mayonnaise
1 tablespoon chopped fresh celery stalks
Cooking spray

1. Spritz the air flow racks with cooking spray.
2. Put the peppers on the air flow racks.
3. Slide the racks into the air fryer oven. Press the Power Button and cook at 400ºF (205ºC) for 10 minutes.
4. Flip the peppers halfway through.
5. When cooking is complete, the peppers should be crisp-tender.
6. Remove from the air fryer oven to a plate and season with salt and pepper.
7. Mix the cream cheese, mayo, and celery in a small bowl and stir to incorporate. Evenly stuff the peppers with the cream cheese mixture with a spoon. Serve immediately.

Ratatouille

Prep time: 15 minutes | Cook time: 16 minutes | Serves 2

2 Roma tomatoes, thinly sliced
1 zucchini, thinly sliced
2 yellow bell peppers, sliced
2 garlic cloves, minced
2 tablespoons olive oil
2 tablespoons herbes de Prair fryer ovence
1 tablespoon vinegar
Salt and black pepper, to taste

1. Put the tomatoes, zucchini, bell peppers, garlic, olive oil, herbes de Prair fryer ovence, and vinegar in a large bowl and toss until the vegetables are evenly coated. Sprinkle with salt and pepper and toss again. Pour the vegetable mixture into a baking dish.
2. Slide the baking dish into the air fryer oven. Press the Power Button and cook at 390ºF (199ºC) for 16 minutes.
3. Stir the vegetables halfway through.
4. When cooking is complete, the vegetables should be tender.
5. Let the vegetable mixture stand for 5 minutes in the air fryer oven before removing and serving.

Fried Zucchini and Eggplant

Prep time: 5 minutes | Cook time: 14 minutes | Serves 2

2 zucchinis, cut into even chunks
1 large eggplant, peeled, cut into chunks
1 large carrot, cut into chunks
6 ounces (170 g)
halloumi cheese, cubed
2 teaspoons olive oil
Salt and black pepper, to taste
1 teaspoon dried mixed herbs

1. Combine the zucchinis, eggplant, carrot, cheese, olive oil, salt, and pepper in a large bowl and toss to coat well.
2. Spread the mixture evenly on the air flow racks.
3. Slide the racks into the air fryer oven. Press the Power Button and cook at 340ºF (171ºC) for 14 minutes.
4. Stir the mixture once during cooking.
5. When cooking is complete, they should be crispy and golden. Remove from the air fryer oven and serve topped with mixed herbs.

Winter Vegetables

Prep time: 5 minutes | Cook time: 16 minutes | Serves 2

1 parsnip, sliced
1 cup sliced butternut squash
1 small red onion, cut into wedges
½ chopped celery
stalk
1 tablespoon chopped fresh thyme
2 teaspoons olive oil
Salt and black pepper, to taste

1. Toss all the ingredients in a large bowl until the vegetables are well coated.
2. Transfer the vegetables to the air flow racks.
3. Slide the racks into the air fryer oven. Press the Power Button and cook at 380ºF (193ºC) for 16 minutes.
4. Stir the vegetables halfway through the cooking time.
5. When cooking is complete, the vegetables should be golden brown and tender. Remove from the air fryer oven and serve warm.

Kung Pao Tofu

Prep time: 10 minutes | Cook time: 10 minutes | Serves 4

1/3 cup Asian-Style sauce
1 teaspoon cornstarch
½ teaspoon red pepper flakes, or more to taste
1 pound (454 g) firm or extra-firm tofu, cut into 1-inch cubes
1 small carrot, peeled
and cut into ¼-inch-thick coins
1 small green bell pepper, cut into bite-size pieces
3 scallions, sliced, whites and green parts separated
3 tablespoons roasted unsalted peanuts

1. In a large bowl, whisk together the sauce, cornstarch, and red pepper flakes. Fold in the tofu, carrot, pepper, and the white parts of the scallions and toss to coat. Spread the mixture evenly on a sheet pan.
2. Slide the pan into the air flow racks. Press the Power Button and cook at 375ºF (190ºC) for 10 minutes.
3. Stir the ingredients once halfway through the cooking time.
4. When done, remove from the air fryer oven. Serve sprinkled with the peanuts and scallion greens.

Parmesan Brussels Sprouts

Prep time: 10 minutes | Cook time: 20 minutes | Serves 4

1 pound (454 g) fresh Brussels sprouts, trimmed
1 tablespoon olive oil
½ teaspoon salt
⅛ teaspoon pepper
¼ cup grated Parmesan cheese

1. In a large bowl, combine the Brussels sprouts with olive oil, salt, and pepper and toss until evenly coated.
2. Spread the Brussels sprouts evenly on the air flow racks.
3. Slide the racks into the air fryer oven. Press the Power Button and cook at 330ºF (166ºC) for 20 minutes.
4. Stir the Brussels sprouts twice during cooking.
5. When cooking is complete, the Brussels sprouts should be golden brown and crisp. Remove from the air fryer oven. Sprinkle the grated Parmesan cheese on top and serve warm.

Basil Eggplant and Bell Peppers

Prep time: 15 minutes | Cook time: 20 minutes | Serves 2

1 small eggplant, halved and sliced
1 yellow bell pepper, cut into thick strips
1 red bell pepper, cut into thick strips
2 garlic cloves, quartered
1 red onion, sliced
1 tablespoon extra-virgin olive oil
Salt and freshly ground black pepper, to taste
½ cup chopped fresh basil, for garnish
Cooking spray

1. Grease a nonstick baking dish with cooking spray.
2. Put the eggplant, bell peppers, garlic, and red onion in the greased baking dish. Drizzle with the olive oil and toss to coat well. Spritz any uncoated surfaces with cooking spray.
3. Slide the baking dish into the air fryer oven. Press the Power Button and cook at 350ºF (180ºC) for 20 minutes.
4. Flip the vegetables halfway through the cooking time.
5. When done, remove from the air fryer oven and sprinkle with salt and pepper.
6. Sprinkle the basil on top for garnish and serve.

Vegetable Bowl

Prep time: 5 minutes | Cook time: 12 minutes | Serves 4

2 teaspoons melted butter
1 cup chopped mushrooms
1 cup cooked rice
1 cup peas
1 carrot, chopped
1 red onion, chopped
1 garlic clove, minced
Salt and black pepper, to taste
2 hard-boiled eggs, grated
1 tablespoon soy sauce

1. Coat a baking dish with melted butter.
2. Stir together the mushrooms, cooked rice, peas, carrot, onion, garlic, salt, and pepper in a large bowl until well mixed. Pour the mixture into the prepared baking dish.
3. Slide the baking dish into the air fryer oven. Press the Power Button and cook at 380ºF (193ºC) for 12 minutes.
4. When cooking is complete, remove from the air fryer oven. Divide the mixture among four plates. Serve warm with a sprinkle of grated eggs and a drizzle of soy sauce.

Sesame Baby Carrots

Prep time: 5 minutes | Cook time: 16 minutes | Serves 4 to 6

1 pound (454 g) baby carrots
1 tablespoon sesame oil
½ teaspoon dried dill
Pinch salt
Freshly ground black pepper, to taste
6 cloves garlic, peeled
3 tablespoons sesame seeds

1. In a medium bowl, drizzle the baby carrots with the sesame oil. Sprinkle with the dill, salt, and pepper and toss to coat well.
2. Put the baby carrots on the air flow racks.
3. Slide the racks into the air fryer oven. Press the Power Button and cook at 380ºF (193ºC) for 16 minutes.
4. After 8 minutes, remove from the air fryer oven and stir in the garlic. Return to the air fryer oven and continue cooking for 8 minutes more.
5. When cooking is complete, the carrots should be lightly browned. Remove the racks from the air fryer oven and serve sprinkled with the sesame seeds.

Crunchy Eggplant Slices

Prep time: 5 minutes | Cook time: 12 minutes | Serves 4

1 cup all-purpose flour
4 eggs
Salt, to taste
2 cups bread crumbs
1 teaspoon Italian seasoning
2 medium eggplants, sliced
2 garlic cloves, sliced
2 tablespoons chopped parsley
Cooking spray

1. Spritz the air flow racks with cooking spray. Set aside.
2. On a plate, place the flour. In a shallow bowl, whisk the eggs with salt. In another shallow bowl, combine the bread crumbs and Italian seasoning.
3. Dredge the eggplant slices, one at a time, in the flour, then in the whisked eggs, finally in the bread crumb mixture to coat well.
4. Lay the coated eggplant slices on the air flow racks.
5. Slide the racks into the air fryer oven. Press the Power Button and cook at 390ºF (199ºC) for 12 minutes.
6. Flip the eggplant slices halfway through the cooking time.
7. When cooking is complete, the eggplant slices should be golden brown and crispy. Transfer the eggplant slices to a plate and sprinkle the garlic and parsley on top before serving.

Eggplant with Yogurt Sauce

Prep time: 5 minutes | Cook time: 15 minutes | Serves 2

1 medium eggplant, quartered and cut crosswise into ½-inch-thick slices
2 tablespoons
vegetable oil
Kosher salt and freshly ground black pepper, to taste

Yogurt Sauce:
½ cup plain yogurt (not Greek)
2 tablespoons Harissa
paste
1 garlic clove, grated
2 teaspoons honey

1. Toss the eggplant slices with the vegetable oil, salt, and pepper in a large bowl until well coated.
2. Lay the eggplant slices on the air flow racks.

3. Slide the racks into the air fryer oven. Press the Power Button and cook at 400ºF (205ºC) for 15 minutes.
4. Stir the slices two to three times during cooking.
5. Meanwhile, make the yogurt sauce by whisking together the yogurt, Harissa paste, and garlic in a small bowl.
6. When cooking is complete, the eggplant slices should be golden brown. Spread the yogurt sauce on a platter, and pile the eggplant slices over the top. Serve drizzled with the honey.

Turmeric Vegetable Salad

Prep time: 5 minutes | Cook time: 20 minutes | Serves 2

1 potato, chopped
1 carrot, sliced diagonally
1 cup cherry tomatoes
½ small beetroot, sliced
¼ onion, sliced
½ teaspoon turmeric
½ teaspoon cumin
¼ teaspoon sea salt
2 tablespoons olive oil, divided
A handful of arugula
A handful of baby spinach
Juice of 1 lemon
3 tablespoons canned chickpeas, for serving
Parmesan shavings, for serving

1. Combine the potato, carrot, cherry tomatoes, beetroot, onion, turmeric, cumin, salt, and 1 tablespoon of olive oil in a large bowl and toss until well coated.
2. Arrange the vegetables on the air flow racks.
3. Slide the racks into the air fryer oven. Press the Power Button and cook at 370ºF (188ºC) for 20 minutes.
4. Stir the vegetables halfway through.
5. When cooking is complete, the potatoes should be golden brown.
6. Let the vegetables cool for 5 to 10 minutes in the air fryer oven.
7. Put the arugula, baby spinach, lemon juice, and remaining 1 tablespoon of olive oil in a salad bowl and stir to combine. Mix in the roasted vegetables and toss well.
8. Scatter the chickpeas and Parmesan shavings on top and serve immediately.

Root Vegetable Medley

Prep time: 10 minutes | Cook time: 22 minutes | Serves 4

2 carrots, sliced
2 potatoes, cut into chunks
1 rutabaga, cut into chunks
1 turnip, cut into chunks
1 beet, cut into chunks

8 shallots, halved
2 tablespoons olive oil
Salt and black pepper, to taste
2 tablespoons tomato pesto
2 tablespoons water
2 tablespoons chopped fresh thyme

1. Toss the carrots, potatoes, rutabaga, turnip, beet, shallots, olive oil, salt, and pepper in a large mixing bowl until the root vegetables are evenly coated.
2. Put the root vegetables on the air flow racks.
3. Slide the racks into the air fryer oven. Press the Power Button and cook at 400ºF (205ºC) for 22 minutes.
4. Stir the vegetables twice during cooking.
5. When cooking is complete, the vegetables should be tender.
6. Meanwhile, in a small bowl, whisk together the tomato pesto and water until smooth.
7. When ready, remove the root vegetables from the air fryer oven to a platter. Drizzle with the tomato pesto mixture and sprinkle with the thyme. Serve immediately.

Roasted Bell Peppers

Prep time: 10 minutes | Cook time: 22 minutes | Serves 4

1 green bell pepper, sliced into 1-inch strips
1 red bell pepper, sliced into 1-inch strips
1 orange bell pepper, sliced into 1-inch strips
1 yellow bell pepper,

sliced into 1-inch strips
2 tablespoons olive oil, divided
½ teaspoon dried marjoram
Pinch salt
Freshly ground black pepper, to taste
1 head garlic

1. Toss the bell peppers with 1 tablespoon of olive oil in a large bowl until well coated. Season with the marjoram, salt, and pepper. Toss again and set aside.
2. Cut off the top of a head of garlic. Put the garlic cloves on a large square of aluminum foil. Drizzle the top with the remaining 1 tablespoon of olive oil and wrap the garlic cloves in foil.
3. Transfer the garlic to the air flow racks.
4. Slide the racks into the air fryer oven. Press the Power Button and cook at 330ºF (166ºC) for 15 minutes.
5. After 15 minutes, remove the air flow racks from the air fryer oven and add the bell peppers. Return to the air fryer oven for 7 minutes.
6. When cooking is complete or until the garlic is soft and the bell peppers are tender.
7. Transfer the cooked bell peppers to a plate. Remove the garlic and unwrap the foil. Let the garlic rest for a few minutes. Once cooled, squeeze the garlic cloves out of their skins and add them to the plate of bell peppers. Stir well and serve immediately.

Tofu Sticks

Prep time: 5 minutes | Cook time: 14 minutes | Serves 4

2 tablespoons olive oil, divided
½ cup flour
½ cup crushed cornflakes

Salt and black pepper, to taste
14 ounces (397 g) firm tofu, cut into ½-inch-thick strips

1. Grease the air flow racks with 1 tablespoon of olive oil.
2. Combine the flour, cornflakes, salt, and pepper on a plate.
3. Dredge the tofu strips in the flour mixture until they are completely coated. Transfer the tofu strips to the greased air flow racks.
4. Drizzle the remaining 1 tablespoon of olive oil over the top of tofu strips.
5. Slide the racks into the air fryer oven. Press the Power Button and cook at 360ºF (182ºC) for 14 minutes.
6. Flip the tofu strips halfway through the cooking time.
7. When cooking is complete, the tofu strips should be crispy. Remove from the air fryer oven and serve warm.

Rice Stuffed Bell Peppers

Prep time: 5 minutes | Cook time: 16 to 17 minutes | Serves 4

ell peppers, tops sliced off
2 cups cooked rice
1 cup crumbled feta cheese
1 onion, chopped
¼ cup sliced kalamata olives

¾ cup tomato sauce
1 tablespoon Greek seasoning
Salt and black pepper, to taste
2 tablespoons chopped fresh dill, for serving

1. Microwave the red bell peppers for 1 to 2 minutes until tender.
2. When ready, transfer the red bell peppers to a plate to cool.
3. Mix the cooked rice, feta cheese, onion, kalamata olives, tomato sauce, Greek seasoning, salt, and pepper in a medium bowl and stir until well combined.
4. Divide the rice mixture among the red bell peppers and transfer to a greased baking dish.
5. Slide the baking dish into the air fryer oven. Press the Power Button and cook at 360°F (182°C) for 15 minutes.
6. When cooking is complete, the rice should be heated through and the vegetables should be soft.
7. Remove from the air fryer oven and serve with the dill sprinkled on top.

Rosemary Butternut Squash

Prep time: 5 minutes | Cook time: 20 minutes | Serves 2

1 pound (454 g) butternut squash, cut into wedges
2 tablespoons olive oil
1 tablespoon dried rosemary

Salt, to salt
1 cup crumbled goat cheese
1 tablespoon maple syrup

1. Toss the squash wedges with the olive oil, rosemary, and salt in a large bowl until well coated.
2. Transfer the squash wedges to the air flow racks, spreading them out in as even a layer as possible.
3. Slide the racks into the air fryer oven. Press the Power Button and cook at 350°F (180°C) for 20 minutes.
4. After 10 minutes, remove from the air fryer oven and flip the squash. Return to the air fryer oven and continue cooking for 10 minutes.
5. When cooking is complete, the squash should be golden brown. Remove from the air fryer oven. Sprinkle the goat cheese on top and serve drizzled with the maple syrup.

Lush Vegetable Balls

Prep time: 15 minutes | Cook time: 18 minutes | Serves 3

½ cup grated carrots
½ cup sweet onions
2 tablespoons olive oil
1 cup rolled oats
½ cup roasted cashews
2 cups cooked chickpeas
Juice of 1 lemon

2 tablespoons soy sauce
1 tablespoon flax meal
1 teaspoon garlic powder
1 teaspoon cumin
½ teaspoon turmeric

1. Mix the carrots, onions, and olive oil in a baking dish and stir to combine.
2. Slide the baking dish into the air fryer oven. Press the Power Button and cook at 350°F (180°C) for 6 minutes.
3. Stir the vegetables halfway through.
4. When cooking is complete, the vegetables should be tender.
5. Meanwhile, put the oats and cashews in a food processor or blender and pulse until coarsely ground. Transfer the mixture to a large bowl. Add the chickpeas, lemon juice, and soy sauce to the food processor and pulse until smooth. Transfer the chickpea mixture to the bowl of oat and cashew mixture.
6. Remove the carrots and onions from the air fryer oven to the bowl of chickpea mixture. Add the flax meal, garlic powder, cumin, and turmeric and stir to incorporate.
7. Scoop tablespoon-sized portions of the veggie mixture and roll them into balls with your hands. Transfer the balls to the air flow racks.
8. Increase the temperature to 370°F (188°C) and cook for 12 minutes. Flip the balls halfway through the cooking time.
9. When cooking is complete, the balls should be golden brown.
10. Serve warm.

Asparagus and Tomato Frittata

Prep time: 10 minutes | Cook time: 12 minutes | Serves 4

2 pounds (907 g) asparagus, trimmed
3 tablespoons extra-virgin olive oil, divided
1 teaspoon kosher salt, divided
1 pint cherry tomatoes
4 large eggs
¼ teaspoon freshly ground black pepper

1. Put the asparagus on a sheet pan and drizzle with 2 tablespoons of olive oil, tossing to coat. Season with ½ teaspoon of kosher salt.
2. Slide the pan into the air fryer oven. Press the Power Button and cook at 375ºF (190ºC) for 12 minutes.
3. Meanwhile, toss the cherry tomatoes with the remaining 1 tablespoon of olive oil in a medium bowl until well coated.
4. After 6 minutes, remove the pan and toss the asparagus. Evenly spread the asparagus in the middle of the sheet pan. Add the tomatoes around the perimeter of the pan. Return to the air fryer oven and continue cooking.
5. After 2 minutes, remove from the air fryer oven.
6. Carefully crack the eggs, one at a time, over the asparagus, spacing them out. Season with the remaining ½ teaspoon of kosher salt and the pepper. Return to the air fryer oven and continue cooking. Cook for an additional 3 to 7 minutes, or until the eggs are cooked to your desired doneness.
7. When done, divide the asparagus and eggs among four plates. Top each plate evenly with the tomatoes and serve.

Salsa Black Bean and Cheese Tacos

Prep time: 12 minutes | Cook time: 7 minutes | Serves 4

1 (15-ounce / 425-g) can black beans, drained and rinsed
½ cup prepared salsa
1½ teaspoons chili powder
4 ounces (113 g) grated Monterey Jack cheese
2 tablespoons minced onion
8 (6-inch) flour tortillas
2 tablespoons vegetable or extra-virgin olive oil
Shredded lettuce, for serving

1. In a medium bowl, add the beans, salsa and chili powder. Coarsely mash them with a potato masher. Fold in the cheese and onion and stir until combined.
2. Arrange the flour tortillas on a cutting board and spoon 2 to 3 tablespoons of the filling into each tortilla. Fold the tortillas over, pressing lightly to even out the filling. Brush the tacos on one side with half the olive oil and put them, oiled side down, on a sheet pan. Brush the top side with the remaining olive oil.
3. Slide the pan into the air fryer oven. Press the Power Button and cook at 400ºF (205ºC) for 7 minutes.
4. Flip the tacos halfway through the cooking time.
5. Remove the pan from the air fryer oven and allow to cool for 5 minutes. Serve with the shredded lettuce on the side.

Zucchini Chips

Prep time: 5 minutes | Cook time: 14 minutes | Serves 4

2 egg whites
Salt and black pepper, to taste
½ cup seasoned bread crumbs
2 tablespoons grated
Parmesan cheese
¼ teaspoon garlic powder
2 medium zucchini, sliced
Cooking spray

1. Spritz the air flow racks with cooking spray.
2. In a bowl, beat the egg whites with salt and pepper. In a separate bowl, thoroughly combine the bread crumbs, Parmesan cheese, and garlic powder.
3. Dredge the zucchini slices in the egg white, then coat in the bread crumb mixture.
4. Arrange the zucchini slices on the air flow racks.
5. Slide the racks into the air fryer oven. Press the Power Button and cook at 400ºF (205ºC) for 14 minutes.
6. Flip the zucchini halfway through.
7. When cooking is complete, the zucchini should be tender.
8. Remove from the air fryer oven to a plate and serve.

Sesame Maitake Mushrooms

Prep time: 5 minutes | Cook time: 15 minutes | Serves 2

1 tablespoon soy sauce	maitake (hen of the woods) mushrooms
2 teaspoons toasted sesame oil	½ teaspoon sea salt
3 teaspoons vegetable oil, divided	½ teaspoon sesame seeds
1 garlic clove, minced	½ teaspoon finely chopped fresh thyme leaves
7 ounces (198 g)	

1. Whisk together the soy sauce, sesame oil, 1 teaspoon of vegetable oil, and garlic in a small bowl.
2. Arrange the mushrooms on the air flow racks. Drizzle the soy sauce mixture over the mushrooms.
3. Slide the racks into the air fryer oven. Press the Power Button and cook at 300ºF (150ºC) for 15 minutes.
4. After 10 minutes, remove from the air fryer oven. Flip the mushrooms and sprinkle the sea salt, sesame seeds, and thyme leaves on top. Drizzle the remaining 2 teaspoons of vegetable oil all over. Return to the air fryer oven and continue cooking for an additional 5 minutes.
5. When cooking is complete, remove the mushrooms from the air fryer oven to a plate and serve hot.

Teriyaki Cauliflower

Prep time: 5 minutes | Cook time: 14 minutes | Serves 4

½ cup soy sauce	2 cloves garlic, chopped
1/3 cup water	½ teaspoon chili powder
1 tablespoon brown sugar	1 big cauliflower head, cut into florets
1 teaspoon sesame oil	
1 teaspoon cornstarch	

1. Make the teriyaki sauce: In a small bowl, whisk together the soy sauce, water, brown sugar, sesame oil, cornstarch, garlic, and chili powder until well combined.
2. Put the cauliflower florets in a large bowl and drizzle the top with the prepared teriyaki sauce and toss to coat well.
3. Put the cauliflower florets on the air flow racks.
4. Slide the racks into the air fryer oven. Press the Power Button and cook at 340ºF (171ºC) for 14 minutes.
5. Stir the cauliflower halfway through.
6. When cooking is complete, the cauliflower should be crisp-tender.
7. Let the cauliflower cool for 5 minutes before serving.

Spicy and Sweet Broccoli

Prep time: 10 minutes | Cook time: 15 to 20 minutes | Serves 4

½ teaspoon olive oil, plus more for greasing	florets
	½ tablespoon minced garlic
1 pound (454 g) fresh broccoli, cut into	Salt, to taste
Sauce:	
1½ tablespoons soy sauce	1 teaspoon white vinegar
2 teaspoons hot sauce or sriracha	Freshly ground black pepper, to taste
1½ teaspoons honey	

1. Grease the air flow racks with olive oil.
2. Add the broccoli florets, ½ teaspoon of olive oil, and garlic to a large bowl and toss well. Season with salt to taste.
3. Put the broccoli on the air flow racks.
4. Slide the racks into the air fryer oven. Press the Power Button and cook at 400ºF (205ºC) for 15 minutes.
5. Stir the broccoli florets three times during cooking.
6. Meanwhile, whisk together all the ingredients for the sauce in a small bowl until well incorporated. If the honey doesn't incorporate well, microwave the sauce for 10 to 20 seconds until the honey is melted.
7. When cooking is complete, the broccoli should be lightly browned and crispy. Continue cooking for 5 minutes, if desired. Remove from the air fryer oven to a serving bowl. Pour over the sauce and toss to combine. Add more salt and pepper, if needed. Serve warm.

Stuffed Beefsteak Tomatoes

Prep time: 10 minutes | Cook time: 18 minutes | Serves 4

4 medium beefsteak tomatoes, rinsed
½ cup grated carrot
1 medium onion, chopped
1 garlic clove, minced
2 teaspoons olive oil

2 cups fresh baby spinach
¼ cup crumbled low-sodium feta cheese
½ teaspoon dried basil

1. On your cutting board, cut a thin slice off the top of each tomato. Scoop out a ¼- to ½-inch-thick tomato pulp and place the tomatoes upside down on paper towels to drain. Set aside.
2. Stir together the carrot, onion, garlic, and olive oil in a baking pan.
3. Slide the pan into the air fryer oven. Press the Power Button and cook at 350°F (180°C) for 5 minutes.
4. Stir the vegetables halfway through.
5. When cooking is complete, the carrot should be crisp-tender.
6. Remove the pan from the air fryer oven and stir in the spinach, feta cheese, and basil.
7. Spoon ¼ of the vegetable mixture into each tomato and transfer the stuffed tomatoes to the air fryer oven. Set time to 13 minutes.
8. When cooking is complete, the filling should be hot and the tomatoes should be lightly caramelized.
9. Let the tomatoes cool for 5 minutes and serve.

Tahini Kale

Prep time: 5 minutes | Cook time: 15 minutes | Serves 2 to 4

Dressing:
¼ cup tahini
¼ cup fresh lemon juice
2 tablespoons olive oil
1 teaspoon sesame

seeds
½ teaspoon garlic powder
¼ teaspoon cayenne pepper

Kale:
4 cups packed torn kale leaves, stems and ribs removed and leaves torn into palm-

size pieces
Kosher salt and freshly ground black pepper, to taste

1. Make the dressing: Whisk together the tahini, lemon juice, olive oil, sesame seeds, garlic powder, and cayenne pepper in a large bowl until well mixed.
2. Add the kale and massage the dressing thoroughly all over the leaves. Sprinkle the salt and pepper to season.
3. Put the kale on the air flow racks.
4. Slide the racks into the air fryer oven. Press the Power Button and cook at 350°F (180°C) for 15 minutes.
5. When cooking is complete, the leaves should be slightly wilted and crispy. Remove from the air fryer oven and serve on a plate.

Walnut Stuffed Portobello Mushrooms

Prep time: 5 minutes | Cook time: 10 minutes | Serves 4

4 large portobello mushrooms
1 tablespoon canola oil
½ cup shredded Mozzarella cheese

$1/3$ cup minced walnuts
2 tablespoons chopped fresh parsley
Cooking spray

1. Spritz the air flow racks with cooking spray.
2. On a clean work surface, remove the mushroom stems. Scoop out the gills with a spoon and discard. Coat the mushrooms with canola oil. Top each mushroom evenly with the shredded Mozzarella cheese, followed by the minced walnuts.
3. Arrange the mushrooms on the air flow racks.
4. Slide the racks into the air fryer oven. Press the Power Button and cook at 350°F (180°C) for 10 minutes.
5. When cooking is complete, the mushroom should be golden brown.
6. Transfer the mushrooms to a plate and sprinkle the parsley on top for garnish before serving.

Lush Ratatouille

Prep time: 10 minutes | Cook time: 12 minutes | Serves 6

1 medium zucchini, sliced ½-inch thick
1 small eggplant, peeled and sliced ½-inch thick
2 teaspoons kosher salt, divided
4 tablespoons extra-virgin olive oil, divided
3 garlic cloves, minced
1 small onion, chopped
1 small red bell pepper, cut into ½-inch chunks
1 small green bell pepper, cut into ½-inch chunks
½ teaspoon dried oregano
¼ teaspoon freshly ground black pepper
1 pint cherry tomatoes
2 tablespoons minced fresh basil
1 cup panko bread crumbs
½ cup grated Parmesan cheese (optional)

1. Season one side of the zucchini and eggplant slices with ¾ teaspoon of salt. Put the slices, salted side down, over a baking sheet. Sprinkle the other sides with ¾ teaspoon of salt. Allow to sit for 10 minutes, or until the slices begin to exude water. When ready, rinse and dry them. Cut the zucchini slices into quarters and the eggplant slices into eighths.
2. Pour the zucchini and eggplant into a large bowl, along with 2 tablespoons of olive oil, garlic, onion, bell peppers, oregano, and black pepper. Toss to coat well. Arrange the vegetables on a sheet pan.
3. Slide the pan into the air fryer oven. Press the Power Button and cook at 375°F (190°C) for 12 minutes.
4. Meanwhile, add the tomatoes and basil to the large bowl. Sprinkle with the remaining ½ teaspoon of salt and 1 tablespoon of olive oil. Toss well and set aside.
5. Stir together the remaining 1 tablespoon of olive oil, panko, and Parmesan cheese (if desired) in a small bowl.
6. After 6 minutes, remove the pan and add the tomato mixture to the sheet pan and stir to mix well. Scatter the panko mixture on top. Return to the air fryer oven and continue cooking for 6 minutes, or until the vegetables are softened and the topping is golden brown.
7. Cool for 5 minutes before serving.

Vegetable Stuffed Mushrooms

Prep time: 5 minutes | Cook time: 8 minutes | Serves 4

4 portobello mushrooms, stem removed
1 tablespoon olive oil
1 tomato, diced
½ green bell pepper, diced
½ small red onion, diced
½ teaspoon garlic powder
Salt and black pepper, to taste
½ cup grated Mozzarella cheese

1. Using a spoon to scoop out the gills of the mushrooms and discard them. Brush the mushrooms with the olive oil.
2. In a mixing bowl, stir together the remaining ingredients except the Mozzarella cheese. Using a spoon to stuff each mushroom with the filling and scatter the Mozzarella cheese on top.
3. Arrange the mushrooms on the air flow racks.
4. Slide the racks into the air fryer oven. Press the Power Button and cook at 330°F (166°C) for 8 minutes.
5. When cooking is complete, the cheese should be melted.
6. Serve warm.

Zucchini and Bell Pepper Quesadilla

Prep time: 5 minutes | Cook time: 10 minutes | Serves 1

1 teaspoon olive oil
2 flour tortillas
¼ zucchini, sliced
¼ yellow bell pepper, sliced
¼ cup shredded gouda cheese
1 tablespoon chopped cilantro
½ green onion, sliced

1. Coat the air flow racks with 1 teaspoon of olive oil.
2. Arrange a flour tortilla on the air flow racks and scatter the top with zucchini, bell pepper, gouda cheese, cilantro, and green onion. Put the other flour tortilla on top.
3. Slide the racks into the air fryer oven. Press the Power Button and cook at 390°F (199°C) for 10 minutes.
4. When cooking is complete, the tortillas should be lightly browned and the vegetables should be tender. Remove from the air fryer oven and cool for 5 minutes before slicing into wedges.

Yogurt Cauliflower with Cashews

Prep time: 5 minutes | Cook time: 12 minutes | Serves 2

4 cups cauliflower florets (about half a large head)
1 tablespoon olive oil
1 teaspoon curry

Yogurt Sauce:
¼ cup plain yogurt
2 tablespoons sour cream
1 teaspoon honey
1 teaspoon lemon juice

powder
Salt, to taste
½ cup toasted, chopped cashews, for garnish

Pinch cayenne pepper
Salt, to taste
1 tablespoon chopped fresh cilantro, plus leaves for garnish

1. In a large mixing bowl, toss the cauliflower florets with the olive oil, curry powder, and salt.
2. Put the cauliflower florets on the air flow racks.
3. Slide the racks into the air fryer oven. Press the Power Button and cook at 400ºF (205ºC) for 12 minutes.
4. Stir the cauliflower florets twice during cooking.
5. When cooking is complete, the cauliflower should be golden brown.
6. Meanwhile, mix all the ingredients for the yogurt sauce in a small bowl and whisk to combine.
7. Remove the cauliflower from the air fryer oven and drizzle with the yogurt sauce. Scatter the toasted cashews and cilantro on top and serve immediately.

Thai Vegetables with Mangoes and Nuts

Prep time: 10 minutes | Cook time: 8 minutes | Serves 4

1 small head Napa cabbage, shredded, divided
1 medium carrot, cut into thin coins
8 ounces (227 g) snow peas
1 red or green bell pepper, sliced into thin strips
1 tablespoon vegetable oil
2 tablespoons soy sauce
1 tablespoon sesame

oil
2 tablespoons brown sugar
2 tablespoons freshly squeezed lime juice
2 teaspoons red or green Thai curry paste
1 serrano chile, deseeded and minced
1 cup frozen mango slices, thawed
½ cup chopped roasted peanuts or cashews

1. Put half the Napa cabbage in a large bowl, along with the carrot, snow peas, and bell pepper. Drizzle with the vegetable oil and toss to coat. Spread them evenly on a sheet pan.
2. Slide the pan into the air fryer oven. Press the Power Button and cook at 375ºF (190ºC) for 8 minutes.
3. Meanwhile, whisk together the soy sauce, sesame oil, brown sugar, lime juice, and curry paste in a small bowl.
4. When done, the vegetables should be tender and crisp. Remove the pan and put the vegetables back into the bowl. Add the chile, mango slices, and the remaining cabbage. Pour over the dressing and toss to coat. Top with the roasted nuts and serve.

Chapter 6 Vegetable Sides

Cheese Crusted Brussels Sprouts

Prep time: 5 minutes | Cook time: 15 minutes | Serves 4

1 pound (454 g) Brussels sprouts, halved
1 cup bread crumbs
2 tablespoons grated Grana Padano cheese

1 tablespoon paprika
2 tablespoons canola oil
1 tablespoon chopped sage

1. Line the air flow racks with parchment paper. Set aside.
2. In a small bowl, thoroughly mix the bread crumbs, cheese, and paprika. In a large bowl, place the Brussels sprouts and drizzle the canola oil over the top. Sprinkle with the bread crumb mixture and toss to coat.
3. Transfer the Brussels sprouts to the prepared air flow racks.
4. Slide the racks into the air fryer oven. Press the Power Button and cook at 400ºF (205ºC) for 15 minutes.
5. Stir the Brussels a few times during cooking.
6. When cooking is complete, the Brussels sprouts should be lightly browned and crisp. Transfer the Brussels sprouts to a plate and sprinkle the sage on top before serving.

Scalloped Potatoes

Prep time: 5 minutes | Cook time: 15 to 20 minutes | Serves 4

2 cup sliced frozen potatoes, thawed
3 cloves garlic, minced

Pinch salt
Freshly ground black pepper, to taste
¾ cup heavy cream

1. Toss the potatoes with the garlic, salt, and black pepper in a baking pan until evenly coated. Pour the heavy cream over the top.
2. Slide the pan into the air fryer oven. Press the Power Button and cook at 380ºF (193ºC) for 15 minutes.
3. When cooking is complete, the potatoes should be tender and the top golden brown. Check for doneness and cook for another 5 minutes if needed. Remove from the air fryer oven and serve hot.

Yogurt Potatoes

Prep time: 5 minutes | Cook time: 35 minutes | Serves 4

4 (7-ounce / 198-g) russet potatoes, rinsed
Olive oil spray
½ teaspoon kosher salt, divided

½ cup 2% plain Greek yogurt
¼ cup minced fresh chives
Freshly ground black pepper, to taste

1. Pat the potatoes dry and pierce them all over with a fork. Spritz the potatoes with olive oil spray. Sprinkle with ¼ teaspoon of the salt.
2. Transfer the potatoes to the air flow racks.
3. Slide the racks into the air fryer oven. Press the Power Button and cook at 400ºF (205ºC) for 35 minutes.
4. When cooking is complete, the potatoes should be fork-tender. Remove from the air fryer oven and split open the potatoes. Top with the yogurt, chives, the remaining ¼ teaspoon of salt, and finish with the black pepper. Serve immediately.

Zucchini Crisps

Prep time: 5 minutes | Cook time: 14 minutes | Serves 4

2 zucchini, sliced into ¼- to ½-inch-thick rounds (about 2 cups)
¼ teaspoon garlic granules

⅛ teaspoon sea salt
Freshly ground black pepper, to taste (optional)
Cooking spray

1. Spritz the air flow racks with cooking spray.
2. Put the zucchini rounds on the air flow racks, spreading them out as much as possible. Top with a sprinkle of garlic granules, sea salt, and black pepper (if desired). Spritz the zucchini rounds with cooking spray.
3. Slide the racks into the air fryer oven. Press the Power Button and cook at 392ºF (200ºC) for 14 minutes.
4. Flip the zucchini rounds halfway through.
5. When cooking is complete, the zucchini rounds should be crisp-tender. Remove from the air fryer oven. Let them rest for 5 minutes and serve.

Parmesan Asparagus Fries

Prep time: 15 minutes | Cook time: 6 minutes | Serves 4

2 egg whites	crumbs
¼ cup water	¼ teaspoon salt
¼ cup plus 2 tablespoons grated Parmesan cheese, divided	12 ounces (340 g) fresh asparagus spears, woody ends trimmed
¾ cup panko bread	Cooking spray

1. In a shallow dish, whisk together the egg whites and water until slightly foamy. In a separate shallow dish, thoroughly combine ¼ cup of Parmesan cheese, bread crumbs, and salt.
2. Dip the asparagus in the egg white, then roll in the cheese mixture to coat well.
3. Put the asparagus on the air flow racks, leaving space between each spear. Spritz the asparagus with cooking spray.
4. Slide the racks into the air fryer oven. Press the Power Button and cook at 390ºF (199ºC) for 6 minutes.
5. When cooking is complete, the asparagus should be golden brown and crisp. Remove from the air fryer oven. Sprinkle with the remaining 2 tablespoons of cheese and serve hot.

Parmesan Broccoli

Prep time: 5 minutes | Cook time: 4 minutes | Serves 4

1 pound (454 g) broccoli florets	unsalted butter, melted
1 medium shallot, minced	2 teaspoons minced garlic
2 tablespoons olive oil	¼ cup grated Parmesan cheese
2 tablespoons	

1. Combine the broccoli florets with the shallot, olive oil, butter, garlic, and Parmesan cheese in a medium bowl and toss until the broccoli florets are thoroughly coated.
2. Put the broccoli florets on the air flow racks.
3. Slide the racks into the air fryer oven. Press the Power Button and cook at 360ºF (182ºC) for 4 minutes.
4. When cooking is complete, the broccoli florets should be crisp-tender. Remove from the air fryer oven and serve warm.

Rosemary Garlic Red Potatoes

Prep time: 5 minutes | Cook time: 20 minutes | Serves 4

1½ pounds (680 g) small red potatoes, cut into 1-inch cubes	garlic
2 tablespoons olive oil	1 teaspoon salt, plus additional as needed
2 tablespoons minced fresh rosemary	½ teaspoon freshly ground black pepper, plus additional as needed
1 tablespoon minced	

1. Toss the potato cubes with the olive oil, rosemary, garlic, salt, and pepper in a large bowl until thoroughly coated.
2. Arrange the potato cubes on the air flow racks.
3. Slide the racks into the air fryer oven. Press the Power Button and cook at 400ºF (205ºC) for 20 minutes.
4. Stir the potatoes a few times during cooking for even cooking.
5. When cooking is complete, the potatoes should be tender. Remove from the air fryer oven to a plate. Taste and add additional salt and pepper as needed.

Charred Green Beans

Prep time: 5 minutes | Cook time: 8 minutes | Serves 4

1 tablespoon soy sauce	sesame oil, divided
½ tablespoon Sriracha sauce	12 ounces (340 g) trimmed green beans
4 teaspoons toasted	½ tablespoon toasted sesame seeds

1. Whisk together the soy sauce, Sriracha sauce, and 1 teaspoon of sesame oil in a small bowl until smooth. Set aside.
2. Toss the green beans with the remaining sesame oil in a large bowl until evenly coated.
3. Put the green beans on the air flow racks.
4. Slide the racks into the air fryer oven. Press the Power Button and cook at 375ºF (190ºC) for 8 minutes.
5. Stir the green beans halfway through the cooking time.
6. When cooking is complete, the green beans should be lightly charred and tender. Remove from the air fryer oven to a platter. Pour the prepared sauce over the top of green beans and toss well. Serve sprinkled with the toasted sesame seeds.

Brown Sugar Acorn Squash

Prep time: 5 minutes | Cook time: 15 minutes | Serves 2

1 medium acorn squash, halved crosswise and deseeded
1 teaspoon coconut oil
1 teaspoon light brown sugar
Few dashes of ground cinnamon
Few dashes of ground nutmeg

1. On a clean work surface, rub the cut sides of the acorn squash with coconut oil. Scatter with the brown sugar, cinnamon, and nutmeg.
2. Put the squash halves on the air flow racks, cut-side up.
3. Slide the racks into the air fryer oven. Press the Power Button and cook at 325ºF (163ºC) for 15 minutes.
4. When cooking is complete, the squash halves should be just tender when pierced in the center with a paring knife. Remove from the air fryer oven. Rest for 5 to 10 minutes and serve warm.

Orange and Balsamic Glazed Carrots

Prep time: 5 minutes | Cook time: 18 minutes | Serves 3

3 medium-size carrots, cut into 2-inch × ½-inch sticks
1 tablespoon orange juice
2 teaspoons balsamic vinegar
1 teaspoon maple
syrup
1 teaspoon avocado oil
½ teaspoon dried rosemary
¼ teaspoon sea salt
¼ teaspoon lemon zest

1. Put the carrots in a baking pan and sprinkle with the orange juice, balsamic vinegar, maple syrup, avocado oil, rosemary, sea salt, finished by the lemon zest. Toss well.
2. Slide the pan into the air fryer oven. Press the Power Button and cook at 392ºF (200ºC) for 18 minutes.
3. Stir the carrots several times during the cooking process.
4. When cooking is complete, the carrots should be nicely glazed and tender. Remove from the air fryer oven and serve hot.

Sweet Potatoes with Tamarind Paste

Prep time: 5 minutes | Cook time: 22 minutes | Serves 4

5 sweet potatoes, peeled and diced
1½ tablespoons fresh lime juice
1 tablespoon butter, melted
2 teaspoons tamarind paste
1½ teaspoon ground allspice
$1/_3$ teaspoon white pepper
½ teaspoon turmeric powder
A few drops liquid stevia

1. In a large mixing bowl, combine all the ingredients and toss until the sweet potatoes are evenly coated. Put the sweet potatoes on the air flow racks.
2. Slide the racks into the air fryer oven. Press the Power Button and cook at 400ºF (205ºC) for 22 minutes.
3. Stir the potatoes twice during cooking.
4. When cooking is complete, the potatoes should be crispy on the outside and soft on the inside. Let the potatoes cool for 5 minutes before serving.

Corn Casserole

Prep time: 5 minutes | Cook time: 15 minutes | Serves 4

2 cups frozen corn, thawed
1 egg, beaten
3 tablespoons flour
½ cup grated Swiss cheese
½ cup light cream
¼ cup milk
Pinch salt
Freshly ground black pepper, to taste
2 tablespoons butter, cut into cubes
Nonstick cooking spray

1. Spritz a baking pan with nonstick cooking spray.
2. Stir together the remaining ingredients except the butter in a medium bowl until well incorporated. Transfer the mixture to the prepared baking pan and scatter with the butter cubes.
3. Slide the pan into the air fryer oven. Press the Power Button and cook at 320ºF (160ºC) for 15 minutes.
4. When cooking is complete, the top should be golden brown and a toothpick inserted in the center should come out clean. Remove from the air fryer oven. Let the casserole cool for 5 minutes before slicing into wedges and serving.

Broccoli with Hot Sauce

Prep time: 5 minutes | Cook time: 14 minutes | Serves 6

Broccoli:

1 medium head broccoli, cut into florets	grated lemon zest
1½ tablespoons olive oil	½ teaspoon hot paprika
1 teaspoon shallot powder	½ teaspoon granulated garlic
1 teaspoon porcini powder	⅓ teaspoon fine sea salt
½ teaspoon freshly	⅓ teaspoon celery seeds

Hot Sauce:

½ cup tomato sauce	½ teaspoon ground allspice
1 tablespoon balsamic vinegar	

1. In a mixing bowl, combine all the ingredients for the broccoli and toss to coat. Transfer the broccoli to the air flow racks.
2. Slide the racks into the air fryer oven. Press the Power Button and cook at 360ºF (182ºC) for 14 minutes.
3. Meanwhile, make the hot sauce by whisking together the tomato sauce, balsamic vinegar, and allspice in a small bowl.
4. When cooking is complete, remove the broccoli from the air fryer oven and serve with the hot sauce.

Brussels Sprouts with Miso Sauce

Prep time: 10 minutes | Cook time: 11 minutes | Serves 4

2½ cups trimmed Brussels sprouts

Sauce:

1½ teaspoons mellow white miso	1 teaspoon grated fresh ginger
1½ tablespoons maple syrup	2 large garlic cloves, finely minced
1 teaspoon toasted sesame oil	¼ to ½ teaspoon red chili flakes
1 teaspoons tamari	Cooking spray

1. Spritz the air flow racks with cooking spray.
2. Arrange the Brussels sprouts on the air flow racks and spray them with cooking spray.
3. Slide the racks into the air fryer oven. Press the Power Button and cook at 392ºF (200ºC) for 11 minutes.
4. After 6 minutes, remove from the air fryer oven. Flip the Brussels sprouts and spritz with cooking spray again. Return to the air fryer oven and continue cooking for 5 minutes more.
5. Meanwhile, make the sauce: Stir together the miso and maple syrup in a medium bowl. Add the sesame oil, tamari, ginger, garlic, and red chili flakes and whisk to combine.
6. When cooking is complete, the Brussels sprouts should be crisp-tender. Transfer the Brussels sprouts to the bowl of sauce, tossing to coat well. If you prefer a saltier taste, you can add additional ½ teaspoon tamari to the sauce. Serve immediately.

Spiced and Cheesy Corn on the Cob

Prep time: 10 minutes | Cook time: 15 minutes | Serves 4

2 tablespoon olive oil, divided	1 teaspoon ground cumin
2 tablespoons grated Parmesan cheese	1 teaspoon paprika
1 teaspoon garlic powder	1 teaspoon salt
1 teaspoon chili powder	¼ teaspoon cayenne pepper (optional)
	4 ears fresh corn, shucked

1. Grease the air flow racks with 1 tablespoon of olive oil. Set aside.
2. Combine the Parmesan cheese, garlic powder, chili powder, cumin, paprika, salt, and cayenne pepper (if desired) in a small bowl and stir to mix well.
3. Lightly coat the ears of corn with the remaining 1 tablespoon of olive oil. Rub the cheese mixture all over the ears of corn until completely coated.
4. Arrange the ears of corn on the greased air flow racks.
5. Slide the racks into the air fryer oven. Press the Power Button and cook at 400ºF (205ºC) for 15 minutes.
6. Flip the ears of corn halfway through the cooking time.
7. When cooking is complete, they should be lightly browned. Remove from the air fryer oven and let them cool for 5 minutes before serving.

Butternut Squash Croquettes

Prep time: 5 minutes | Cook time: 17 minutes | Serves 4

⅓ butternut squash, peeled and grated
⅓ cup all-purpose flour
2 eggs, whisked
4 cloves garlic, minced
1½ tablespoons olive oil
1 teaspoon fine sea salt
⅓ teaspoon freshly ground black pepper, or more to taste
⅓ teaspoon dried sage
Pinch of ground allspice

1. Line the air flow racks with parchment paper. Set aside.
2. In a mixing bowl, stir together all the ingredients until well combined.
3. Make the squash croquettes: Use a small cookie scoop to drop tablespoonfuls of the squash mixture onto a lightly floured surface and shape into balls with your hands. Transfer them to the air flow racks.
4. Slide the racks into the air fryer oven. Press the Power Button and cook at 345ºF (174ºC) for 17 minutes.
5. When cooking is complete, the squash croquettes should be golden brown. Remove from the air fryer oven to a plate and serve warm.

Hot Cabbage

Prep time: 5 minutes | Cook time: 7 minutes | Serves 4

1 head cabbage, sliced into 1-inch-thick ribbons
1 tablespoon olive oil
1 teaspoon garlic powder
1 teaspoon red pepper flakes
1 teaspoon salt
1 teaspoon freshly ground black pepper

1. Toss the cabbage with the olive oil, garlic powder, red pepper flakes, salt, and pepper in a large mixing bowl until well coated.
2. Transfer the cabbage to the air flow racks.
3. Slide the racks into the air fryer oven. Press the Power Button and cook at 350ºF (180ºC) for 7 minutes.
4. Flip the cabbage with tongs halfway through the cooking time.
5. When cooking is complete, the cabbage should be crisp. Remove from the air fryer oven to a plate and serve warm.

Broccoli Gratin

Prep time: 5 minutes | Cook time: 14 minutes | Serves 2

⅓ cup fat-free milk
1 tablespoon all-purpose or gluten-free flour
½ tablespoon olive oil
½ teaspoon ground sage
¼ teaspoon kosher salt
⅛ teaspoon freshly ground black pepper
2 cups roughly chopped broccoli florets
6 tablespoons shredded Cheddar cheese
2 tablespoons panko bread crumbs
1 tablespoon grated Parmesan cheese
Olive oil spray

1. Spritz a baking dish with olive oil spray.
2. Mix the milk, flour, olive oil, sage, salt, and pepper in a medium bowl and whisk to combine. Stir in the broccoli florets, Cheddar cheese, bread crumbs, and Parmesan cheese and toss to coat.
3. Pour the broccoli mixture into the prepared baking dish.
4. Slide the baking dish into the air fryer oven. Press the Power Button and cook at 330ºF (166ºC) for 14 minutes.
5. When cooking is complete, the top should be golden brown and the broccoli should be tender. Remove from the air fryer oven and serve immediately.

Garlic Asparagus

Prep time: 5 minutes | Cook time: 10 minutes | Serves 4

1 pound (454 g) asparagus, woody ends trimmed
2 tablespoons olive oil
1 tablespoon balsamic vinegar
2 teaspoons minced garlic
Salt and freshly ground black pepper, to taste

1. In a large shallow bowl, toss the asparagus with the olive oil, balsamic vinegar, garlic, salt, and pepper until thoroughly coated. Put the asparagus on the air flow racks.
2. Slide the racks into the air fryer oven. Press the Power Button and cook at 400ºF (205ºC) for 10 minutes.
3. Flip the asparagus with tongs halfway through the cooking time.
4. When cooking is complete, the asparagus should be crispy. Remove the racks from the air fryer oven and serve warm.

Chapter 7 Fish and Seafood

Cajun Cod

Prep time: 5 minutes | Cook time: 12 minutes | Makes 2 cod fillets

1 tablespoon Cajun seasoning	cod fillets, cut to fit into the air flow racks
1 teaspoon salt	Cooking spray
½ teaspoon lemon pepper	2 tablespoons unsalted butter, melted
½ teaspoon freshly ground black pepper	1 lemon, cut into 4 wedges
2 (8-ounce / 227-g)	

1. Spritz the air flow racks with cooking spray.
2. Thoroughly combine the Cajun seasoning, salt, lemon pepper, and black pepper in a small bowl. Rub this mixture all over the cod fillets until coated.
3. Put the fillets on the air flow racks and brush the melted butter over both sides of each fillet.
4. Slide the racks into the air fryer oven. Press the Power Button and cook at 360ºF (182ºC) for 12 minutes.
5. Flip the fillets halfway through the cooking time.
6. When cooking is complete, the fish should flake apart with a fork. Remove the fillets from the air fryer oven and serve with fresh lemon wedges.

Lemon Shrimp

Prep time: 10 minutes | Cook time: 8 minutes | Serves 4

1 pound (454 g) shrimp, deveined	2 cloves garlic, finely minced
4 tablespoons olive oil	1 teaspoon crushed red pepper flakes, or more to taste
1½ tablespoons lemon juice	
1½ tablespoons fresh parsley, roughly chopped	Garlic pepper, to taste
	Sea salt, to taste

1. Toss all the ingredients in a large bowl until the shrimp are coated on all sides.
2. Arrange the shrimp on the air flow racks.
3. Slide the racks into the air fryer oven. Press the Power Button and cook at 385ºF (196ºC) for 8 minutes.
4. When cooking is complete, the shrimp should be pink and cooked through. Remove from the air fryer oven and serve warm.

Simple Piri-Piri King Prawns

Prep time: 10 minutes | Cook time: 8 minutes | Serves 2

12 king prawns, rinsed	1 teaspoon garlic paste
1 tablespoon coconut oil	1 teaspoon curry powder
Salt and ground black pepper, to taste	½ teaspoon piri piri powder
1 teaspoon onion powder	½ teaspoon cumin powder

1. Combine all the ingredients in a large bowl and toss until the prawns are completely coated. Put the prawns on the air flow racks.
2. Slide the racks into the air fryer oven. Press the Power Button and cook at 360ºF (182ºC) for 8 minutes.
3. Flip the prawns halfway through the cooking time.
4. When cooking is complete, the prawns will turn pink. Remove from the air fryer oven and serve hot.

Italian Milky Cod Fillets

Prep time: 15 minutes | Cook time: 12 minutes | Serves 4

4 cod fillets	chopped
¼ teaspoon fine sea salt	½ cup non-dairy milk
1 teaspoon cayenne pepper	4 garlic cloves, minced
¼ teaspoon ground black pepper, or more to taste	1 Italian pepper, chopped
½ cup fresh Italian parsley, coarsely	1 teaspoon dried basil
	½ teaspoon dried oregano
	Cooking spray

1. Lightly spritz a baking dish with cooking spray.
2. Season the fillets with salt, cayenne pepper, and black pepper.
3. Pulse the remaining ingredients in a food processor, then transfer the mixture to a shallow bowl. Coat the fillets with the mixture.
4. Slide the baking dish into the air fryer oven. Press the Power Button and cook at 375ºF (190ºC) for 12 minutes.
5. When cooking is complete, the fish will be flaky. Remove from the air fryer oven and serve on a plate.

Bacon-Wrapped Scallops

Prep time: 5 minutes | Cook time: 10 minutes | Serves 4

8 slices bacon, cut in half
16 sea scallops, patted dry
Salt and freshly ground black pepper, to taste
Cooking spray

Special Equipment:
16 toothpicks, soaked in water for at least 30 minutes

1. On a clean work surface, wrap half of a slice of bacon around each scallop and secure with a toothpick.
2. Lay the bacon-wrapped scallops on the air flow racks.
3. Spritz the scallops with cooking spray and sprinkle the salt and pepper to season.
4. Slide the racks into the air fryer oven. Press the Power Button and cook at 370ºF (188ºC) for 10 minutes.
5. Flip the scallops halfway through the cooking time.
6. When cooking is complete, the bacon should be cooked through and the scallops should be firm. Remove the scallops from the air fryer oven to a plate Serve warm.

Golden Cod Sticks

Prep time: 10 minutes | Cook time: 8 minutes | Makes 8 cod sticks

8 ounces (227 g) cod fillets, cut into ½×3-inch strips
Salt, to taste
(optional)
½ cup plain bread crumbs
Cooking spray

1. Season the cod strips with salt to taste, if desired.
2. Put the bread crumbs on a plate. Roll the cod strips in the bread crumbs to coat. Spritz the cod strips with cooking spray.
3. Arrange the cod strips on the air flow racks.
4. Slide the racks into the air fryer oven. Press the Power Button and cook at 390ºF (199ºC) for 8 minutes.
5. When cooking is complete, they should be golden brown. Remove from the air fryer oven and cool for 5 minutes before serving.

Lemon Tilapia

Prep time: 10 minutes | Cook time: 12 minutes | Serves 4

1 tablespoon olive oil
1 tablespoon lemon juice
1 teaspoon minced
garlic
½ teaspoon chili powder
4 tilapia fillets

1. Line a baking pan with parchment paper.
2. In a shallow bowl, stir together the olive oil, lemon juice, garlic, and chili powder to make a marinade. Put the tilapia fillets in the bowl, turning to coat evenly.
3. Put the fillets in the baking pan in a single layer.
4. Slide the pan into the air fryer oven. Press the Power Button and cook at 375ºF (190ºC) for 12 minutes.
5. When cooked, the fish will flake apart with a fork. Remove from the air fryer oven to a plate and serve hot.

Lemon Garlic Swordfish Steaks

Prep time: 10 minutes | Cook time: 8 minutes | Serves 4

4 (4-ounce / 113-g) swordfish steaks
½ teaspoon toasted sesame oil
1 jalapeño pepper, finely minced
2 garlic cloves, grated
2 tablespoons freshly
squeezed lemon juice
1 tablespoon grated fresh ginger
½ teaspoon Chinese five-spice powder
⅛ teaspoon freshly ground black pepper

1. On a clean work surface, place the swordfish steaks and brush both sides of the fish with the sesame oil.
2. Combine the jalapeño, garlic, lemon juice, ginger, five-spice powder, and black pepper in a small bowl and stir to mix well. Rub the mixture all over the fish until coated. Allow to sit for 10 minutes.
3. When ready, arrange the swordfish steaks on the air flow racks.
4. Slide the racks into the air fryer oven. Press the Power Button and cook at 380ºF (193ºC) for 8 minutes.
5. Flip the steaks halfway through.
6. When cooking is complete, remove from the air fryer oven and cool for 5 minutes before serving.

Salmon Patties

Prep time: 5 minutes | Cook time: 11 minutes | Makes 6 patties

1 (14.75-ounce / 418-g) can Alaskan pink salmon, drained and bones removed
½ cup bread crumbs
1 egg, whisked

2 scallions, diced
1 teaspoon garlic powder
Salt and pepper, to taste
Cooking spray

1. Stir together the salmon, bread crumbs, whisked egg, scallions, garlic powder, salt, and pepper in a large bowl until well incorporated.
2. Divide the salmon mixture into six equal portions and form each into a patty with your hands.
3. Arrange the salmon patties on the air flow racks and spritz them with cooking spray.
4. Slide the racks into the air fryer oven. Press the Power Button and cook at 400°F (205°C) for 10 minutes.
5. Flip the patties once halfway through.
6. When cooking is complete, the patties should be golden brown and cooked through. Remove the patties from the air fryer oven and serve on a plate.

Salsa Salmon and Pepper Bowl

Prep time: 115 minutes | Cook time: 12 minutes | Serves 4

12 ounces (340 g) salmon fillets, cut into 1½-inch cubes
1 red onion, chopped
1 jalapeño pepper, minced
1 red bell pepper, chopped

¼ cup salsa
2 teaspoons peanut oil or safflower oil
2 tablespoons tomato juice
1 teaspoon chili powder

1. Mix the salmon cubes, red onion, jalapeño, red bell pepper, salsa, peanut oil, tomato juice, chili powder in a medium metal bowl and stir until well incorporated.
2. Put the metal bowl into the air fryer oven. Press the Power Button and cook at 370°F (188°C) for 12 minutes.
3. Stir the ingredients once halfway through the cooking time.
4. When cooking is complete, the salmon should be cooked through and the veggies should be fork-tender. Serve warm.

Worcestershire Halibut

Prep time: 5 minutes | Cook time: 10 minutes | Serves 4

1 pound (454 g) halibut steaks
¼ cup vegetable oil
2½ tablespoons Worcestershire sauce
2 tablespoons honey
2 tablespoons vermouth

1 tablespoon freshly squeezed lemon juice
1 tablespoon fresh parsley leaves, coarsely chopped
Salt and pepper, to taste
1 teaspoon dried basil

1. Put all the ingredients in a large mixing dish and gently stir until the fish is coated evenly. Transfer the fish to the air flow racks.
2. Slide the racks into the air fryer oven. Press the Power Button and cook at 390°F (199°C) for 10 minutes.
3. Flip the fish halfway through cooking time.
4. When cooking is complete, the fish should reach an internal temperature of at least 145°F (63°C) on a meat thermometer. Remove from the air fryer oven and let the fish cool for 5 minutes before serving.

Hot Prawns

Prep time: 10 minutes | Cook time: 8 minutes | Serves 2

8 prawns, cleaned
Salt and black pepper, to taste
½ teaspoon ground cayenne pepper
½ teaspoon garlic

powder
½ teaspoon ground cumin
½ teaspoon red chili flakes
Cooking spray

1. Spritz the air flow racks with cooking spray.
2. Toss the remaining ingredients in a large bowl until the prawns are well coated.
3. Spread the coated prawns evenly on the air flow racks and spray them with cooking spray.
4. Slide the racks into the air fryer oven. Press the Power Button and cook at 340°F (171°C) for 8 minutes.
5. Flip the prawns halfway through the cooking time.
6. When cooking is complete, the prawns should be pink. Remove the prawns from the air fryer oven to a plate.

Air Fried Scallops

Prep time: 5 minutes | Cook time: 4 minutes | Serves 2

12 medium sea scallops, rinsed and patted dry
1 teaspoon fine sea salt
¾ teaspoon ground

black pepper, plus more for garnish
Fresh thyme leaves, for garnish (optional)
Avocado oil spray

1. Coat the air flow racks with avocado oil spray.
2. Put the scallops in a medium bowl and spritz with avocado oil spray. Sprinkle the salt and pepper to season.
3. Transfer the seasoned scallops to the air flow racks, spacing them apart.
4. Slide the racks into the air fryer oven. Press the Power Button and cook at 390ºF (199ºC) for 4 minutes.
5. Flip the scallops halfway through the cooking time.
6. When cooking is complete, the scallops should reach an internal temperature of just 145ºF (63ºC) on a meat thermometer. Remove from the air fryer oven. Sprinkle the pepper and thyme leaves on top for garnish, if desired. Serve immediately.

Crab Sticks with Mayo Sauce

Prep time: 5 minutes | Cook time: 12 minutes | Serves 4

Crab Sticks:
2 eggs
1 cup flour
1/3 cup panko bread crumbs
1 tablespoon old bay

seasoning
1 pound (454 g) crab sticks
Cooking spray

Mayo Sauce:
½ cup mayonnaise
1 lime, juiced

2 garlic cloves, minced

1. In a bowl, beat the eggs. In a shallow bowl, place the flour. In another shallow bowl, thoroughly combine the panko bread crumbs and old bay seasoning.
2. Dredge the crab sticks in the flour, shaking off any excess, then in the beaten eggs, finally press them in the bread crumb mixture to coat well.
3. Arrange the crab sticks on the air flow racks and spray with cooking spray.
4. Slide the racks into the air fryer oven. Press the Power Button and cook at 390ºF (199ºC) for 12 minutes.
5. Flip the crab sticks halfway through the cooking time.
6. Meanwhile, make the sauce by whisking together the mayo, lime juice, and garlic in a small bowl.
7. When cooking is complete, remove from the air fryer oven. Serve the crab sticks with the mayo sauce on the side.

Sole and Veg Fritters

Prep time: 5 minutes | Cook time: 24 minutes | Serves 2

½ pound (227 g) sole fillets
½ pound (227 g) mashed cauliflower
½ cup red onion, chopped
1 bell pepper, finely chopped
1 egg, beaten
2 garlic cloves, minced
2 tablespoons fresh

parsley, chopped
1 tablespoon olive oil
1 tablespoon coconut aminos
½ teaspoon scotch bonnet pepper, minced
½ teaspoon paprika
Salt and white pepper, to taste
Cooking spray

1. Spray the air flow racks with cooking spray. Put the sole fillets on the racks.
2. Slide the racks into the air fryer oven. Press the Power Button and cook at 395ºF (202ºC) for 10 minutes.
3. Flip the fillets halfway through.
4. When cooking is complete, transfer the fish fillets to a large bowl. Mash the fillets into flakes. Add the remaining ingredients and stir to combine.
5. Make the fritters: Scoop out 2 tablespoons of the fish mixture and shape into a patty about ½ inch thick with your hands. Repeat with the remaining fish mixture. Put the patties on the air flow racks.
6. Slide the racks into the air fryer oven. Press the Power Button and cook at 380ºF (193ºC) for 14 minutes.
7. Flip the patties halfway through.
8. When cooking is complete, they should be golden brown and cooked through. Remove the racks from the air fryer oven and cool for 5 minutes before serving.

Catfish Nuggets

Prep time: 10 minutes | Cook time: 7 to 8 minutes | Serves 4

2 medium catfish fillets, cut into chunks
Salt and pepper, to taste
2 eggs
2 tablespoons skim

milk
½ cup cornstarch
1 cup panko bread crumbs
Cooking spray

1. In a medium bowl, season the fish chunks with salt and pepper to taste.
2. In a small bowl, beat together the eggs with milk until well combined.
3. Put the cornstarch and bread crumbs into separate shallow dishes.
4. Dredge the fish chunks one at a time in the cornstarch, coating well on both sides, then dip in the egg mixture, shaking off any excess, finally press well into the bread crumbs. Spritz the fish chunks with cooking spray.
5. Arrange the fish chunks on the air flow racks.
6. Slide the racks into the air fryer oven. Press the Power Button and cook at 390ºF (199ºC) for 8 minutes.
7. Flip the fish chunks halfway through the cooking time.
8. When cooking is complete, they should be no longer translucent in the center and golden brown. Remove the fish chunks from the air fryer oven to a plate. Serve warm.

Hoisin Scallops with Roasted Mushrooms

Prep time: 10 minutes | Cook time: 8 minutes | Serves 4

1 pound (454 g) sea scallops
3 tablespoons hoisin sauce
½ cup toasted sesame seeds
6 ounces (170 g) snow peas, trimmed

3 teaspoons vegetable oil, divided
1 teaspoon soy sauce
1 teaspoon sesame oil
1 cup roasted mushrooms

1. Brush the scallops with the hoisin sauce. Put the sesame seeds in a shallow dish. Roll the scallops in the sesame seeds until evenly coated.

2. Combine the snow peas with 1 teaspoon of vegetable oil, the sesame oil, and soy sauce in a medium bowl and toss to coat.
3. Grease a sheet pan with the remaining 2 teaspoons of vegetable oil. Put the scallops in the middle of the pan and arrange the snow peas around the scallops in a single layer.
4. Slide the pan into the air fryer oven. Press the Power Button and cook at 375ºF (190ºC) for 8 minutes.
5. After 5 minutes, remove the pan and flip the scallops. Fold in the mushrooms and stir well. Return to the air fryer oven and continue cooking.
6. When done, remove from the air fryer oven and cool for 5 minutes. Serve warm.

Parmesan Pollock

Prep time: 8 minutes | Cook time: 17 minutes | Serves 4

$1/_3$ cup grated Parmesan cheese
½ teaspoon fennel seed
½ teaspoon tarragon
$1/_3$ teaspoon mixed peppercorns

2 eggs, beaten
4 (4-ounce / 113-g) pollock fillets, halved
2 tablespoons dry white wine
1 teaspoon seasoned salt

1. Put the grated Parmesan cheese, fennel seed, tarragon, and mixed peppercorns in a food processor and pulse for about 20 seconds until well combined. Transfer the cheese mixture to a shallow dish.
2. Put the beaten eggs in another shallow dish.
3. Drizzle the dry white wine over the top of pollock fillets. Dredge each fillet in the beaten eggs on both sides, shaking off any excess, then roll them in the cheese mixture until fully coated. Season with the salt.
4. Arrange the fillets on the air flow racks.
5. Slide the racks into the air fryer oven. Press the Power Button and cook at 345ºF (174ºC) for 17 minutes.
6. Flip the fillets once halfway through the cooking time.
7. When cooking is complete, the pollock should be cooked through no longer translucent. Remove from the air fryer oven and cool for 5 minutes before serving.

Crab Cakes with Bell Pepper

Prep time: 5 minutes | Cook time: 10 minutes | Serves 4

8 ounces (227 g) jumbo lump crab meat
1 egg, beaten
Juice of ½ lemon
1/3 cup bread crumbs
¼ cup diced green bell pepper
¼ cup diced red bell pepper
¼ cup mayonnaise
1 tablespoon Old Bay seasoning
1 teaspoon flour
Cooking spray

1. Make the crab cakes: Put all the ingredients except the flour and oil in a large bowl and stir until well incorporated.
2. Divide the crab mixture into four equal portions and shape each portion into a patty with your hands. Top each patty with a sprinkle of ¼ teaspoon of flour.
3. Arrange the crab cakes on the air flow racks and spritz them with cooking spray.
4. Slide the racks into the air fryer oven. Press the Power Button and cook at 375ºF (190ºC) for 10 minutes.
5. Flip the crab cakes halfway through.
6. When cooking is complete, the cakes should be cooked through. Remove from the air fryer oven. Divide the crab cakes among four plates and serve.

Parmesan Salmon Patties

Prep time: 10 minutes | Cook time: 13 minutes | Serves 4

1 pound (454 g) salmon, chopped into ½-inch pieces
2 tablespoons coconut flour
2 tablespoons grated Parmesan cheese
1½ tablespoons milk
½ white onion, peeled and finely chopped
½ teaspoon butter, at room temperature
½ teaspoon chipotle powder
½ teaspoon dried parsley flakes
1/3 teaspoon ground black pepper
1/3 teaspoon smoked cayenne pepper
1 teaspoon fine sea salt

1. Put all the ingredients for the salmon patties in a bowl and stir to combine well.
2. Scoop out 2 tablespoons of the salmon mixture and shape into a patty with your palm, about ½ inch thick. Repeat until all the mixture is used. Transfer to the refrigerator for about 2 hours until firm.

3. When ready, arrange the salmon patties on the air flow racks.
4. Slide the racks into the air fryer oven. Press the Power Button and cook at 395ºF (202ºC) for 13 minutes.
5. Flip the patties halfway through the cooking time.
6. When cooking is complete, the patties should be golden brown. Remove from the air fryer oven and cool for 5 minutes before serving.

Tilapia Meunière

Prep time: 10 minutes | Cook time: 20 minutes | Serves 4

10 ounces (283 g) Yukon Gold potatoes, sliced ¼-inch thick
5 tablespoons unsalted butter, melted, divided
1 teaspoon kosher salt, divided
4 (8-ounce / 227-g) tilapia fillets
½ pound (227 g) green beans, trimmed
Juice of 1 lemon
2 tablespoons chopped fresh parsley, for garnish

1. In a large bowl, drizzle the potatoes with 2 tablespoons of melted butter and ¼ teaspoon of kosher salt. Transfer the potatoes to a sheet pan.
2. Slide the pan into the air fryer oven. Press the Power Button and cook at 375ºF (190ºC) for 20 minutes.
3. Meanwhile, season both sides of the fillets with ½ teaspoon of kosher salt. Put the green beans in the medium bowl and sprinkle with the remaining ¼ teaspoon of kosher salt and 1 tablespoon of butter, tossing to coat.
4. After 10 minutes, remove the pan and push the potatoes to one side. Put the fillets in the middle of the pan and add the green beans on the other side. Drizzle the remaining 2 tablespoons of butter over the fillets. Return to the air fryer oven and continue cooking, or until the fish flakes easily with a fork and the green beans are crisp-tender.
5. When cooked, remove from the air fryer oven. Drizzle the lemon juice over the fillets and sprinkle the parsley on top for garnish. Serve hot.

Cod with Parsley

Prep time: 10 minutes | Cook time: 12 minutes | Serves 4

1 teaspoon olive oil
4 cod fillets
¼ teaspoon fine sea salt
¼ teaspoon ground black pepper, or more to taste
1 teaspoon cayenne pepper
½ cup fresh Italian

parsley, coarsely chopped
½ cup nondairy milk
1 Italian pepper, chopped
4 garlic cloves, minced
1 teaspoon dried basil
½ teaspoon dried oregano

1. Lightly coat the sides and bottom of a baking dish with the olive oil. Set aside.
2. In a large bowl, sprinkle the fillets with salt, black pepper, and cayenne pepper.
3. In a food processor, pulse the remaining ingredients until smoothly puréed.
4. Add the purée to the bowl of fillets and toss to coat, then transfer to the prepared baking dish.
5. Slide the baking dish into the air fryer oven. Press the Power Button and cook at 380ºF (193ºC) for 12 minutes.
6. When cooking is complete, the fish should flake when pressed lightly with a fork. Remove from the air fryer oven and serve warm.

Salmon Fillets with Cherry Tomatoes

Prep time: 10 minutes | Cook time: 15 minutes | Serves 4

4 (6-ounce / 170-g) salmon fillets, patted dry
1 teaspoon kosher salt, divided
1 pound (454 g) cherry tomatoes, halved, divided
3 tablespoons extra-

virgin olive oil, divided
2 garlic cloves, minced
1 small red bell pepper, deseeded and chopped
2 tablespoons chopped fresh basil, divided

1. Season both sides of the salmon with ½ teaspoon of kosher salt.
2. Put about half of the tomatoes in a large bowl, along with the remaining ½ teaspoon of kosher salt, 2 tablespoons of olive oil, garlic, bell pepper, and 1 tablespoon of basil. Toss to coat and then transfer to the sheet pan.

3. Arrange the salmon fillets on the sheet pan, skin-side down. Brush them with the remaining 1 tablespoon of olive oil.
4. Slide the pan into the air fryer oven. Press the Power Button and cook at 375ºF (190ºC) for 15 minutes.
5. After 7 minutes, remove the pan and fold in the remaining tomatoes. Return to the air fryer oven and continue cooking.
6. When cooked, remove from the air fryer oven. Serve sprinkled with the remaining 1 tablespoon of basil.

Snapper Fillets with Tomatoes

Prep time: 9 minutes | Cook time: 18 minutes | Serves 4

2 tablespoons extra-virgin olive oil
2 large garlic cloves, minced
½ onion, finely chopped
1 (14.5-ounce / 411-g) can diced tomatoes, drained
¼ cup sliced green olives

3 tablespoons capers, divided
2 tablespoons chopped fresh parsley, divided
½ teaspoon dried oregano
4 (6-ounce / 170-g) snapper fillets
½ teaspoon kosher salt

1. Grease a sheet pan generously with olive oil, then Press the Power Button and cook at 375ºF (190ºC) for 18 minutes.
2. Remove the pan and add the garlic and onion to the olive oil in the pan, stirring to coat. Return to the air fryer oven and continue cooking.
3. After 2 minutes, remove from the air fryer oven. Stir in the tomatoes, olives, 1½ tablespoons of capers, 1 tablespoon of parsley, and oregano. Return to the air fryer oven and continue cooking for 6 minutes until heated through.
4. Meanwhile, rub the fillets with the salt on both sides.
5. After another 6 minutes, remove the pan. Put the fillets in the center of the sheet pan and spoon some of the sauce over them. Return to the air fryer oven and continue cooking, or until the fish is flaky.
6. When cooked, remove from the air fryer oven. Scatter the remaining 1½ tablespoons of capers and 1 tablespoon of parsley on top of the fillets, then serve.

Tilapia with Aioli

Prep time: 5 minutes | Cook time: 15 minutes | Serves 4

Tilapia:

4 tilapia fillets
1 tablespoon extra-virgin olive oil
1 teaspoon garlic powder

1 teaspoon paprika
1 teaspoon dried basil
Pinch of lemon-pepper seasoning

Aioli:

2 garlic cloves, minced
1 tablespoon mayonnaise
Juice of ½ lemon

1 teaspoon extra-virgin olive oil
Salt and pepper, to taste

1. On a clean work surface, brush both sides of each fillet with the olive oil. Sprinkle with the garlic powder, paprika, basil, and lemon-pepper seasoning. Put the fillets on the air flow racks.
2. Slide the racks into the air fryer oven. Press the Power Button and cook at 400°F (205°C) for 15 minutes.
3. Flip the fillets halfway through.
4. Meanwhile, make the aioli: Whisk together the garlic, mayo, lemon juice, olive oil, salt, and pepper in a small bowl until smooth.
5. When cooking is complete, the fish should flake apart with a fork and no longer translucent in the center. Remove the fish from the air fryer oven and serve with the aioli on the side.

Tuna and Chili Casserole

Prep time: 10 minutes | Cook time: 16 minutes | Serves 4

½ tablespoon sesame oil
⅓ cup yellow onions, chopped
½ bell pepper, deveined and chopped
2 cups canned tuna, chopped
Cooking spray
5 eggs, beaten
½ chili pepper,

deveined and finely minced
1½ tablespoons sour cream
⅓ teaspoon dried basil
⅓ teaspoon dried oregano
Fine sea salt and ground black pepper, to taste

1. Heat the sesame oil in a nonstick skillet over medium heat until it shimmers.
2. Add the onions and bell pepper and sauté for 4 minutes, stirring occasionally, or until tender.
3. Add the canned tuna and keep stirring until the tuna is heated through.
4. Meanwhile, coat a baking dish lightly with cooking spray.
5. Transfer the tuna mixture to the baking dish, along with the beaten eggs, chili pepper, sour cream, basil, and oregano. Stir to combine well. Season with sea salt and black pepper.
6. Slide the baking dish into the air fryer oven. Press the Power Button and cook at 325°F (160°C) for 12 minutes.
7. When cooking is complete, the eggs should be completely set and the top lightly browned. Remove from the air fryer oven and serve on a plate.

Tuna Wraps

Prep time: 10 minutes | Cook time: 4 to 7 minutes | Serves 4

1 pound (454 g) fresh tuna steak, cut into 1-inch cubes
2 garlic cloves, minced
1 tablespoon grated fresh ginger
½ teaspoon toasted

sesame oil
4 low-sodium whole-wheat tortillas
2 cups shredded romaine lettuce
1 red bell pepper, thinly sliced
¼ cup mayonnaise

1. Combine the tuna cubes, garlic, ginger, and sesame oil in a medium bowl and toss until well coated. Allow to sit for 10 minutes.
2. When ready, place the tuna cubes on the air flow racks.
3. Slide the racks into the air fryer oven. Press the Power Button and cook at 390°F (199°C) for 6 minutes.
4. When cooking is complete, the tuna cubes should be cooked through and golden brown. Remove the tuna cubes from the air fryer oven to a plate.
5. Make the wraps: Put the tortillas on a flat work surface and top each tortilla evenly with the cooked tuna, lettuce, bell pepper, and finish with the mayonnaise. Roll them up and serve immediately.

Mediterranean Scallops

Prep time: 10 minutes | Cook time: 12 minutes | Serves 2

⅓ cup shallots, chopped	balsamic vinegar
1½ tablespoons olive oil	½ teaspoon ginger, grated
1½ tablespoons coconut aminos	1 clove garlic, chopped
1 tablespoon Mediterranean seasoning mix	1 pound (454 g) scallops, cleaned
½ tablespoon	Cooking spray
	Belgian endive, for garnish

1. Put all the ingredients except the scallops and Belgian endive in a small skillet over medium heat and stir to combine. Let this mixture simmer for about 2 minutes.
2. Remove the mixture from the skillet to a large bowl and set aside to cool.
3. Add the scallops, coating them all over, then transfer to the refrigerator to marinate for at least 2 hours.
4. When ready, place the scallops on the air flow racks and spray with cooking spray.
5. Slide the racks into the air fryer oven. Press the Power Button and cook at 345ºF (174ºC) for 10 minutes.
6. Flip the scallops halfway through the cooking time.
7. When cooking is complete, the scallops should be tender and opaque. Remove from the air fryer oven and serve garnished with the Belgian endive.

Tuna, Pineapple, and Grape Kebabs

Prep time: 15 minutes | Cook time: 10 minutes | Serves 4

Kebabs:

1 pound (454 g) tuna steaks, cut into 1-inch cubes	drained, juice reserved
½ cup canned pineapple chunks,	½ cup large red grapes

Marinade:

1 tablespoon honey	fresh ginger
1 teaspoon olive oil	Pinch cayenne pepper
2 teaspoons grated	

Special Equipment:
4 metal skewers

1. Make the kebabs: Thread, alternating tuna cubes, pineapple chunks, and red grapes, onto the metal skewers.
2. Make the marinade: Whisk together the honey, olive oil, ginger, and cayenne pepper in a small bowl. Brush generously the marinade over the kebabs and allow to sit for 10 minutes.
3. When ready, transfer the kebabs to the air flow racks.
4. Slide the racks into the air fryer oven. Press the Power Button and cook at 370ºF (188ºC) for 10 minutes.
5. After 5 minutes, remove from the air fryer oven and flip the kebabs and brush with the remaining marinade. Return to the air fryer oven and continue cooking for an additional 5 minutes.
6. When cooking is complete, the kebabs should reach an internal temperature of 145ºF (63ºC) on a meat thermometer. Remove from the air fryer oven and discard any remaining marinade. Serve hot.

Ritzy Crab Ratatouille

Prep time: 15 minutes | Cook time: 13 minutes | Serves 4

1½ cups peeled and cubed eggplant	basil
2 large tomatoes, chopped	½ teaspoon dried thyme
1 red bell pepper, chopped	Pinch salt
1 onion, chopped	Freshly ground black pepper, to taste
1 tablespoon olive oil	1½ cups cooked crab meat
½ teaspoon dried	

1. In a metal bowl, stir together the eggplant, tomatoes, bell pepper, onion, olive oil, basil and thyme. Season with salt and pepper.
2. Put the metal bowl into the air fryer oven. Press the Power Button and cook at 400ºF (205ºC) for 13 minutes.
3. After 9 minutes, remove the bowl from the air fryer oven. Add the crab meat and stir well and continue cooking for another 4 minutes, or until the vegetables are softened and the ratatouille is bubbling.
4. When cooking is complete, remove from the air fryer oven and serve warm.

Sriracha Shrimp and Tomato Skewers

Prep time: 15 minutes | Cook time: 5 minutes | Serves 4

1½ pounds (680 g) jumbo shrimp, cleaned, shelled and deveined
1 pound (454 g) cherry tomatoes
2 tablespoons butter, melted
1 tablespoons Sriracha sauce
Sea salt and ground
black pepper, to taste
1 teaspoon dried parsley flakes
½ teaspoon dried basil
½ teaspoon dried oregano
½ teaspoon mustard seeds
½ teaspoon marjoram

Special Equipment:
4 to 6 wooden skewers, soaked in water for 30 minutes

1. Put all the ingredients in a large bowl and toss to coat well.
2. Make the kebabs: Thread, alternating jumbo shrimp and cherry tomatoes, onto the wooden skewers. Put the kebabs on the air flow racks.
3. Slide the racks into the air fryer oven. Press the Power Button and cook at 400°F (205°C) for 5 minutes.
4. When cooking is complete, the shrimp should be pink and the cherry tomatoes should be softened. Remove from the air fryer oven. Let the shrimp and cherry tomato kebabs cool for 5 minutes and serve hot.

Scampi with Lemony Basil Sauce

Prep time: 5 minutes | Cook time: 8 minutes | Serves 4

Lemony Basil Sauce:
¼ cup unsalted butter
2 tablespoons fish stock
2 cloves garlic, minced
2 tablespoons chopped fresh basil leaves
1 tablespoon lemon juice
1 tablespoon chopped fresh parsley, plus more for garnish
1 teaspoon red pepper flakes

Shrimp:
1 pound (454 g) scampi, peeled and deveined, tails removed
Fresh basil sprigs, for garnish

1. Put all the ingredients for the sauce in a baking pan and stir to incorporate.
2. Slide the pan into the air fryer oven. Press the Power Button and cook at 350°F (180°C) for 8 minutes.
3. After 3 minutes, remove from the air fryer oven and add the scampi to the baking pan, flipping to coat in the sauce. Return to the air fryer oven and continue cooking for 5 minutes until the scampi are pink and opaque. Stir the scampi twice during cooking.
4. When cooking is complete, remove from the air fryer oven. Serve garnished with the parsley and basil sprigs.

Shrimp Patties

Prep time: 15 minutes | Cook time: 12 minutes | Serves 4

½ pound (227 g) raw shrimp, shelled, deveined, and chopped finely
2 cups cooked sushi rice
¼ cup chopped red bell pepper
¼ cup chopped celery
¼ cup chopped green onion
2 teaspoons Worcestershire sauce
½ teaspoon salt
½ teaspoon garlic powder
½ teaspoon Old Bay seasoning
½ cup plain bread crumbs
Cooking spray

1. Put all the ingredients except the bread crumbs and oil in a large bowl and stir to incorporate.
2. Scoop out the shrimp mixture and shape into 8 equal-sized patties with your hands, no more than ½-inch thick. Roll the patties in the bread crumbs on a plate and spray both sides with cooking spray. Put the patties on the air flow racks.
3. Slide the racks into the air fryer oven. Press the Power Button and cook at 390°F (199°C) for 12 minutes.
4. Flip the patties halfway through the cooking time.
5. When cooking is complete, the outside should be crispy brown. Remove from the air fryer oven. Divide the patties among four plates and serve warm.

Calamari Rings

Prep time: 5 minutes | Cook time: 12 minutes | Serves 4

2 large eggs
2 garlic cloves, minced
½ cup cornstarch
1 cup bread crumbs
1 pound (454 g) calamari rings
Cooking spray
1 lemon, sliced

1. In a small bowl, whisk the eggs with minced garlic. Put the cornstarch and bread crumbs into separate shallow dishes.
2. Dredge the calamari rings in the cornstarch, then dip in the egg mixture, shaking off any excess, finally roll them in the bread crumbs to coat well. Let the calamari rings sit for 10 minutes in the refrigerator.
3. Spritz the air flow racks with cooking spray. Transfer the calamari rings to the pan.
4. Slide the racks into the air fryer oven. Press the Power Button and cook at 390ºF (199ºC) for 12 minutes.
5. Stir the calamari rings once halfway through the cooking time.
6. When cooking is complete, remove from the air fryer oven. Serve the calamari rings with the lemon slices sprinkled on top.

Worcestershire Flounder Fillets

Prep time: 8 minutes | Cook time: 12 minutes | Serves 2

2 flounder fillets, patted dry
1 egg
½ teaspoon Worcestershire sauce
¼ cup almond flour
¼ cup coconut flour
½ teaspoon coarse sea salt
½ teaspoon lemon pepper
¼ teaspoon chili powder
Cooking spray

1. In a shallow bowl, beat together the egg with Worcestershire sauce until well incorporated.
2. In another bowl, thoroughly combine the almond flour, coconut flour, sea salt, lemon pepper, and chili powder.
3. Dredge the fillets in the egg mixture, shaking off any excess, then roll in the flour mixture to coat well.

4. Spritz the air flow racks with cooking spray. Put the fillets on the racks.
5. Slide the racks into the air fryer oven. Press the Power Button and cook at 390ºF (199ºC) for 12 minutes.
6. After 7 minutes, remove from the air fryer oven and flip the fillets and spray with cooking spray. Return to the air fryer oven and continue cooking for 5 minutes, or until the fish is flaky.
7. When cooking is complete, remove from the air fryer oven and serve warm.

Dijon Haddock with Asparagus

Prep time: 10 minutes | Cook time: 15 minutes | Serves 4

4 (6-ounce / 170 g) haddock fillets, patted dry
1 teaspoon kosher salt, divided
1 tablespoon honey
2 tablespoons unsalted butter,
melted
2 teaspoons Dijon mustard
2 pounds (907 g) asparagus, trimmed
Lemon wedges, for serving

1. Season both sides of the haddock fillets with ½ teaspoon of kosher salt.
2. Whisk together the honey, 1 tablespoon of butter, and mustard in a small bowl. Set aside.
3. Arrange the asparagus on a sheet pan. Drizzle the remaining 1 tablespoon of butter all over and season with the remaining ½ teaspoon of salt, tossing to coat. Move the asparagus to the outside of the sheet pan.
4. Put the haddock fillets on the sheet pan, skin-side down. Brush the fillets generously with the honey mixture.
5. Slide the pan into the air fryer oven. Press the Power Button and cook at 375ºF (190ºC) for 15 minutes.
6. Toss the asparagus once halfway through the cooking time.
7. When done, transfer the haddock fillets and asparagus to a plate. Serve warm with a squeeze of lemon juice.

Hoisin Tuna with Rice

Prep time: 15 minutes | Cook time: 5 minutes | Serves 4

½ cup hoisin sauce
2 tablespoons rice wine vinegar
2 teaspoons sesame oil
2 teaspoons dried lemongrass
1 teaspoon garlic powder
¼ teaspoon red

pepper flakes
½ small onion, quartered and thinly sliced
8 ounces (227 g) fresh tuna, cut into 1-inch cubes
Cooking spray
3 cups cooked jasmine rice

1. In a small bowl, whisk together the hoisin sauce, vinegar, sesame oil, lemongrass, garlic powder, and red pepper flakes.
2. Add the sliced onion and tuna cubes and gently toss until the fish is evenly coated.
3. Arrange the coated tuna cubes on the air flow racks.
4. Slide the racks into the air fryer oven. Press the Power Button and cook at 390ºF (199ºC) for 5 minutes.
5. Flip the fish halfway through the cooking time.
6. When cooking is complete, the fish should be flaked. Continue cooking for 1 minute, if necessary. Remove from the air fryer oven and serve over hot jasmine rice.

Salmon Fillets with Asparagus

Prep time: 5 minutes | Cook time: 12 minutes | Serves 2

2 teaspoons olive oil, plus additional for drizzling
2 (5-ounce / 142-g) salmon fillets, with skin
Salt and freshly ground black pepper, to taste

1 bunch asparagus, trimmed
1 teaspoon dried tarragon
1 teaspoon dried chives
Fresh lemon wedges, for serving

1. Rub the olive oil all over the salmon fillets. Sprinkle with salt and pepper to taste.
2. Put the asparagus on a foil-lined baking sheet and place the salmon fillets on top, skin-side down.
3. Slide the baking sheet into the air fryer oven. Press the Power Button and cook at 425ºF (220ºC) for 12 minutes.

4. When cooked, the fillets should register 145ºF (63ºC) on an instant-read thermometer. Remove from the air fryer oven and cut the salmon fillets in half crosswise, then use a metal spatula to lift flesh from skin and transfer to a serving plate. Discard the skin and drizzle the salmon fillets with additional olive oil. Scatter with the herbs.
5. Serve the salmon fillets with asparagus spears and lemon wedges on the side.

Scallops with Peas, Beans, and Broccoli

Prep time: 15 minutes | Cook time: 9 minutes | Serves 4

1 cup frozen peas, thawed
1 cup green beans
1 cup frozen chopped broccoli
2 teaspoons olive oil
½ teaspoon dried

oregano
½ teaspoon dried basil
12 ounces (340 g) sea scallops, rinsed and patted dry

1. Put the peas, green beans, and broccoli in a large bowl. Drizzle with the olive oil and toss to coat well. Transfer the vegetables to the air flow racks.
2. Slide the racks into the air fryer oven. Press the Power Button and cook at 400ºF (205ºC) for 5 minutes.
3. When cooking is complete, the vegetables should be fork-tender. Transfer the vegetables to a serving bowl. Scatter with the oregano and basil and set aside.
4. Put the scallops on the air flow racks.
5. Slide the racks into the air fryer oven. Press the Power Button and cook at 400ºF (205ºC) for 4 minutes.
6. When cooking is complete, the scallops should be firm and just opaque in the center. Remove from the air fryer oven to the bowl of vegetables and toss well. Serve warm.

Shrimp with Mayo Sauce

Prep time: 5 minutes | Cook time: 7 minutes | Serves 4

Shrimp
12 jumbo shrimp
½ teaspoon garlic salt
Mayo Sauce:
4 tablespoons mayonnaise
1 teaspoon grated lemon rind
1 teaspoon Dijon

¼ teaspoon freshly cracked mixed peppercorns

mustard
1 teaspoon chipotle powder
½ teaspoon cumin powder

1. In a medium bowl, season the shrimp with garlic salt and cracked mixed peppercorns.
2. Put the shrimp on the air flow racks.
3. Slide the racks into the air fryer oven. Press the Power Button and cook at 395ºF (202ºC) for 7 minutes.
4. After 5 minutes, remove from the air fryer oven and flip the shrimp. Return to the air fryer oven and continue cooking for 2 minutes more, or until they are pink and no longer opaque.
5. Meanwhile, stir together all the ingredients for the sauce in a small bowl until well mixed.
6. When cooking is complete, remove the shrimp from the air fryer oven and serve alongside the sauce.

Gold Fillets

Prep time: 20 minutes | Cook time: 7 minutes | Serves 4

1 pound (454 g) fish fillets
1 tablespoon coarse brown mustard
1 teaspoon
Crumb Coating:
¾ cup panko bread crumbs
¼ cup stone-ground

Worcestershire sauce
½ teaspoon hot sauce
Salt, to taste
Cooking spray

cornmeal
¼ teaspoon salt

1. On your cutting board, cut the fish fillets crosswise into slices, about 1 inch wide.
2. In a small bowl, stir together the mustard, Worcestershire sauce, and hot sauce to make a paste and rub this paste on all sides of the fillets. Season with salt to taste.

3. In a shallow bowl, thoroughly combine all the ingredients for the crumb coating and spread them on a sheet of wax paper.
4. Roll the fish fillets in the crumb mixture until thickly coated. Spritz all sides of the fish with cooking spray, then arrange them on the air flow racks.
5. Slide the racks into the air fryer oven. Press the Power Button and cook at 400ºF (205ºC) for 7 minutes.
6. When cooking is complete, the fish should flake apart with a fork. Remove from the air fryer oven and serve warm.

Hot Halibut

Prep time: 5 minutes | Cook time: 10 minutes | Serves 4

2 medium halibut fillets
Dash of tabasco sauce
1 teaspoon curry powder
½ teaspoon ground coriander
½ teaspoon hot

paprika
Kosher salt and freshly cracked mixed peppercorns, to taste
2 eggs
1½ tablespoons olive oil
½ cup grated Parmesan cheese

1. On a clean work surface, drizzle the halibut fillets with the tabasco sauce. Sprinkle with the curry powder, coriander, hot paprika, salt, and cracked mixed peppercorns. Set aside.
2. In a shallow bowl, beat the eggs until frothy. In another shallow bowl, combine the olive oil and Parmesan cheese.
3. One at a time, dredge the halibut fillets in the beaten eggs, shaking off any excess, then roll them over the Parmesan cheese until evenly coated.
4. Arrange the halibut fillets on the air flow racks.
5. Slide the racks into the air fryer oven. Press the Power Button and cook at 365ºF (185ºC) for 10 minutes.
6. When cooking is complete, the fish should be golden brown and crisp. Cool for 5 minutes before serving.

Snapper Fillets with Fruit

Prep time: 15 minutes | Cook time: 12 minutes | Serves 4

4 (4-ounce / 113-g) red snapper fillets
2 teaspoons olive oil
3 plums, halved and pitted
3 nectarines, halved and pitted
1 cup red grapes
1 tablespoon freshly squeezed lemon juice
1 tablespoon honey
½ teaspoon dried thyme

1. Arrange the red snapper fillets on the air flow racks and drizzle the olive oil over the top.
2. Slide the racks into the air fryer oven. Press the Power Button and cook at 390ºF (199ºC) for 12 minutes.
3. After 4 minutes, remove from the air fryer oven. Top the fillets with the plums and nectarines. Scatter the red grapes all over the fillets. Drizzle with the lemon juice and honey and sprinkle the thyme on top. Return to the air fryer oven and continue cooking for 8 minutes, or until the fish is flaky.
4. When cooking is complete, remove from the air fryer oven and serve warm.

Lemony Snapper Fillets

Prep time: 13 minutes | Cook time: 10 minutes | Serves 4

1 teaspoon olive oil
1½ teaspoons black pepper
¼ teaspoon garlic powder
¼ teaspoon thyme
⅛ teaspoon cayenne pepper
4 (4-ounce / 113-g) red snapper fillets, skin on
4 thin slices lemon
Nonstick cooking spray

1. Spritz the air flow racks with nonstick cooking spray.
2. In a small bowl, stir together the olive oil, black pepper, garlic powder, thyme, and cayenne pepper. Rub the mixture all over the fillets until coated.
3. Lay the fillets, skin-side down, on the air flow racks and top each fillet with a slice of lemon.
4. Slide the racks into the air fryer oven. Press the Power Button and cook at 390ºF (199ºC) for 10 minutes.
5. Flip the fillets halfway through.

6. When cooking is complete, the fish should be cooked through. Let the fish cool for 5 minutes and serve.

Crab and Haddock Cakes

Prep time: 20 minutes | Cook time: 12 minutes | Serves 4

8 ounces (227 g) imitation crab meat
4 ounces (113 g) leftover cooked haddock fish
2 tablespoons minced celery
2 tablespoons minced green onion
2 tablespoons light mayonnaise
1 tablespoon plus 2 teaspoons Worcestershire sauce
¾ cup crushed saltine cracker crumbs
2 teaspoons dried parsley flakes
1 teaspoon prepared yellow mustard
½ teaspoon garlic powder
½ teaspoon dried dill weed, crushed
½ teaspoon Old Bay seasoning
½ cup panko bread crumbs
Cooking spray

1. Pulse the crab meat and fish in a food processor until finely chopped.
2. Transfer the meat mixture to a large bowl, along with the celery, green onion, mayo, Worcestershire sauce, cracker crumbs, parsley flakes, mustard, garlic powder, dill weed, and Old Bay seasoning. Stir to mix well.
3. Scoop out the meat mixture and form into 8 equal-sized patties with your hands.
4. Put the panko bread crumbs on a plate. Roll the patties in the bread crumbs until they are evenly coated on both sides. Put the patties on the air flow racks and spritz them with cooking spray.
5. Slide the racks into the air fryer oven. Press the Power Button and cook at 390ºF (199ºC) for 12 minutes.
6. Flip the patties halfway through the cooking time.
7. When cooking is complete, they should be golden brown and cooked through. Remove from the air fryer oven. Divide the patties among four plates and serve.

Lemon Shrimp

Prep time: 10 minutes | Cook time: 5 minutes | Serves 4

18 shrimp, shelled and deveined
2 garlic cloves, peeled and minced
2 tablespoons extra-virgin olive oil
2 tablespoons freshly squeezed lemon juice
½ cup fresh parsley, coarsely chopped
1 teaspoon onion powder
1 teaspoon lemon-pepper seasoning
½ teaspoon hot paprika
½ teaspoon salt
¼ teaspoon cumin powder

1. Toss all the ingredients in a mixing bowl until the shrimp are well coated.
2. Cover and allow to marinate in the refrigerator for 30 minutes.
3. When ready, transfer the shrimp to the air flow racks.
4. Slide the racks into the air fryer oven. Press the Power Button and cook at 400ºF (205ºC) for 5 minutes.
5. When cooking is complete, the shrimp should be pink on the outside and opaque in the center. Remove from the air fryer oven and serve warm.

Orange Shrimp

Prep time: 40 minutes | Cook time: 12 minutes | Serves 4

⅓ cup orange juice
3 teaspoons minced garlic
1 teaspoon Old Bay seasoning
¼ to ½ teaspoon cayenne pepper
1 pound (454 g) medium shrimp, thawed, deveined, peeled, with tails off, and patted dry
Cooking spray

1. Stir together the orange juice, garlic, Old Bay seasoning, and cayenne pepper in a medium bowl. Add the shrimp to the bowl and toss to coat well.
2. Cover the bowl with plastic wrap and marinate in the refrigerator for 30 minutes.
3. Spritz the air flow racks with cooking spray. Put the shrimp on the racks and spray with cooking spray.
4. Slide the racks into the air fryer oven. Press the Power Button and cook at 400ºF (205ºC) for 12 minutes.

5. Flip the shrimp halfway through the cooking time.
6. When cooked, the shrimp should be opaque and crisp. Remove from the air fryer oven and serve hot.

Yellow Mustard Sole

Prep time: 5 minutes | Cook time: 10 minutes | Serves 4

5 teaspoons low-sodium yellow mustard
1 tablespoon freshly squeezed lemon juice
4 (3.5-ounce / 99-g) sole fillets
2 teaspoons olive oil
½ teaspoon dried marjoram
½ teaspoon dried thyme
⅛ teaspoon freshly ground black pepper
1 slice bread, crumbled

1. Whisk together the mustard and lemon juice in a small bowl until thoroughly mixed and smooth. Spread the mixture evenly over the sole fillets, then transfer the fillets to the air flow racks.
2. In a separate bowl, combine the olive oil, marjoram, thyme, black pepper, and bread crumbs and stir to mix well. Gently but firmly press the mixture onto the top of fillets, coating them completely.
3. Slide the racks into the air fryer oven. Press the Power Button and cook at 320ºF (160ºC) for 10 minutes.
4. When cooking is complete, the fish should reach an internal temperature of 145ºF (63ºC) on a meat thermometer. Remove the racks from the air fryer oven and serve on a plate.

Crispy Scallops

Prep time: 5 minutes | Cook time: 7 minutes | Serves 4

1 egg
3 tablespoons all-purpose flour
1 cup bread crumbs
1 pound (454 g) fresh scallops
2 tablespoons olive oil
Salt and black pepper, to taste

1. In a bowl, lightly beat the egg. Put the flour and bread crumbs into separate shallow dishes.
2. Dredge the scallops in the flour and shake off any excess. Dip the flour-coated scallops in the beaten egg and roll in the bread crumbs.
3. Brush the scallops generously with olive oil and season with salt and pepper, to taste. Transfer the scallops to the air flow racks.
4. Slide the racks into the air fryer oven. Press the Power Button and cook at 360°F (182°C) for 7 minutes.
5. Flip the scallops halfway through the cooking time.
6. When cooking is complete, the scallops should reach an internal temperature of just 145°F (63°C) on a meat thermometer. Remove from the air fryer oven. Let the scallops cool for 5 minutes and serve.

Pecan Catfish

Prep time: 5 minutes | Cook time: 12 minutes | Serves 4

½ cup pecan meal
1 teaspoon fine sea salt
¼ teaspoon ground
For Garnish (Optional):
Fresh oregano
Pecan halves
black pepper
4 (4-ounce / 113-g) catfish fillets
Avocado oil spray

1. Spray the air flow racks with avocado oil spray.
2. Combine the pecan meal, sea salt, and black pepper in a large bowl. Dredge each catfish fillet in the meal mixture, turning until well coated. Spritz the fillets with avocado oil spray, then transfer to the air flow racks.
3. Slide the racks into the air fryer oven. Press the Power Button and cook at 375°F (190°C) for 12 minutes.
4. Flip the fillets halfway through the cooking time.
5. When cooking is complete, the fish should be cooked through and no longer translucent. Remove from the air fryer oven and sprinkle the oregano sprigs and pecan halves on top for garnish, if desired. Serve immediately.

Teriyaki Salmon with Bok Choy

Prep time: 15 minutes | Cook time: 15 minutes | Serves 4

¾ cup Teriyaki Sauce, divided
4 (6-ounce / 170-g) skinless salmon fillets
4 heads baby bok choy, root ends trimmed off and cut in half lengthwise
through the root
1 teaspoon sesame oil
1 tablespoon vegetable oil
1 tablespoon toasted sesame seeds

1. Set aside ¼ cup of Teriyaki Sauce and pour the remaining sauce into a resealable plastic bag. Put the salmon into the bag and seal, squeezing as much air out as possible. Allow the salmon to marinate for at least 10 minutes.
2. Arrange the bok choy halves on a sheet pan. Drizzle the oils over the vegetables, tossing to coat. Drizzle about 1 tablespoon of the reserved Teriyaki Sauce over the bok choy, then push them to the sides of the sheet pan.
3. Put the salmon fillets in the middle of the sheet pan.
4. Slide the pan into the air fryer oven. Press the Power Button and cook at 375°F (190°C) for 15 minutes.
5. When done, remove the pan and brush the salmon with the remaining Teriyaki Sauce. Serve garnished with the sesame seeds.

Coconut Fish Curry

Prep time: 10 minutes | Cook time: 22 minutes | Serves 4

2 tablespoons sunflower oil, divided
1 pound (454 g) fish, chopped
1 ripe tomato, pureéd
2 red chilies, chopped
1 shallot, minced
1 garlic clove, minced
1 cup coconut milk

1 tablespoon coriander powder
1 teaspoon red curry paste
½ teaspoon fenugreek seeds
Salt and white pepper, to taste

1. Coat the air flow racks with 1 tablespoon of sunflower oil. Put the fish on the air flow racks.
2. Slide the racks into the air fryer oven. Press the Power Button and cook at 380ºF (193ºC) for 10 minutes.
3. Flip the fish halfway through the cooking time.
4. When cooking is complete, transfer the cooked fish to a baking pan greased with the remaining 1 tablespoon of sunflower oil. Stir in the remaining ingredients.
5. Slide the pan into the air fryer oven. Press the Power Button and cook at 350ºF (180ºC) for 12 minutes.
6. When cooking is complete, they should be heated through. Cool for 5 to 8 minutes before serving.

Shrimp and Artichoke Paella

Prep time: 5 minutes | Cook time: 16 minutes | Serves 4

1 (10-ounce / 284-g) package frozen cooked rice, thawed
1 (6-ounce / 170-g) jar artichoke hearts, drained and chopped
¼ cup vegetable broth

½ teaspoon dried thyme
½ teaspoon turmeric
1 cup frozen cooked small shrimp
½ cup frozen baby peas
1 tomato, diced

1. Mix the cooked rice, chopped artichoke hearts, vegetable broth, thyme, and turmeric in a baking pan and stir to combine.
2. Slide the pan into the air fryer oven. Press the Power Button and cook at 340ºF (171ºC) for 16 minutes.

3. After 9 minutes, remove from the air fryer oven and add the shrimp, baby peas, and diced tomato to the baking pan. Mix well. Return to the air fryer oven and continue cooking for 7 minutes more, or until the shrimp are done and the paella is bubbling.
4. When cooking is complete, remove from the air fryer oven. Cool for 5 minutes before serving.

Pollock Sticks

Prep time: 10 minutes | Cook time: 6 minutes | Serves 8

8 ounces (227 g) pollock fillets, cut into ½ × 3 inches strips
Salt, to taste

(optional)
½ cup plain bread crumbs
Cooking spray

1. Season the fish strips with salt to taste, if desired.
2. Put the bread crumbs on a plate, then roll the fish in the bread crumbs until well coated. Spray all sides of the fish with cooking spray. Transfer to the air flow racks.
3. Slide the racks into the air fryer oven. Press the Power Button and cook at 400ºF (205ºC) for 6 minutes.
4. When cooked, the fish sticks should be golden brown and crispy. Remove from the air fryer oven to a plate and serve hot.

Malty-Beer-Breaded Cod Fillets

Prep time: 5 minutes | Cook time: 15 minutes | Serves 4

2 eggs
1 cup malty beer
1 cup all-purpose flour
½ cup cornstarch
1 teaspoon garlic powder
Salt and ground black pepper, to taste
4 (4-ounce / 113-g) cod fillets
Cooking spray

1. In a shallow bowl, beat together the eggs with the beer. In another shallow bowl, thoroughly combine the flour and cornstarch. Sprinkle with the garlic powder, salt, and pepper.
2. Dredge each cod fillet in the flour mixture, then in the egg mixture. Dip each piece of fish in the flour mixture a second time.
3. Spritz the air flow racks with cooking spray. Arrange the cod fillets on the racks.
4. Slide the racks into the air fryer oven. Press the Power Button and cook at 400°F (205°C) for 15 minutes.
5. Flip the fillets halfway through the cooking time.
6. When cooking is complete, the cod should reach an internal temperature of 145°F (63°C) on a meat thermometer and the outside should be crispy. Let the fish cool for 5 minutes and serve.

Tilapia Tacos

Prep time: 10 minutes | Cook time: 10 to 15 minutes | Serves 6

1 tablespoon avocado oil
1 tablespoon Cajun seasoning
4 (5 to 6 ounce / 142 to 170 g) tilapia fillets
1 (14-ounce / 397-g) package coleslaw mix
12 corn tortillas
2 limes, cut into wedges

1. Line a baking pan with parchment paper.
2. In a shallow bowl, stir together the avocado oil and Cajun seasoning to make a marinade. Put the tilapia fillets into the bowl, turning to coat evenly.
3. Put the fillets in the baking pan in a single layer.
4. Slide the pan into the air fryer oven. Press the Power Button and cook at 375°F (190°C) for 10 minutes.

5. When cooked, the fish should be flaky. If necessary, continue cooking for 5 minutes more. Remove the fish from the air fryer oven to a plate.
6. Assemble the tacos: Spoon some coleslaw mix into each tortilla and top each with ⅓ of a tilapia fillet. Squeeze some lime juice over the top of each taco and serve immediately.

Paprika Tiger Prawn

Prep time: 5 minutes | Cook time: 10 minutes | Serves 4

1 pound (454 g) tiger prawn
2 tablespoons olive oil
½ tablespoon old bay seasoning
¼ tablespoon smoked paprika
¼ teaspoon cayenne pepper
Pinch of sea salt

1. Toss all the ingredients in a large bowl until the prawn are evenly coated.
2. Arrange the prawn on the air flow racks.
3. Slide the racks into the air fryer oven. Press the Power Button and cook at 380°F (193°C) for 10 minutes.
4. When cooking is complete, the prawn should be pink and cooked through. Remove from the air fryer oven and serve hot.

Chapter 8 Meats

Beef Stroganoff with Mushrooms

Prep time: 15 minutes | Cook time: 14 minutes | Serves 4

1 pound (454 g) beef steak, thinly sliced
8 ounces (227 g) mushrooms, sliced
1 whole onion, chopped

2 cups beef broth
1 cup sour cream
4 tablespoons butter, melted
2 cups cooked egg noodles

1. Combine the mushrooms, onion, beef broth, sour cream and butter in a bowl until well blended. Add the beef steak to another bowl.
2. Spread the mushroom mixture over the steak and let marinate for 10 minutes.
3. Pour the marinated steak in a baking pan.
4. Slide the pan into the air fryer oven. Press the Power Button and cook at 400ºF (205ºC) for 14 minutes.
5. Flip the steak halfway through the cooking time.
6. When cooking is complete, the steak should be browned and the vegetables should be tender.
7. Serve hot with the cooked egg noodles.

Herby Beef and Zucchini

Prep time: 5 minutes | Cook time: 12 minutes | Serves 4

1½ pounds (680 g) ground beef
1 pound (454 g) chopped zucchini
2 tablespoons extra-virgin olive oil
1 teaspoon dried

oregano
1 teaspoon dried basil
1 teaspoon dried rosemary
2 tablespoons fresh chives, chopped

1. In a large bowl, combine all the ingredients, except for the chives, until well blended.
2. Put the beef and zucchini mixture in a baking pan.
3. Slide the pan into the air fryer oven. Press the Power Button and cook at 400ºF (205ºC) for 12 minutes.
4. When cooking is complete, the beef should be browned and the zucchini should be tender.
5. Divide the beef and zucchini mixture among four serving dishes. Top with fresh chives and serve hot.

Roasted Pork Chops

Prep time: 5 minutes | Cook time: 20 minutes | Serves 2

2 (10-ounce / 284-g) bone-in, center cut pork chops, 1-inch thick
2 teaspoons

Worcestershire sauce
Salt and ground black pepper, to taste
Cooking spray

1. Rub the Worcestershire sauce on both sides of pork chops.
2. Season with salt and pepper to taste.
3. Spritz the air flow racks with cooking spray and place the chops on the air flow racks side by side.
4. Press the Power Button and cook at 350ºF (180ºC) for 20 minutes.
5. After 10 minutes, remove from the air fryer oven. Flip the pork chops with tongs. Return to the air fryer oven and continue cooking.
6. When cooking is complete, the pork should be well browned on both sides.
7. Let rest for 5 minutes before serving.

Cauliflower Sausage Casserole

Prep time: 5 minutes | Cook time: 27 minutes | Serves 6

1 pound (454 g) cauliflower, chopped
6 pork sausages, chopped
½ onion, sliced
3 eggs, beaten
⅓ cup Colby cheese

1 teaspoon cumin powder
½ teaspoon tarragon
½ teaspoon sea salt
½ teaspoon ground black pepper
Cooking spray

1. Spritz a baking pan with cooking spray.
2. In a saucepan over medium heat, boil the cauliflower until tender. Put the boiled cauliflower in a food processor and pulse until puréed. Transfer to a large bowl and combine with remaining ingredients until well blended.
3. Pour the cauliflower and sausage mixture into the pan.
4. Slide the pan into the air fryer oven. Press the Power Button and cook at 365ºF (185ºC) for 27 minutes.
5. When cooking is complete, the sausage should be lightly browned.
6. Divide the mixture among six serving dishes and serve warm.

Marinara Beef Meatballs

Prep time: 5 minutes | Cook time: 8 minutes | Serves 4

1 pound (454 g) lean ground sirloin beef
2 tablespoons seasoned bread crumbs
¼ teaspoon kosher
salt
1 large egg, beaten
1 cup Marinara sauce, for serving
Cooking spray

1. Spritz the air flow racks with cooking spray.
2. Mix all the ingredients, except for the Marinara sauce, into a bowl until well blended. Shape the mixture into sixteen meatballs.
3. Arrange the meatballs on the prepared air flow racks and mist with cooking spray.
4. Slide the racks into the air fryer oven. Press the Power Button and cook at 360ºF (182ºC) for 8 minutes.
5. Flip the meatballs halfway through.
6. When cooking is complete, the meatballs should be well browned.
7. Divide the meatballs among four plates and serve warm with the Marinara sauce.

Worcestershire Ribeye Steaks

Prep time: 35 minutes | Cook time: 10 to 12 minutes | Serves 2 to 4

2 (8-ounce / 227-g) boneless ribeye steaks
4 teaspoons Worcestershire sauce
½ teaspoon garlic powder
Salt and ground black pepper, to taste
4 teaspoons olive oil

1. Brush the steaks with Worcestershire sauce on both sides. Sprinkle with garlic powder and coarsely ground black pepper. Drizzle the steaks with olive oil. Allow steaks to marinate for 30 minutes.
2. Transfer the steaks on the air flow racks.
3. Press the Power Button and cook at 400ºF (205ºC) for 4 minutes.
4. After 2 minutes, remove from the air fryer oven. Flip the steaks. Return to the air fryer oven and continue cooking.
5. When cooking is complete, the steaks should be well browned.
6. Remove the steaks from the air flow racks and let sit for 5 minutes. Salt and serve.

Thai Curry Beef Meatballs

Prep time: 5 minutes | Cook time: 15 minutes | Serves 4

1 pound (454 g) ground beef
1 tablespoon sesame oil
2 teaspoons chopped lemongrass
1 teaspoon red Thai
curry paste
1 teaspoon Thai seasoning blend
Juice and zest of ½ lime
Cooking spray

1. Spritz the air flow racks with cooking spray.
2. In a medium bowl, combine all the ingredients until well blended.
3. Shape the meat mixture into 24 meatballs and arrange them on the racks.
4. Slide the racks into the air fryer oven. Press the Power Button and cook at 380ºF (193ºC) for 15 minutes.
5. Flip the meatballs halfway through.
6. When cooking is complete, the meatballs should be browned.
7. Transfer the meatballs to plates. Let cool for 5 minutes before serving.

Crusted Wasabi Spam

Prep time: 5 minutes | Cook time: 12 minutes | Serves 3

⅔ cup all-purpose flour
2 large eggs
1½ tablespoons wasabi paste
2 cups panko bread crumbs
6 ½-inch-thick spam slices
Cooking spray

1. Spritz the air flow racks with cooking spray.
2. Pour the flour in a shallow plate. Whisk the eggs with wasabi in a large bowl. Pour the panko in a separate shallow plate.
3. Dredge the spam slices in the flour first, then dunk in the egg mixture, and then roll the spam over the panko to coat well. Shake the excess off.
4. Arrange the spam slices on the racks and spritz with cooking spray.
5. Slide the racks into the air fryer oven. Press the Power Button and cook at 400ºF (205ºC) for 12 minutes.
6. Flip the spam slices halfway through.
7. When cooking is complete, the spam slices should be golden and crispy.
8. Serve immediately.

Beef Kofta

Prep time: 10 minutes | Cook time: 13 minutes | Makes 12 koftas

1½ pounds (680 g) lean ground beef
1 teaspoon onion powder
¾ teaspoon ground cinnamon
¾ teaspoon ground dried turmeric
1 teaspoon ground cumin
¾ teaspoon salt
¼ teaspoon cayenne
12 (3½- to 4-inch-long) cinnamon sticks
Cooking spray

1. Spritz the air flow racks with cooking spray.
2. Combine all the ingredients, except for the cinnamon sticks, in a large bowl. Toss to mix well.
3. Divide and shape the mixture into 12 balls, then wrap each ball around each cinnamon stick and leave a quarter of the length uncovered.
4. Arrange the beef-cinnamon sticks on the prepared racks and spritz with cooking spray.
5. Slide the racks into the air fryer oven. Press the Power Button and cook at 375ºF (190ºC) for 13 minutes.
6. Flip the sticks halfway through the cooking.
7. When cooking is complete, the beef should be browned.
8. Serve immediately.

Beef Satay with Peanut Dipping Sauce

Prep time: 30 minutes | Cook time: 5 minutes | Serves 4

8 ounces (227 g) London broil, sliced into 8 strips
2 teaspoons curry
powder
½ teaspoon kosher salt
Cooking spray
Peanut Dipping Sauce:
2 tablespoons creamy peanut butter
1 tablespoon reduced-sodium soy sauce
2 teaspoons rice vinegar
1 teaspoon honey
1 teaspoon grated ginger

Special Equipment:
4 bamboo skewers, cut into halves and soaked in water for 20 minutes to keep them from burning while cooking

1. Spritz the air flow racks with cooking spray.
2. In a bowl, place the London broil strips and sprinkle with the curry powder and kosher salt to season. Thread the strips onto the soaked skewers.
3. Arrange the skewers on the prepared air flow racks and spritz with cooking spray.
4. Slide the racks into the air fryer oven. Press the Power Button and cook at 360ºF (182ºC) for 5 minutes.
5. Flip the beef halfway through the cooking time.
6. When cooking is complete, the beef should be well browned.
7. In the meantime, stir together the peanut butter, soy sauce, rice vinegar, honey, and ginger in a bowl to make the dipping sauce.
8. Transfer the beef to the serving dishes and let rest for 5 minutes. Serve with the peanut dipping sauce on the side.

Golden Venison

Prep time: 10 minutes | Cook time: 10 minutes | Serves 4

2 eggs
¼ cup milk
1 cup whole wheat flour
½ teaspoon salt
¼ teaspoon ground
black pepper
1 pound (454 g) venison backstrap, sliced
Cooking spray

1. Spritz the air flow racks with cooking spray.
2. Whisk the eggs with milk in a large bowl. Combine the flour with salt and ground black pepper in a shallow dish.
3. Dredge the venison in the flour first, then into the egg mixture. Shake the excess off and roll the venison back over the flour to coat well.
4. Arrange the venison on the racks and spritz with cooking spray.
5. Slide the racks into the air fryer oven. Press the Power Button and cook at 360ºF (182ºC) for 10 minutes.
6. Flip the venison halfway through.
7. When cooking is complete, the internal temperature of the venison should reach at least 145ºF (63ºC) for medium rare.
8. Serve immediately.

Teriyaki Ribs

Prep time: 5 minutes | Cook time: 30 minutes | Serves 4

¼ cup soy sauce	dried ginger
¼ cup honey	4 (8-ounce / 227-
1 teaspoon garlic powder	g) boneless country-style pork ribs
1 teaspoon ground	Cooking spray

1. Spritz the air flow racks with cooking spray.
2. Make the teriyaki sauce: combine the soy sauce, honey, garlic powder, and ginger in a bowl. Stir to mix well.
3. Brush the ribs with half of the teriyaki sauce, then arrange the ribs on the racks. Spritz with cooking spray.
4. Slide the racks into the air fryer oven. Press the Power Button and cook at 350ºF (180ºC) for 30 minutes.
5. After 15 minutes, remove from the air fryer oven. Flip the ribs and brush with remaining teriyaki sauce. Return to the air fryer oven and continue cooking.
6. When cooking is complete, the internal temperature of the ribs should reach at least 145ºF (63ºC).
7. Serve immediately.

Pork with Coriander-Parsley Sauce

Prep time: 1 hour 15 minutes | Cook time: 30 minutes | Serves 4

1 teaspoon golden flaxseeds meal	freshly squeezed
1 egg white, well whisked	1 tablespoon olive oil
1 tablespoon soy sauce	1 pound (454 g) pork butt, cut into pieces 2-inches long
1 teaspoon lemon juice, preferably	Salt and ground black pepper, to taste

Coriander-Parsley Sauce:

3 garlic cloves, minced	1 teaspoon lemon juice
⅓ cup fresh coriander leaves	½ tablespoon salt
⅓ cup fresh parsley leaves	⅓ cup extra-virgin olive oil

1. Combine the flaxseeds meal, egg white, soy sauce, lemon juice, salt, black pepper, and olive oil in a large bowl. Dunk the pork strips in and press to submerge.
2. Wrap the bowl in plastic and refrigerate to marinate for at least an hour.
3. Arrange the marinated pork strips on the air flow racks.
4. Slide the racks into the air fryer oven. Press the Power Button and cook at 380ºF (193ºC) for 30 minutes.
5. After 15 minutes, remove from the air fryer oven. Flip the pork. Return to the air fryer oven and continue cooking.
6. When cooking is complete, the pork should be well browned.
7. Meanwhile, combine the ingredients for the sauce in a small bowl. Stir to mix well. Arrange the bowl in the refrigerator to chill until ready to serve.
8. Serve the air fried pork strips with the chilled sauce.

Macadamia-Breaded Pork

Prep time: 5 minutes | Cook time: 35 minutes | Serves 2

1 clove garlic, minced	crumbs
2 tablespoons olive oil	1 tablespoon
1 pound (454 g) pork rack	rosemary, chopped
	1 egg
1 cup chopped macadamia nuts	Salt and ground black pepper, to taste
1 tablespoon bread	

1. Combine the garlic and olive oil in a small bowl. Stir to mix well.
2. On a clean work surface, rub the pork rack with the garlic oil and sprinkle with salt and black pepper on both sides.
3. Combine the macadamia nuts, bread crumbs, and rosemary in a shallow dish. Whisk the egg in a large bowl.
4. Dredge the pork in the egg, then roll the pork over the macadamia nut mixture to coat well. Shake the excess off.
5. Arrange the pork on the air flow racks.
6. Slide the racks into the air fryer oven. Press the Power Button and cook at 350ºF (180ºC) for 30 minutes.
7. After 30 minutes, remove from the air fryer oven. Flip the pork rack. Return to the air fryer oven and increase temperature to 390ºF (199ºC) for 5 minutes. Keep cooking.
8. When cooking is complete, the pork should be browned.
9. Serve immediately.

Crispy Liver Strips

Prep time: 15 minutes | Cook time: 4 to 5 minutes | Serves 4

1 pound (454 g) sliced calf's liver, cut into about ½-inch-wide strips
Salt and ground black pepper, to taste
2 eggs
2 tablespoons milk
½ cup whole wheat flour
1½ cups panko bread crumbs
½ cup plain bread crumbs
½ teaspoon salt
¼ teaspoon ground black pepper
Cooking spray

1. Sprinkle the liver strips with salt and pepper.
2. Beat together the egg and milk in a bowl. Put wheat flour in a shallow dish. In a second shallow dish, mix panko, plain bread crumbs, ½ teaspoon salt, and ¼ teaspoon pepper.
3. Dip liver strips in flour, egg wash, and then bread crumbs, pressing in coating slightly to make crumbs stick.
4. Spritz the air flow racks with cooking spray. Put strips in a single layer on the air flow racks.
5. Press the Power Button and cook at 400ºF (205ºC) for 4 minutes.
6. After 2 minutes, remove from the air fryer oven. Flip the strips with tongs. Return to the air fryer oven and continue cooking.
7. When cooking is complete, the liver strips should be crispy and golden.
8. Serve immediately.

Pork Schnitzel

Prep time: 15 minutes | Cook time: 15 minutes | Serves 4

4 thin boneless pork loin chops
2 tablespoons lemon juice
½ cup flour
¼ teaspoon marjoram
1 teaspoon salt
1 cup panko bread crumbs
2 eggs
Lemon wedges, for serving
Cooking spray

1. On a clean work surface, drizzle the pork chops with lemon juice on both sides.
2. Combine the flour with marjoram and salt on a shallow plate. Pour the bread crumbs on a separate shallow dish. Beat the eggs in a large bowl.
3. Dredge the pork chops in the flour, then dunk in the beaten eggs to coat well. Shake the excess off and roll over the bread crumbs. Arrange the pork chops on the air flow racks and spritz with cooking spray.
4. Slide the racks into the air fryer oven. Press the Power Button and cook at 400ºF (205ºC) for 15 minutes.
5. After 7 minutes, remove from the air fryer oven. Flip the pork. Return to the air fryer oven and continue cooking.
6. When cooking is complete, the pork should be crispy and golden.
7. Squeeze the lemon wedges over the fried chops and serve immediately.

Pistachio-Crusted Lamb

Prep time: 10 minutes | Cook time: 20 minutes | Serves 2

½ cup finely chopped pistachios
1 teaspoon chopped fresh rosemary
3 tablespoons panko bread crumbs
2 teaspoons chopped fresh oregano
1 tablespoon olive oil
Salt and freshly ground black pepper, to taste
1 lamb rack, bones fat trimmed and frenched
1 tablespoon Dijon mustard

1. Put the pistachios, rosemary, bread crumbs, oregano, olive oil, salt, and black pepper in a food processor. Pulse to combine until smooth.
2. Rub the lamb rack with salt and black pepper on a clean work surface, then place it on the air flow racks.
3. Slide the racks into the air fryer oven. Press the Power Button and cook at 380ºF (193ºC) for 12 minutes.
4. Flip the lamb halfway through.
5. When cooking is complete, the lamb should be lightly browned.
6. Transfer the lamb on a plate and brush with Dijon mustard on the fat side, then sprinkle with the pistachios mixture over the lamb rack to coat well.
7. Put the lamb rack back to the air fryer oven and air fry for 8 more minutes or until the internal temperature of the rack reaches at least 145ºF (63ºC).
8. Remove the lamb rack from the air fryer oven with tongs and allow to cool for 5 minutes before slicing to serve.

Pork and Vegetable Rice Bowl

Prep time: 10 minutes | Cook time: 12 minutes | Serves 4

3 scallions, diced (about ½ cup)
½ red bell pepper, diced (about ½ cup)
2 teaspoons sesame oil
½ pound (227 g) pork tenderloin, diced
½ cup frozen peas, thawed
½ cup roasted mushrooms
½ cup soy sauce
2 cups cooked rice
1 egg, beaten

1. Put the scallions and red pepper on a baking pan. Drizzle with the sesame oil and toss the vegetables to coat them in the oil.
2. Slide the pan into the air fryer oven. Press the Power Button and cook at 375ºF (190ºC) for 12 minutes.
3. While the vegetables are cooking, place the pork in a large bowl. Add the peas, mushrooms, soy sauce, and rice and toss to coat the ingredients with the sauce.
4. After about 4 minutes, remove from the air fryer oven. Put the pork mixture on the pan and stir the scallions and peppers into the pork and rice. Return to the air fryer oven and continue cooking.
5. After another 6 minutes, remove from the air fryer oven. Move the rice mixture to the sides to create an empty circle in the middle of the pan. Pour the egg in the circle. Return to the air fryer oven and continue cooking.
6. When cooking is complete, remove from the air fryer oven and stir the egg to scramble it. Stir the egg into the fried rice mixture. Serve immediately.

Honey Dijon Pork Tenderloin

Prep time: 15 minutes | Cook time: 15 minutes | Serves 4

3 tablespoons Dijon mustard
3 tablespoons honey
1 teaspoon dried rosemary
1 tablespoon olive oil
1 pound (454 g) pork tenderloin, rinsed and drained
Salt and freshly ground black pepper, to taste

1. In a small bowl, combine the Dijon mustard, honey, and rosemary. Stir to combine.
2. Rub the pork tenderloin with salt and pepper on all sides on a clean work surface.
3. Heat the olive oil in an air fryer oven-safe skillet over high heat. Sear the pork loin on all sides in the skillet for 6 minutes or until golden brown. Flip the pork halfway through.
4. Remove from the heat and spread honey-mustard mixture evenly to coat the pork loin.
5. Slide the skillet into the air fryer oven. Press the Power Button and cook at 425ºF (220ºC) for 15 minutes.
6. When cooking is complete, an instant-read thermometer inserted in the pork should register at least 145ºF (63ºC).
7. Remove from the air fryer oven and allow to rest for 3 minutes. Slice the pork into ½-inch slices and serve.

Dijon Pork Tenderloin

Prep time: 5 minutes | Cook time: 10 minutes | Serves 6

2 large egg whites
1½ tablespoons Dijon mustard
2 cups crushed pretzel crumbs
1½ pounds (680 g) pork tenderloin, cut into ¼-pound (113-g) sections
Cooking spray

1. Spritz the air flow racks with cooking spray.
2. Whisk the egg whites with Dijon mustard in a bowl until bubbly. Pour the pretzel crumbs in a separate bowl.
3. Dredge the pork tenderloin in the egg white mixture and press to coat. Shake the excess off and roll the tenderloin over the pretzel crumbs.
4. Arrange the well-coated pork tenderloin on the racks and spritz with cooking spray.
5. Slide the racks into the air fryer oven. Press the Power Button and cook at 350ºF (180ºC) for 10 minutes.
6. After 5 minutes, remove from the air fryer oven. Flip the pork. Return to the air fryer oven and continue cooking.
7. When cooking is complete, the pork should be golden brown and crispy.
8. Serve immediately.

Lechon Carajay

Prep time: 10 minutes | Cook time: 30 minutes | Serves 4

1 pound (454 g) pork belly, cut into three thick chunks
6 garlic cloves
2 bay leaves
2 tablespoons soy sauce
1 teaspoon kosher salt
1 teaspoon ground black pepper
3 cups water
Cooking spray

1. Put all the ingredients in a pressure cooker, then put the lid on and cook on high for 15 minutes.
2. Natural release the pressure and release any remaining pressure, transfer the tender pork belly on a clean work surface. Allow to cool under room temperature until you can handle.
3. Generously spritz the air flow racks with cooking spray.
4. Cut each chunk into two slices, then put the pork slices on the racks.
5. Slide the racks into the air fryer oven. Press the Power Button and cook at 400ºF (205ºC) for 15 minutes.
6. After 7 minutes, remove from the air fryer oven. Flip the pork. Return to the air fryer oven and continue cooking.
7. When cooking is complete, the pork fat should be crispy.
8. Serve immediately.

Caraway Beef Steaks

Prep time: 5 minutes | Cook time: 10 minutes | Serves 4

4 beef steaks
2 teaspoons caraway seeds
2 teaspoons garlic powder
Sea salt and cayenne
pepper, to taste
1 tablespoon melted butter
1/3 cup almond flour
2 eggs, beaten

1. Add the beef steaks to a large bowl and toss with the caraway seeds, garlic powder, salt and pepper until well coated.
2. Stir together the melted butter and almond flour in a bowl. Whisk the eggs in a different bowl.
3. Dredge the seasoned steaks in the eggs, then dip in the almond and butter mixture.

4. Arrange the coated steaks on the air flow racks.
5. Slide the racks into the air fryer oven. Press the Power Button and cook at 355ºF (179ºC) for 10 minutes.
6. Flip the steaks once halfway through to ensure even cooking.
7. When cooking is complete, the internal temperature of the beef steaks should reach at least 145ºF (63ºC) on a meat thermometer.
8. Transfer the steaks to plates. Let cool for 5 minutes and serve hot.

Pork, Bell Pepper, and Pineapple Kebabs

Prep time: 10 minutes | Cook time: 12 minutes | Serves 4

¼ teaspoon kosher salt
1 medium pork tenderloin (about 1 pound / 454 g), cut into 1½-inch chunks
1 green bell pepper, seeded and cut into 1-inch pieces
1 red bell pepper, seeded and cut into 1-inch pieces
2 cups fresh pineapple chunks
¾ cup Teriyaki Sauce or store-bought variety, divided

Special Equipment:
12 (9- to 12-inch) wooden skewers, soaked in water for about 30 minutes

1. Sprinkle the pork cubes with the salt.
2. Thread the pork, bell peppers, and pineapple onto a skewer. Repeat until all skewers are complete. Brush the skewers generously with about half of the Teriyaki Sauce. Put them on a sheet pan.
3. Slide the pan into the air fryer oven. Press the Power Button and cook at 375ºF (190ºC) for 10 minutes.
4. After about 5 minutes, remove from the air fryer oven. Turn over the skewers and brush with the remaining half of Teriyaki Sauce. Transfer the pan back to the air fryer oven and continue cooking until the vegetables are tender and browned in places and the pork is browned and cooked through.
5. Remove the pan from the air fryer oven and serve.

Orange Pork Carnitas

Prep time: 1 hour 10 minutes | Cook time: 25 minutes | Serves 6

2½ pounds (1.1 kg) boneless country-style pork ribs, cut into 2-inch pieces
3 tablespoons olive brine
1 tablespoon minced fresh oregano leaves
⅓ cup orange juice
1 teaspoon ground cumin
1 tablespoon minced garlic
1 teaspoon salt
1 teaspoon ground black pepper
Cooking spray

1. Combine all the ingredients in a large bowl. Toss to coat the pork ribs well. Wrap the bowl in plastic and refrigerate for at least an hour to marinate.
2. Spritz the air flow racks with cooking spray.
3. Arrange the marinated pork ribs on the racks and spritz with cooking spray.
4. Slide the racks into the air fryer oven. Press the Power Button and cook at 400ºF (205ºC) for 25 minutes.
5. Flip the ribs halfway through.
6. When cooking is complete, the ribs should be well browned.
7. Serve immediately.

Honey New York Strip

Prep time: 5 minutes | Cook time: 14 minutes | Serves 4

2 pounds (907 g) New York strip
1 teaspoon cayenne pepper
1 tablespoon honey
1 tablespoon Dijon mustard
½ stick butter, softened
Sea salt and freshly ground black pepper, to taste
Cooking spray

1. Spritz the air flow racks with cooking spray.
2. Sprinkle the New York strip with cayenne pepper, salt, and black pepper on a clean work surface.
3. Arrange the New York strip on the prepared racks and spritz with cooking spray.
4. Slide the racks into the air fryer oven. Press the Power Button and cook at 400ºF (205ºC) for 14 minutes.
5. Flip the New York strip halfway through.

6. When cooking is complete, the strips should be browned.
7. Meanwhile, combine the honey, mustard, and butter in a small bowl. Stir to mix well.
8. Transfer the air fried New York strip onto a plate and baste with the honey-mustard butter before serving.

Sriracha Beef and Broccoli

Prep time: 10 minutes | Cook time: 15 minutes | Serves 4

12 ounces (340 g) broccoli, cut into florets (about 4 cups)
1 pound (454 g) flat iron steak, cut into thin strips
½ teaspoon kosher salt
¾ cup soy sauce
1 teaspoon Sriracha sauce
3 tablespoons freshly squeezed orange juice
1 teaspoon cornstarch
1 medium onion, thinly sliced

1. Line a baking pan with aluminum foil. Put the broccoli on top and sprinkle with 3 tablespoons of water. Seal the broccoli in the foil in a single layer.
2. Slide the pan into the air fryer oven. Press the Power Button and cook at 375ºF (190ºC) for 6 minutes.
3. While the broccoli steams, sprinkle the steak with the salt. In a small bowl, whisk together the soy sauce, Sriracha, orange juice, and cornstarch. Put the onion and beef in a large bowl.
4. When cooking is complete, remove from the air fryer oven. Open the packet of broccoli and use tongs to transfer the broccoli to the bowl with the beef and onion, discarding the foil and remaining water. Pour the sauce over the beef and vegetables and toss to coat. Put the mixture in the baking pan.
5. Slide the pan into the air fryer oven. Press the Power Button and cook at 375ºF (190ºC) for 9 minutes.
6. After about 4 minutes, remove from the air fryer oven and gently toss the ingredients. Return the pan to air fryer oven and continue cooking.
7. When cooking is complete, the sauce should be thickened, the vegetables tender, and the beef barely pink in the center. Serve warm.

Kielbasa with Pineapples

Prep time: 15 minutes | Cook time: 10 minutes | Serves 2 to 4

¾ pound (340 g) kielbasa sausage, cut into ½-inch slices
1 (8-ounce / 227-g) can pineapple chunks in juice, drained
1 cup bell pepper chunks
1 tablespoon barbecue seasoning
1 tablespoon soy sauce
Cooking spray

1. Spritz the air flow racks with cooking spray.
2. Combine all the ingredients in a large bowl. Toss to mix well.
3. Pour the sausage mixture on the air flow racks.
4. Slide the racks into the air fryer oven. Press the Power Button and cook at 390ºF (199ºC) for 10 minutes.
5. After 5 minutes, remove from the air fryer oven. Stir the sausage mixture. Return to the air fryer oven and continue cooking.
6. When cooking is complete, the sausage should be lightly browned and the bell pepper and pineapple should be soft.
7. Serve immediately.

Thyme Lamb with Asparagus

Prep time: 10 minutes | Cook time: 15 minutes | Serves 4

4 asparagus spears, trimmed
2 tablespoons olive oil, divided
1 pound (454 g) lamb chops
1 garlic clove, minced
2 teaspoons chopped fresh thyme, for serving
Salt and ground black pepper, to taste

1. Spritz the air flow racks with cooking spray.
2. On a large plate, brush the asparagus with 1 tablespoon olive oil, then sprinkle with salt. Set aside.
3. On a separate plate, brush the lamb chops with remaining olive oil and sprinkle with salt and ground black pepper.
4. Arrange the lamb chops on the racks.
5. Slide the racks into the air fryer oven. Press the Power Button and cook at 400ºF (205ºC) for 15 minutes.
6. Flip the lamb chops and add the asparagus and garlic halfway through.
7. When cooking is complete, the lamb should be well browned and the asparagus should be tender.
8. Serve them on a plate with thyme on top.

Pork with Butternut Squash

Prep time: 15 minutes | Cook time: 13 minutes | Serves 4

4 boneless pork loin chops, ¾- to 1-inch thick
1 teaspoon kosher salt, divided
2 tablespoons Dijon mustard
2 tablespoons brown sugar
1 pound (454 g) butternut squash, cut into 1-inch cubes
1 large apple, peeled and cut into 12 to 16 wedges
1 medium onion, thinly sliced
½ teaspoon dried thyme
¼ teaspoon freshly ground black pepper
1 tablespoon unsalted butter, melted
½ cup chicken stock

1. Sprinkle the pork chops on both sides with ½ teaspoon of kosher salt. In a small bowl, whisk together the mustard and brown sugar. Baste about half of the mixture on one side of the pork chops. Put the chops, basted-side up, on a baking pan.
2. Put the squash in a large bowl. Add the apple, onion, thyme, remaining kosher salt, pepper, and butter and toss to coat. Arrange the squash-fruit mixture around the chops on the pan. Pour the chicken stock over the mixture, avoiding the chops.
3. Slide the pan into the air fryer oven. Press the Power Button and cook at 350ºF (180ºC) for 13 minutes.
4. After about 7 minutes, remove from the air fryer oven. Gently toss the squash mixture and turn over the chops. Baste the chops with the remaining mustard mixture. Return to the air fryer oven and continue cooking.
5. When cooking is complete, the pork chops should register at least 145ºF (63ºC) in the center on a meat thermometer, and the squash and apples should be tender. If necessary, continue cooking for up to 3 minutes more.
6. Remove from the air fryer oven. Spoon the squash and apples onto four plates, and place a pork chop on top. Serve immediately.

Pork Schnitzel

Prep time: 5 minutes | Cook time: 14 minutes | Serves 2

½ cup pork rinds
½ tablespoon fresh parsley
½ teaspoon fennel seed
½ teaspoon mustard
⅓ tablespoon cider vinegar
1 teaspoon garlic salt
⅓ teaspoon ground black pepper
2 eggs
2 pork schnitzel, halved
Cooking spray

1. Spritz the air flow racks with cooking spray.
2. Put the pork rinds, parsley, fennel seeds, and mustard in a food processor. Pour in the vinegar and sprinkle with salt and ground black pepper. Pulse until well combined and smooth.
3. Pour the pork rind mixture in a large bowl. Whisk the eggs in a separate bowl.
4. Dunk the pork schnitzel in the whisked eggs, then dunk in the pork rind mixture to coat well. Shake the excess off.
5. Arrange the schnitzel on the racks and spritz with cooking spray.
6. Slide the racks into the air fryer oven. Press the Power Button and cook at 350ºF (180ºC) for 14 minutes.
7. After 7 minutes, remove from the air fryer oven. Flip the schnitzel. Return to the air fryer oven and continue cooking.
8. When cooking is complete, the schnitzel should be golden and crispy.
9. Serve immediately.

Pork Meatballs with Chili

Prep time: 5 minutes | Cook time: 15 minutes | Serves 4

1 pound (454 g) ground pork
2 cloves garlic, finely minced
1 cup scallions, finely chopped
1½ tablespoons Worcestershire sauce
½ teaspoon freshly
grated ginger root
1 teaspoon turmeric powder
1 tablespoon oyster sauce
1 small sliced red chili, for garnish
Cooking spray

1. Spritz the air flow racks with cooking spray.
2. Combine all the ingredients, except for the red chili in a large bowl. Toss to mix well.
3. Shape the mixture into equally sized balls, then arrange them on the air flow racks and spritz with cooking spray.
4. Slide the racks into the air fryer oven. Press the Power Button and cook at 350ºF (180ºC) for 15 minutes.
5. After 7 minutes, remove from the air fryer oven. Flip the balls. Return to the air fryer oven and continue cooking.
6. When cooking is complete, the balls should be lightly browned.
7. Serve the pork meatballs with red chili on top.

Pork and Vegetable Kabobs

Prep time: 25 minutes | Cook time: 15 minutes | Serves 4

1 pound (454 g) pork tenderloin, cubed
1 teaspoon smoked paprika
Salt and ground black pepper, to taste
1 green bell pepper,
cut into chunks
1 zucchini, cut into chunks
1 red onion, sliced
1 tablespoon oregano
Cooking spray

Special Equipment:
Small bamboo skewers, soaked in water for 20 minutes

1. Spritz the air flow racks with cooking spray.
2. Add the pork to a bowl and season with the smoked paprika, salt and black pepper. Thread the seasoned pork cubes and vegetables alternately onto the soaked skewers. Arrange the skewers on the racks.
3. Slide the racks into the air fryer oven. Press the Power Button and cook at 350ºF (180ºC) for 15 minutes.
4. After 7 minutes, remove from the air fryer oven. Flip the pork skewers. Return to the air fryer oven and continue cooking.
5. When cooking is complete, the pork should be browned and vegetables are tender.
6. Transfer the skewers to the serving dishes and sprinkle with oregano. Serve hot.

Red Grapes with Italian Sausages

Prep time: 10 minutes | Cook time: 20 minutes | Serves 6

2 pounds (905 g) seedless red grapes
3 shallots, sliced
2 teaspoons fresh thyme
2 tablespoons olive oil
½ teaspoon kosher salt
Freshly ground black pepper, to taste
6 links (about 1½ pounds / 680 g) hot Italian sausage
3 tablespoons balsamic vinegar

1. Put the grapes in a large bowl. Add the shallots, thyme, olive oil, salt, and pepper. Gently toss. Put the grapes in a baking pan. Arrange the sausage links evenly in the pan.
2. Slide the pan into the air fryer oven. Press the Power Button and cook at 375ºF (190ºC) for 20 minutes.
3. After 10 minutes, remove the pan. Turn over the sausages and sprinkle the vinegar over the sausages and grapes. Gently toss the grapes and move them to one side of the pan. Return to the air fryer oven and continue cooking.
4. When cooking is complete, the grapes should be soft and the sausages browned. Serve immediately.

Ritzy Pork Sausage Ratatouille

Prep time: 10 minutes | Cook time: 25 minutes | Serves 4

4 pork sausages
Ratatouille:
2 zucchinis, sliced
1 eggplant, sliced
15 ounces (425 g) tomatoes, sliced
1 red bell pepper, sliced
1 medium red onion, sliced
1 cup canned butter
beans, drained
1 tablespoon balsamic vinegar
2 garlic cloves, minced
1 red chili, chopped
2 tablespoons fresh thyme, chopped
2 tablespoons olive oil

1. Put the sausages on the air flow racks.
2. Slide the racks into the air fryer oven. Press the Power Button and cook at 390ºF (199ºC) for 10 minutes.
3. After 7 minutes, remove from the air fryer oven. Flip the sausages. Return to the air fryer oven and continue cooking.

4. When cooking is complete, the sausages should be lightly browned.
5. Meanwhile, make the ratatouille: arrange the vegetable slices on a baking pan alternatively, then add the remaining ingredients on top.
6. Transfer the air fried sausage to a plate, then arrange the baking pan in the air fryer oven.
7. Cook for 15 minutes until the vegetables are tender. Give the vegetables a stir halfway through the baking.
8. Serve the ratatouille with the sausage on top.

Rosemary Pork Leg

Prep time: 10 minutes | Cook time: 52 minutes | Serves 4

2 teaspoons sesame oil
1 teaspoon dried sage, crushed
1 teaspoon cayenne pepper
1 rosemary sprig, chopped
1 thyme sprig, chopped
Sea salt and ground black pepper, to taste
2 pounds (907 g) pork leg roast, scored
½ pound (227 g) candy onions, sliced
4 cloves garlic, finely chopped
2 chili peppers, minced

1. In a mixing bowl, combine the sesame oil, sage, cayenne pepper, rosemary, thyme, salt and black pepper until well mixed. In another bowl, place the pork leg and brush with the seasoning mixture.
2. Put the seasoned pork leg in a baking pan. Slide the pan into the air fryer oven. Press the Power Button and cook at 400ºF (205ºC) for 40 minutes.
3. After 20 minutes, remove from the air fryer oven. Flip the pork leg. Return to the air fryer oven and continue cooking.
4. After another 20 minutes, add the candy onions, garlic, and chili peppers to the pan and air fry for another 12 minutes.
5. When cooking is complete, the pork leg should be browned.
6. Transfer the pork leg to a plate. Let cool for 5 minutes and slice. Spread the juices left in the pan over the pork and serve warm with the candy onions.

Sage Lamb Shoulder

Prep time: 5 minutes | Cook time: 25 minutes | Serves 4

1 cup all-purpose flour	paprika
2 teaspoons dried sage leaves	1 tablespoon salt
2 teaspoons garlic powder	4 (6-ounce / 170-g) bone-in lamb shoulder chops, fat trimmed
1 tablespoon mild	Cooking spray

1. Spritz the air flow racks with cooking spray.
2. Combine the flour, sage leaves, garlic powder, paprika, and salt in a large bowl. Stir to mix well. Dunk in the lamb chops and toss to coat well.
3. Arrange the lamb chops on the racks and spritz with cooking spray.
4. Slide the racks into the air fryer oven. Press the Power Button and cook at 375ºF (190ºC) for 25 minutes.
5. Flip the chops halfway through.
6. When cooking is complete, the chops should be golden brown and reaches your desired doneness.
7. Serve immediately.

Salsa Beef and Bell Pepper Meatballs

Prep time: 10 minutes | Cook time: 10 minutes | Serves 4

1 pound (454 g) ground beef (85% lean)	powder
	1 clove garlic, minced
½ cup salsa	½ teaspoon ground cumin
¼ cup diced green or red bell peppers	1 teaspoon fine sea salt
1 large egg, beaten	Lime wedges, for serving
¼ cup chopped onions	Cooking spray
½ teaspoon chili	

1. Spritz the air flow racks with cooking spray.
2. Combine all the ingredients in a large bowl. Stir to mix well.
3. Divide and shape the mixture into 1-inch balls. Arrange the balls on the racks and spritz with cooking spray.
4. Slide the racks into the air fryer oven. Press the Power Button and cook at 350ºF (180ºC) for 10 minutes.

5. Flip the balls with tongs halfway through.
6. When cooking is complete, the balls should be well browned.
7. Transfer the balls on a plate and squeeze the lime wedges over before serving.

Prosciutto and Asparagus Tart

Prep time: 10 minutes | Cook time: 25 minutes | Serves 4

All-purpose flour, for dusting	trimmed
1 sheet (½ package) frozen puff pastry, thawed	8 ounces (227 g) thinly sliced prosciutto, sliced into ribbons about ½-inch wide
½ cup grated Parmesan cheese	2 teaspoons aged balsamic vinegar
1 pound (454 g) (or more) asparagus,	

1. On a lightly floured cutting board, unwrap and unfold the puff pastry and roll it lightly with a rolling pin to press the folds together. Put it on a sheet pan.
2. Roll about ½ inch of the pastry edges up to form a ridge around the perimeter. Crimp the corners together to create a solid rim around the pastry. Using a fork, pierce the bottom of the pastry all over. Scatter the cheese over the bottom of the pastry.
3. Arrange the asparagus spears on top of the cheese in a single layer with 4 or 5 spears pointing one way, the next few pointing the opposite direction. You may need to trim them so they fit within the border of the pastry shell. Lay the prosciutto on top more or less evenly.
4. Slide the pan into the air fryer oven. Press the Power Button and cook at 375ºF (190ºC) for 25 minutes.
5. After about 15 minutes, check the tart, rotating the pan if the crust is not browning evenly and continue cooking until the pastry is golden brown and the edges of the prosciutto pieces are browned.
6. Remove from the air fryer oven. Allow to cool for 5 minutes before slicing.
7. Drizzle with the balsamic vinegar just before serving.

Spanish Carne Asada

Prep time: 5 minutes | Cook time: 15 minutes | Serves 4

3 chipotle peppers in adobo, chopped
⅓ cup chopped fresh oregano
⅓ cup chopped fresh parsley
4 cloves garlic, minced

Juice of 2 limes
1 teaspoon ground cumin seeds
⅓ cup olive oil
1 to 1½ pounds (454 g to 680 g) flank steak
Salt, to taste

1. Combine the chipotle, oregano, parsley, garlic, lime juice, cumin, and olive oil in a large bowl. Stir to mix well.
2. Dunk the flank steak in the mixture and press to coat well. Wrap the bowl in plastic and marinate under room temperature for at least 30 minutes.
3. Discard the marinade and place the steak on the air flow racks. Sprinkle with salt.
4. Slide the racks into the air fryer oven. Press the Power Button and cook at 390°F (199°C) for 15 minutes.
5. Flip the steak halfway through the cooking time.
6. When cooking is complete, the steak should be medium-rare or reach your desired doneness.
7. Remove the steak from the air fryer oven and slice to serve.

Pork Chops with Carrots and Mushrooms

Prep time: 10 minutes | Cook time: 15 minutes | Serves 4

2 carrots, cut into sticks
1 cup mushrooms, sliced
2 garlic cloves, minced
2 tablespoons olive oil
1 pound (454 g) boneless pork chops

1 teaspoon dried oregano
1 teaspoon dried thyme
1 teaspoon cayenne pepper
Salt and ground black pepper, to taste
Cooking spray

1. In a mixing bowl, toss together the carrots, mushrooms, garlic, olive oil and salt until well combined.
2. Add the pork chops to a different bowl and season with oregano, thyme, cayenne pepper, salt and black pepper.
3. Place the vegetable mixture on the greased air flow racks. Put the seasoned pork chops on top.
4. Slide the racks into the air fryer oven. Press the Power Button and cook at 360°F (182°C) for 15 minutes.
5. After 7 minutes, remove from the air fryer oven. Flip the pork and stir the vegetables. Return to the air fryer oven and continue cooking.
6. When cooking is complete, the pork chops should be browned and the vegetables should be tender.
7. Transfer the pork chops to the serving dishes and let cool for 5 minutes. Serve warm with vegetable on the side.

Spinach and Beef Meatloaves

Prep time: 15 minutes | Cook time: 45 minutes | Serves 2

1 large egg, beaten
1 cup frozen spinach
⅓ cup almond meal
¼ cup chopped onion
¼ cup plain Greek milk
¼ teaspoon salt
¼ teaspoon dried sage
2 teaspoons olive oil, divided

Freshly ground black pepper, to taste
½ pound (227 g) extra-lean ground beef
¼ cup tomato paste
1 tablespoon granulated stevia
¼ teaspoon Worcestershire sauce
Cooking spray

1. Coat a shallow baking pan with cooking spray.
2. In a large bowl, combine the beaten egg, spinach, almond meal, onion, milk, salt, sage, 1 teaspoon of olive oil, and pepper.
3. Crumble the beef over the spinach mixture. Mix well to combine. Divide the meat mixture in half. Shape each half into a loaf. Put the loaves in the prepared pan.
4. In a small bowl, whisk together the tomato paste, stevia, Worcestershire sauce, and remaining 1 teaspoon of olive oil. Spoon half of the sauce over each meatloaf.
5. Press the Power Button and cook at 350°F (180°C) for 40 minutes.
6. When cooking is complete, an instant-read thermometer inserted in the center of the meatloaves should read at least 165°F (74°C).
7. Serve immediately.

Stuffed Beef Tenderloin with Feta Cheese

Prep time: 10 minutes | Cook time: 10 minutes | Serves 4

1½ pounds (680 g) beef tenderloin, pounded to ¼ inch thick	creamy goat cheese
	½ cup crumbled feta cheese
3 teaspoons sea salt	¼ cup finely chopped onions
1 teaspoon ground black pepper	2 cloves garlic, minced
2 ounces (57 g)	Cooking spray

1. Spritz the air flow racks with cooking spray.
2. Unfold the beef tenderloin on a clean work surface. Rub the salt and pepper all over the beef tenderloin to season.
3. Make the filling for the stuffed beef tenderloins: Combine the goat cheese, feta, onions, and garlic in a medium bowl. Stir until well blended.
4. Spoon the mixture in the center of the tenderloin. Roll the tenderloin up tightly like rolling a burrito and use some kitchen twine to tie the tenderloin.
5. Arrange the tenderloin on the air flow racks.
6. Slide the racks into the air fryer oven. Press the Power Button and cook at 400ºF (205ºC) for 10 minutes.
7. Flip the tenderloin halfway through.
8. When cooking is complete, the instant-read thermometer inserted in the center of the tenderloin should register 135ºF (57ºC) for medium-rare.
9. Transfer to a platter and serve immediately.

Teriyaki Rump Steak with Broccoli and Capsicum

Prep time: 5 minutes | Cook time: 13 minutes | Serves 4

½ pound (227 g) rump steak	into florets
	2 red capsicums, sliced
⅓ cup teriyaki marinade	Fine sea salt and ground black pepper, to taste
1½ teaspoons sesame oil	
½ head broccoli, cut	Cooking spray

1. Toss the rump steak in a large bowl with teriyaki marinade. Wrap the bowl in plastic and refrigerate to marinate for at least an hour.
2. Spritz the air flow racks with cooking spray.
3. Discard the marinade and transfer the steak on the racks. Spritz with cooking spray.
4. Slide the racks into the air fryer oven. Press the Power Button and cook at 400ºF (205ºC) for 13 minutes.
5. Flip the steak halfway through.
6. When cooking is complete, the steak should be well browned.
7. Meanwhile, heat the sesame oil in a nonstick skillet over medium heat. Add the broccoli and capsicum. Sprinkle with salt and ground black pepper. Sauté for 5 minutes or until the broccoli is tender.
8. Transfer the air fried rump steak on a plate and top with the sautéed broccoli and capsicum. Serve hot.

Sumptuous Beef and Pork Sausage Meatloaf

Prep time: 10 minutes | Cook time: 25 minutes | Serves 4

¾ pound (340 g) ground chuck	1 tablespoon fresh parsley
4 ounces (113 g) ground pork sausage	1 teaspoon garlic paste
2 eggs, beaten	1 teaspoon chopped porcini mushrooms
1 cup Parmesan cheese, grated	½ teaspoon cumin powder
1 cup chopped shallot	Seasoned salt and crushed red pepper flakes, to taste
3 tablespoons plain milk	
1 tablespoon oyster sauce	

1. In a large bowl, combine all the ingredients until well blended.
2. Put the meat mixture in a baking pan. Use a spatula to press the mixture to fill the pan.
3. Slide the pan into the air fryer oven. Press the Power Button and cook at 360ºF (182ºC) for 25 minutes.
4. When cooking is complete, the meatloaf should be well browned.
5. Let the meatloaf rest for 5 minutes. Transfer to a serving dish and slice. Serve warm.

Tomato Beef Meatloaf

Prep time: 15 minutes | Cook time: 25 minutes | Serves 4

1½ pounds (680 g) ground beef
1 cup tomato sauce
½ cup bread crumbs
2 egg whites
½ cup grated Parmesan cheese
1 diced onion
2 tablespoons chopped parsley
2 tablespoons minced ginger
2 garlic cloves, minced
½ teaspoon dried basil
1 teaspoon cayenne pepper
Salt and ground black pepper, to taste
Cooking spray

1. Spritz a meatloaf pan with cooking spray.
2. Combine all the ingredients in a large bowl. Stir to mix well.
3. Pour the meat mixture in the prepared meatloaf pan and press with a spatula to make it firm.
4. Slide the pan into the air fryer oven. Press the Power Button and cook at 360ºF (182ºC) for 25 minutes.
5. When cooking is complete, the beef should be well browned.
6. Serve immediately.

Spinach and Cheese Steak Rolls

Prep time: 50 minutes | Cook time: 9 minutes | Serves 4

2 teaspoons dried Italian seasoning
2 cloves garlic, minced
1 tablespoon vegetable oil
1 teaspoon kosher salt
1 teaspoon ground black pepper
1 pound (454 g) flank steak, ¼ to ½ inch thick
1 (10-ounce / 284-g) package frozen spinach, thawed and squeezed dry
½ cup diced jarred roasted red pepper
1 cup shredded Mozzarella cheese
Cooking spray

1. Combine the Italian seasoning, garlic, vegetable oil, salt, and ground black pepper in a large bowl. Stir to mix well.
2. Dunk the steak in the seasoning mixture and toss to coat well. Wrap the bowl in plastic and marinate under room temperature for at least 30 minutes.
3. Spritz the air flow racks with cooking spray.
4. Remove the marinated steak from the bowl and unfold on a clean work surface, then spread the top of the steak with a layer of spinach, a layer of red pepper and a layer of cheese. Leave a ¼-inch edge uncovered.
5. Roll the steak up to wrap the filling, then secure with 3 toothpicks. Cut the roll in half and transfer the rolls onto the prepared air flow racks, seam side down.
6. Slide the racks into the air fryer oven. Press the Power Button and cook at 400ºF (205ºC) for 9 minutes.
7. Flip the rolls halfway through the cooking.
8. When cooking is complete, the steak should be lightly browned and the internal temperature reaches at least 145ºF (63ºC).
9. Remove the rolls from the air fryer oven and slice to serve.

Worcestershire London Broil

Prep time: 8 hours 5 minutes | Cook time: 25 minutes | Serves 6

2 tablespoons Worcestershire sauce
2 tablespoons minced onion
¼ cup honey
⅔ cup ketchup
2 tablespoons apple cider vinegar
½ teaspoon paprika
¼ cup olive oil
1 teaspoon salt
1 teaspoon freshly ground black pepper
2 pounds (907 g) London broil, top round (about 1-inch thick)

1. Combine all the ingredients, except for the London broil, in a large bowl. Stir to mix well.
2. Pierce the meat with a fork generously on both sides, then dunk the meat in the mixture and press to coat well.
3. Wrap the bowl in plastic and refrigerate to marinate for at least 8 hours.
4. Discard the marinade and transfer the London broil to the air flow racks.
5. Slide the racks into the air fryer oven. Press the Power Button and cook at 400ºF (205ºC) for 25 minutes.
6. Flip the meat halfway through the cooking time.
7. When cooking is complete, the meat should be well browned.
8. Transfer the cooked London broil on a plate and allow to cool for 5 minutes before slicing to serve.

Tonkatsu

Prep time: 5 minutes | Cook time: 10 minutes | Serves 4

⅔ cup all-purpose flour
2 large egg whites
1 cup panko bread crumbs

4 (4-ounce / 113-g) center-cut boneless pork loin chops (about ½ inch thick)
Cooking spray

1. Pour the flour in a bowl. Whisk the egg whites in a separate bowl. Spread the bread crumbs on a large plate.
2. Dredge the pork loin chops in the flour first, press to coat well, then shake the excess off and dunk the chops in the eggs whites, and then roll the chops over the bread crumbs. Shake the excess off.
3. Arrange the pork chops on the air flow racks and spritz with cooking spray.
4. Slide the racks into the air fryer oven. Press the Power Button and cook at 375ºF (190ºC) for 10 minutes.
5. After 5 minutes, remove from the air fryer oven. Flip the pork chops. Return to the air fryer oven and continue cooking.
6. When cooking is complete, the pork chops should be crunchy and lightly browned.
7. Serve immediately.

Tuscan Air Fried Veal Loin

Prep time: 1 hour 10 minutes | Cook time: 12 minutes | Makes 3 veal chops

1½ teaspoons crushed fennel seeds
1 tablespoon minced fresh rosemary leaves
1 tablespoon minced garlic
1½ teaspoons lemon zest

1½ teaspoons salt
½ teaspoon red pepper flakes
2 tablespoons olive oil
3 (10-ounce / 284-g) bone-in veal loin, about ½ inch thick

1. Combine all the ingredients, except for the veal loin, in a large bowl. Stir to mix well.
2. Dunk the loin in the mixture and press to submerge. Wrap the bowl in plastic and refrigerate for at least an hour to marinate.
3. Arrange the veal loin on the air flow racks.
4. Slide the racks into the air fryer oven. Press the Power Button and cook at 400ºF (205ºC) for 12 minutes.

5. Flip the veal halfway through.
6. When cooking is complete, the internal temperature of the veal should reach at least 145ºF (63ºC) for medium rare.
7. Serve immediately.

Tomato-Relished Bacon-Wrapped Sausage

Prep time: 1 hour 15 minutes | Cook time: 32 minutes | Serves 4

8 pork sausages
Relish:
8 large tomatoes, chopped
1 small onion, peeled
1 clove garlic, peeled
1 tablespoon white wine vinegar
3 tablespoons

8 bacon strips

chopped parsley
1 teaspoon smoked paprika
2 tablespoons sugar
Salt and ground black pepper, to taste

1. Purée the tomatoes, onion, and garlic in a food processor until well mixed and smooth.
2. Pour the purée in a saucepan and drizzle with white wine vinegar. Sprinkle with salt and ground black pepper. Simmer over medium heat for 10 minutes.
3. Add the parsley, paprika, and sugar to the saucepan and cook for 10 more minutes or until it has a thick consistency. Keep stirring during the cooking. Refrigerate for an hour to chill.
4. Wrap the sausage with bacon strips and secure with toothpicks, then place them on the air flow racks.
5. Slide the racks into the air fryer oven. Press the Power Button and cook at 350ºF (180ºC) for 12 minutes.
6. Flip the bacon-wrapped sausage halfway through.
7. When cooking is complete, the bacon should be crispy and browned.
8. Transfer the bacon-wrapped sausage on a plate and baste with the relish or just serve with the relish alongside.

Chapter 9 Poultry

Honey BBQ Chicken Drumsticks

Prep time: 5 minutes | Cook time: 18 minutes | Serves 5

1 tablespoon olive oil
10 chicken drumsticks
Chicken seasoning or rub, to taste
Salt and ground black pepper, to taste
1 cup barbecue sauce
¼ cup honey

1. Grease the air flow racks with olive oil.
2. Rub the chicken drumsticks with chicken seasoning or rub, salt and ground black pepper on a clean work surface.
3. Arrange the chicken drumsticks on the air flow racks.
4. Slide the racks into the air fryer oven. Press the Power Button and cook at 390ºF (199ºC) for 18 minutes.
5. Flip the drumsticks halfway through.
6. When cooking is complete, the drumsticks should be lightly browned.
7. Meanwhile, combine the barbecue sauce and honey in a small bowl. Stir to mix well.
8. Remove the drumsticks from the air fryer oven and baste with the sauce mixture to serve.

Citrus Balsamic Duck

Prep time: 5 minutes | Cook time: 13 minutes | Serves 4

4 (6-ounce / 170-g) skin-on duck breasts
1 teaspoon salt
¼ cup orange marmalade
1 tablespoon white balsamic vinegar
¾ teaspoon ground black pepper

1. Cut 10 slits into the skin of the duck breasts, then sprinkle with salt on both sides.
2. Put the breasts on the air flow racks, skin side up.
3. Slide the racks into the air fryer oven. Press the Power Button and cook at 400ºF (205ºC) for 10 minutes.
4. Meanwhile, combine the remaining ingredients in a small bowl. Stir to mix well.
5. When cooking is complete, brush the duck skin with the marmalade mixture. Flip the breast and air fry for 3 more minutes or until the skin is crispy and the breast is well browned.
6. Serve immediately.

Crusted Chicken Livers

Prep time: 10 minutes | Cook time: 10 minutes | Serves 4

2 eggs
2 tablespoons water
¾ cup flour
2 cups panko bread crumbs
1 teaspoon salt
½ teaspoon ground black pepper
20 ounces (567 g) chicken livers
Cooking spray

1. Spritz the air flow racks with cooking spray.
2. Whisk the eggs with water in a large bowl. Pour the flour in a separate bowl. Pour the panko on a shallow dish and sprinkle with salt and pepper.
3. Dredge the chicken livers in the flour. Shake the excess off, then dunk the livers in the whisked eggs, and then roll the livers over the panko to coat well.
4. Arrange the livers on the air flow racks and spritz with cooking spray.
5. Slide the racks into the air fryer oven. Press the Power Button and cook at 390ºF (199ºC) for 10 minutes.
6. Flip the livers halfway through.
7. When cooking is complete, the livers should be golden and crispy.
8. Serve immediately.

Easy Chicken Wings

Prep time: 10 minutes | Cook time: 15 minutes | Serves 4

1 tablespoon olive oil
8 whole chicken wings
Chicken seasoning or rub, to taste
1 teaspoon garlic powder
Freshly ground black pepper, to taste

1. Grease the air flow racks with olive oil.
2. On a clean work surface, rub the chicken wings with chicken seasoning and rub, garlic powder, and ground black pepper.
3. Arrange the well-coated chicken wings on the air flow racks.
4. Slide the racks into the air fryer oven. Press the Power Button and cook at 400ºF (205ºC) for 15 minutes.
5. Flip the chicken wings halfway through.
6. When cooking is complete, the internal temperature of the chicken wings should reach at least 165ºF (74ºC).
7. Remove the chicken wings from the air fryer oven. Serve immediately.

Strawberry Turkey

Prep time: 15 minutes | Cook time: 37 minutes | Serves 2

2 pounds (907 g) turkey breast
1 tablespoon olive oil
Salt and ground black pepper, to taste
1 cup fresh strawberries

1. Rub the turkey bread with olive oil on a clean work surface, then sprinkle with salt and ground black pepper.
2. Transfer the turkey on the air flow racks and spritz with cooking spray.
3. Slide the racks into the air fryer oven. Press the Power Button and cook at 375ºF (190ºC) for 30 minutes.
4. Flip the turkey breast halfway through.
5. Meanwhile, put the strawberries in a food processor and pulse until smooth.
6. When cooking is complete, spread the puréed strawberries over the turkey and fry for 7 more minutes.
7. Serve immediately.

Lime Chicken

Prep time: 35 minutes | Cook time: 10 minutes | Serves 4

4 (4-ounce / 113-g) boneless, skinless chicken breasts
½ cup chopped fresh cilantro
Juice of 1 lime
Chicken seasoning or rub, to taste
Salt and ground black pepper, to taste
Cooking spray

1. Put the chicken breasts in the large bowl, then add the cilantro, lime juice, chicken seasoning, salt, and black pepper. Toss to coat well.
2. Wrap the bowl in plastic and refrigerate to marinate for at least 30 minutes.
3. Spritz the air flow racks with cooking spray.
4. Remove the marinated chicken breasts from the bowl and place on the air flow racks. Spritz with cooking spray.
5. Slide the racks into the air fryer oven. Press the Power Button and cook at 400ºF (205ºC) for 10 minutes.
6. Flip the breasts halfway through.
7. When cooking is complete, the internal temperature of the chicken should reach at least 165ºF (74ºC).
8. Serve immediately.

Cajun Drumsticks

Prep time: 5 minutes | Cook time: 18 minutes | Serves 5

1 tablespoon olive oil
10 chicken drumsticks
1½ tablespoons Cajun seasoning
Salt and ground black pepper, to taste

1. Grease the air flow racks with olive oil.
2. On a clean work surface, rub the chicken drumsticks with Cajun seasoning, salt, and ground black pepper.
3. Arrange the seasoned chicken drumsticks on the air flow racks.
4. Slide the racks into the air fryer oven. Press the Power Button and cook at 390ºF (199ºC) for 18 minutes.
5. Flip the drumsticks halfway through.
6. When cooking is complete, the drumsticks should be lightly browned.
7. Remove the chicken drumsticks from the air fryer oven. Serve immediately.

Chicken Nuggets

Prep time: 15 minutes | Cook time: 15 minutes | Serves 4

2 tablespoons panko bread crumbs
¼ cup grated Parmesan cheese
⅛ tablespoon paprika
½ tablespoon garlic powder
2 large eggs
4 chicken cutlets
1 tablespoon parsley
Salt and ground black pepper, to taste
Cooking spray

1. Spritz the air flow racks with cooking spray.
2. Combine the bread crumbs, Parmesan, paprika, garlic powder, salt, and ground black pepper in a large bowl. Stir to mix well. Beat the eggs in a separate bowl.
3. Dredge the chicken cutlets in the beaten eggs, then roll over the bread crumbs mixture to coat well. Shake the excess off.
4. Transfer the chicken cutlets on the air flow racks and spritz with cooking spray.
5. Slide the racks into the air fryer oven. Press the Power Button and cook at 400ºF (205ºC) for 15 minutes. Flip the cutlets halfway through.
6. When cooking is complete, the cutlets should be crispy and golden brown.
7. Serve with parsley on top.

Lemon Chicken

Prep time: 5 minutes | Cook time: 35 minutes | Serves 6

3 (8-ounce / 227-g) boneless, skinless chicken breasts, halved, rinsed
1 cup dried bread crumbs
¼ cup olive oil
¼ cup chicken broth
Zest of 1 lemon
3 medium garlic cloves, minced
½ cup fresh lemon juice
½ cup water
¼ cup minced fresh oregano
1 medium lemon, cut into wedges
¼ cup minced fresh parsley, divided
Cooking spray

1. Pour the bread crumbs in a shadow dish, then roll the chicken breasts in the bread crumbs to coat.
2. Spritz a skillet with cooking spray, and brown the coated chicken breasts over medium heat about 3 minutes on each side. Transfer the browned chicken to a baking pan.
3. In a small bowl, combine the remaining ingredients, except the lemon and parsley. Pour the sauce over the chicken.
4. Slide the baking pan in the air fryer oven. Press the Power Button and cook at 325ºF (163ºC) for 30 minutes.
5. After 15 minutes, remove from the air fryer oven. Flip the breasts. Return to the air fryer oven and continue cooking.
6. When cooking is complete, the chicken should no longer pink.
7. Transfer to a serving platter, and spoon the sauce over the chicken. Garnish with the lemon and parsley.

Turkey Meatloaves

Prep time: 6 minutes | Cook time: 24 minutes | Serves 4

¼ cup grated carrot
2 garlic cloves, minced
2 tablespoons ground almonds
$1/3$ cup minced onion
2 teaspoons olive oil
1 teaspoon dried marjoram
1 egg white
¾ pound (340 g) ground turkey breast

1. In a medium bowl, stir together the carrot, garlic, almonds, onion, olive oil, marjoram, and egg white.
2. Add the ground turkey. Mix until combined.

3. Double 16 foil muffin cup liners to make 8 cups. Divide the turkey mixture evenly among the liners. Put the muffin cups on the air flow racks.
4. Slide the racks into the air fryer oven. Press the Power Button and cook at 400ºF (205ºC) for 24 minutes.
5. When cooking is complete, the meatloaves should reach an internal temperature of 165ºF (74ºC) on a meat thermometer.
6. Serve immediately.

Chicken Taco Lettuce Wraps

Prep time: 10 minutes | Cook time: 6 minutes | Serves 4

1 pound (454 g) ground chicken
2 cloves garlic, minced
¼ cup diced onions
¼ teaspoon sea salt
Cooking spray
Peanut Sauce:
¼ cup creamy peanut butter, at room temperature
2 tablespoons tamari
1½ teaspoons hot sauce
2 tablespoons lime juice
2 tablespoons grated fresh ginger
2 tablespoons chicken broth
2 teaspoons sugar
For Serving:
2 small heads butter lettuce, leaves separated
Lime slices (optional)

1. Spritz a baking pan with cooking spray.
2. Combine the ground chicken, garlic, and onions in the baking pan, then sprinkle with salt. Use a fork to break the ground chicken and combine them well.
3. Slide the pan into the air fryer oven. Press the Power Button and cook at 350ºF (180ºC) for 5 minutes.
4. Stir them halfway through the cooking time.
5. When cooking is complete, the chicken should be lightly browned.
6. Meanwhile, combine the ingredients for the sauce in a small bowl. Stir to mix well.
7. Pour the sauce in the pan of chicken, then cook for 1 more minute or until heated through.
8. Unfold the lettuce leaves on a large serving plate, then divide the chicken mixture on the lettuce leaves. Drizzle with lime juice and serve immediately.

Chicken Fingers

Prep time: 20 minutes | Cook time: 10 minutes | Makes 12 chicken fingers

½ cup all-purpose flour
2 cups panko bread crumbs
2 tablespoons canola oil
1 large egg
3 boneless and

skinless chicken breasts, each cut into 4 strips
Kosher salt and freshly ground black pepper, to taste
Cooking spray

1. Spritz the air flow racks with cooking spray.
2. Pour the flour in a large bowl. Combine the panko and canola oil on a shallow dish. Whisk the egg in a separate bowl.
3. Rub the chicken strips with salt and ground black pepper on a clean work surface, then dip the chicken in the bowl of flour. Shake the excess off and dunk the chicken strips in the bowl of whisked egg, then roll the strips over the panko to coat well.
4. Arrange the strips on the air flow racks.
5. Slide the racks into the air fryer oven. Press the Power Button and cook at 360ºF (182ºC) for 10 minutes.
6. Flip the strips halfway through.
7. When cooking is complete, the strips should be crunchy and lightly browned.
8. Serve immediately.

Bruschetta Chicken

Prep time: 10 minutes | Cook time: 10 minutes | Serves 4

Bruschetta Stuffing:

1 tomato, diced
3 tablespoons balsamic vinegar
1 teaspoon Italian seasoning
2 tablespoons

chopped fresh basil
3 garlic cloves, minced
2 tablespoons extra-virgin olive oil

Chicken:

4 (4-ounce / 113-g) boneless, skinless chicken breasts, cut 4 slits each
1 teaspoon Italian

seasoning
Chicken seasoning or rub, to taste
Cooking spray

1. Spritz the air flow racks with cooking spray.
2. Combine the ingredients for the bruschetta stuffing in a bowl. Stir to mix well. Set aside.
3. Rub the chicken breasts with Italian seasoning and chicken seasoning on a clean work surface.
4. Arrange the chicken breasts, slits side up, on the air flow racks and spritz with cooking spray.
5. Slide the racks into the air fryer oven. Press the Power Button and cook at 370ºF (188ºC) for 10 minutes.
6. Flip the breast and fill the slits with the bruschetta stuffing halfway through.
7. When cooking is complete, the chicken should be well browned.
8. Serve immediately.

Chicken Thigh Yakitori

Prep time: 10 minutes | Cook time: 15 minutes | Serves 4

½ cup mirin
¼ cup dry white wine
½ cup soy sauce
1 tablespoon light brown sugar
1½ pounds (680 g) boneless, skinless

chicken thighs, cut into 1½-inch pieces, fat trimmed
4 medium scallions, trimmed, cut into 1½-inch pieces
Cooking spray

Special Equipment:
4 (4-inch) bamboo skewers, soaked in water for at least 30 minutes

1. Combine the mirin, dry white wine, soy sauce, and brown sugar in a saucepan. Bring to a boil over medium heat. Keep stirring.
2. Boil for another 2 minutes or until it has a thick consistency. Turn off the heat.
3. Spritz the air flow racks with cooking spray.
4. Run the bamboo skewers through the chicken pieces and scallions alternatively.
5. Arrange the skewers on the air flow racks, then brush with mirin mixture on both sides. Spritz with cooking spray.
6. Slide the racks into the air fryer oven. Press the Power Button and cook at 400ºF (205ºC) for 10 minutes.
7. Flip the skewers halfway through.
8. When cooking is complete, the chicken and scallions should be glossy.
9. Serve immediately.

Chicken Nuggets

Prep time: 10 minutes | Cook time: 8 minutes | Serves 4

1 pound (454 g) boneless, skinless chicken breasts, cut into 1-inch pieces
2 tablespoons panko bread crumbs
6 tablespoons bread crumbs
Chicken seasoning or rub, to taste
Salt and ground black pepper, to taste
2 eggs
Cooking spray

1. Spritz the air flow racks with cooking spray.
2. Combine the bread crumbs, chicken seasoning, salt, and black pepper in a large bowl. Stir to mix well. Whisk the eggs in a separate bowl.
3. Dunk the chicken pieces in the egg mixture, then in the bread crumb mixture. Shake the excess off.
4. Arrange the well-coated chicken pieces on the air flow racks. Spritz with cooking spray.
5. Slide the racks into the air fryer oven. Press the Power Button and cook at 400ºF (205ºC) for 8 minutes.
6. Flip the chicken halfway through.
7. When cooking is complete, the chicken should be crispy and golden brown.
8. Serve immediately.

Chicken Schnitzel

Prep time: 15 minutes | Cook time: 5 minutes | Serves 4

½ cup all-purpose flour
1 teaspoon marjoram
½ teaspoon thyme
1 teaspoon dried parsley flakes
½ teaspoon salt
1 egg
1 teaspoon lemon juice
1 teaspoon water
1 cup bread crumbs
4 chicken tenders, pounded thin, cut in half lengthwise
Cooking spray

1. Spritz the air flow racks with cooking spray.
2. Combine the flour, marjoram, thyme, parsley, and salt in a shallow dish. Stir to mix well.
3. Whisk the egg with lemon juice and water in a large bowl. Pour the bread crumbs in a separate shallow dish.
4. Roll the chicken halves in the flour mixture first, then in the egg mixture, and then roll over the bread crumbs to coat well. Shake the excess off.
5. Arrange the chicken halves on the air flow racks and spritz with cooking spray on both sides.
6. Slide the racks into the air fryer oven. Press the Power Button and cook at 390ºF (199ºC) for 5 minutes.
7. Flip the halves halfway through.
8. When cooking is complete, the chicken halves should be golden brown and crispy.
9. Serve immediately.

Oregano Cornish Hens

Prep time: 2 hours 15 minutes | Cook time: 30 minutes | Serves 8

4 (1¼-pound / 567-g) Cornish hens, giblets removed, split lengthwise
2 cups white wine, divided
2 garlic cloves, minced
1 small onion, minced
½ teaspoon celery seeds
½ teaspoon poultry seasoning
½ teaspoon paprika
½ teaspoon dried oregano
¼ teaspoon freshly ground black pepper

1. Put the hens, cavity side up, in a baking pan. Pour 1½ cups of the wine over the hens; set aside.
2. In a shallow bowl, combine the garlic, onion, celery seeds, poultry seasoning, paprika, oregano, and pepper. Sprinkle half of the combined seasonings over the cavity of each split half. Cover and refrigerate. Allow the hens to marinate for 2 hours.
3. Transfer the hens on the air flow racks. Slide the racks into the air fryer oven. Press the Power Button and cook at 350ºF (180ºC) for 90 minutes.
4. Remove the racks from the air fryer oven halfway through the baking, turn breast side up, and remove the skin. Pour the remaining ½ cup of wine over the top, and sprinkle with the remaining seasonings.
5. When cooking is complete, the inner temperature of the hens should be at least 165ºF (74ºC). Transfer the hens to a serving platter and serve hot.

Goulash

Prep time: 5 minutes | Cook time: 17 minutes | Serves 2

2 red bell peppers, chopped
1 pound (454 g) ground chicken
2 medium tomatoes, diced
½ cup chicken broth
Salt and ground black pepper, to taste
Cooking spray

1. Spritz a baking pan with cooking spray.
2. Set the bell pepper in the baking pan.
3. Slide the pan into the air fryer oven. Press the Power Button and cook at 365°F (185°C) for 5 minutes.
4. Stir the bell pepper halfway through.
5. When cooking is complete, the bell pepper should be tender.
6. Add the ground chicken and diced tomatoes in the baking pan and stir to mix well.
7. Set the time of air fryer oven to 12 minutes. Press Start. Stir the mixture and mix in the chicken broth, salt and ground black pepper halfway through.
8. When cooking is complete, the chicken should be well browned.
9. Serve immediately.

Chicken with Gnocchi and Spinach

Prep time: 10 minutes | Cook time: 13 minutes | Serves 4

1 (1-pound / 454-g) package shelf-stable gnocchi
1¼ cups chicken stock
½ teaspoon kosher salt
1 pound (454 g) chicken breast, cut into 1-inch chunks
1 cup heavy whipping cream
2 tablespoons sun-dried tomato purée
1 garlic clove, minced
1 cup frozen spinach, thawed and drained
1 cup grated Parmesan cheese

1. Put the gnocchi in an even layer on a baking pan. Pour the chicken stock over the gnocchi.
2. Slide the pan into the air fryer oven. Press the Power Button and cook at 400°F (205°C) for 7 minutes.
3. While the gnocchi are cooking, sprinkle the salt over the chicken pieces. In a small bowl, mix the cream, tomato purée, and garlic.
4. When cooking is complete, blot off any remaining stock, or drain the gnocchi and return it to the pan. Top the gnocchi with the spinach and chicken. Pour the cream mixture over the ingredients in the pan.
5. Slide the pan into the air fryer oven. Press the Power Button and cook at 400°F (205°C) for 6 minutes.
6. After 4 minutes, remove from the air fryer oven and gently stir the ingredients. Return to the air fryer oven and continue cooking.
7. When cooking is complete, the gnocchi should be tender and the chicken should be cooked through. Remove from the air fryer oven. Stir in the Parmesan cheese until it's melted and serve.

Bacon-Wrapped Chicken

Prep time: 10 minutes | Cook time: 20 minutes | Serves 4

4 (5-ounce / 142-g) boneless, skinless chicken breasts, pounded to ¼ inch thick
1 cup cream cheese
2 tablespoons
chopped fresh chives
8 slices thin-cut bacon
Sprig of fresh cilantro, for garnish
Cooking spray

1. Spritz the air flow racks with cooking spray.
2. On a clean work surface, slice the chicken horizontally to make a 1-inch incision on top of each chicken breast with a knife, then cut into the chicken to make a pocket. Leave a ½-inch border along the sides and bottom.
3. Combine the cream cheese and chives in a bowl. Stir to mix well, then gently pour the mixture into the chicken pockets.
4. Wrap each stuffed chicken breast with 2 bacon slices, then secure the ends with toothpicks.
5. Arrange them on the air flow racks.
6. Slide the racks into the air fryer oven. Press the Power Button and cook at 400°F (205°C) for 20 minutes.
7. Flip the bacon-wrapped chicken halfway through the cooking time.
8. When cooking is complete, the bacon should be browned and crispy.
9. Transfer them on a large plate and serve with cilantro on top.

Ham and Chicken Meatballs

Prep time: 10 minutes | Cook time: 15 minutes | Serves 4

Meatballs:

½ pound (227 g) ham, diced	minced
½ pound (227 g) ground chicken	¼ cup chopped onions
½ cup grated Swiss cheese	1½ teaspoons sea salt
1 large egg, beaten	1 teaspoon ground black pepper
3 cloves garlic,	Cooking spray

Dijon Sauce:

3 tablespoons Dijon mustard	¾ teaspoon sea salt
2 tablespoons lemon juice	¼ teaspoon ground black pepper
¼ cup chicken broth, warmed	Chopped fresh thyme leaves, for garnish

1. Spritz the air flow racks with cooking spray.
2. Combine the ingredients for the meatballs in a large bowl. Stir to mix well, then shape the mixture in twelve 1½-inch meatballs.
3. Arrange the meatballs on the air flow racks.
4. Slide the racks into the air fryer oven. Press the Power Button and cook at 390ºF (199ºC) for 15 minutes.
5. Flip the balls halfway through.
6. When cooking is complete, the balls should be lightly browned.
7. Meanwhile, combine the ingredients, except for the thyme leaves, for the sauce in a small bowl. Stir to mix well.
8. Transfer the cooked meatballs on a large plate, then baste the sauce over. Garnish with thyme leaves and serve.

Peanut Chicken

Prep time: 10 minutes | Cook time: 12 minutes | Serves 4

½ cup grated Parmesan cheese	2 tablespoons peanut oil
½ teaspoon garlic powder	1½ pounds (680 g) chicken tenderloins
1 teaspoon red pepper flakes	2 tablespoons peanuts, roasted and roughly chopped
Sea salt and ground black pepper, to taste	Cooking spray

1. Spritz the air flow racks with cooking spray.
2. Combine the Parmesan cheese, garlic powder, red pepper flakes, salt, black pepper, and peanut oil in a large bow. Stir to mix well.
3. Dip the chicken tenderloins in the cheese mixture, then press to coat well. Shake the excess off.
4. Transfer the chicken tenderloins on the air flow racks.
5. Slide the racks into the air fryer oven. Press the Power Button and cook at 360ºF (182ºC) for 12 minutes.
6. Flip the tenderloin halfway through.
7. When cooking is complete, the tenderloin should be well browned.
8. Transfer the chicken tenderloins on a large plate and top with peanuts before serving.

Buffalo Chicken Wings

Prep time: 10 minutes | Cook time: 20 minutes | Serves 6

16 chicken drumettes (party wings)	Ground black pepper, to taste
Chicken seasoning or rub, to taste	¼ cup buffalo wings sauce
1 teaspoon garlic powder	Cooking spray

1. Spritz the air flow racks with cooking spray.
2. Rub the chicken wings with chicken seasoning, garlic powder, and ground black pepper on a clean work surface.
3. Arrange the chicken wings on the air flow racks. Spritz with cooking spray.
4. Slide the racks into the air fryer oven. Press the Power Button and cook at 400ºF (205ºC) for 10 minutes.
5. Flip the chicken wings halfway through.
6. When cooking is complete, the chicken wings should be lightly browned.
7. Transfer the chicken wings in a large bowl, then pour in the buffalo wings sauce and toss to coat well.
8. Put the wings back to the air fryer oven for 7 minutes. Flip the wings halfway through.
9. When cooking is complete, the wings should be heated through. Serve immediately.

Chicken Veg Curry

Prep time: 10 minutes | Cook time: 20 minutes | Serves 4

1 pound (454 g) boneless, skinless chicken thighs
1 teaspoon kosher salt, divided
¼ cup unsalted butter, melted
1 tablespoon curry powder
2 medium sweet potatoes, peeled and cut in 1-inch cubes
12 ounces (340 g) Brussels sprouts, halved

1. Sprinkle the chicken thighs with ½ teaspoon of kosher salt. Put them in the single layer on a baking pan.
2. In a small bowl, stir together the butter and curry powder.
3. Put the sweet potatoes and Brussels sprouts in a large bowl. Drizzle half the curry butter over the vegetables and add the remaining kosher salt. Toss to coat. Transfer the vegetables to the baking pan and place in a single layer around the chicken. Brush half of the remaining curry butter over the chicken.
4. Slide the pan into the air fryer oven. Press the Power Button and cook at 400ºF (205ºC) for 20 minutes.
5. After 10 minutes, remove from the air fryer oven and turn over the chicken thighs. Baste them with the remaining curry butter. Return to the air fryer oven and continue cooking.
6. Cooking is complete when the sweet potatoes are tender and the chicken is cooked through and reads 165ºF (74ºC) on a meat thermometer.

Turkey Cauliflower Meatloaf

Prep time: 15 minutes | Cook time: 50 minutes | Serves 6

2 pounds (907 g) lean ground turkey
1¹⁄₃ cups riced cauliflower
2 large eggs, lightly beaten
¼ cup almond flour
²⁄₃ cup chopped yellow or white onion
1 teaspoon ground dried turmeric
1 teaspoon ground cumin
1 teaspoon ground coriander
1 tablespoon minced garlic
1 teaspoon salt
1 teaspoon ground black pepper
Cooking spray

1. Spritz a loaf pan with cooking spray.
2. Combine all the ingredients in a large bowl. Stir to mix well. Pour half of the mixture in the prepared loaf pan and press with a spatula to coat the bottom evenly. Spritz the mixture with cooking spray.
3. Slide the pan into the air fryer oven. Press the Power Button and cook at 350ºF (180ºC) for 25 minutes.
4. When cooking is complete, the meat should be well browned and the internal temperature should reach at least 165ºF (74ºC).
5. Remove the loaf pan from the air fryer oven and serve immediately.

Herbed Dijon Turkey

Prep time: 5 minutes | Cook time: 30 minutes | Serves 4

1 teaspoon chopped fresh sage
1 teaspoon chopped fresh tarragon
1 teaspoon chopped fresh thyme leaves
1 teaspoon chopped fresh rosemary leaves
1½ teaspoons sea salt
1 teaspoon ground black pepper
1 (2-pound / 907-g) turkey breast
3 tablespoons Dijon mustard
3 tablespoons butter, melted
Cooking spray

1. Spritz the air flow racks with cooking spray.
2. Combine the herbs, salt, and black pepper in a small bowl. Stir to mix well. Set aside.
3. Combine the Dijon mustard and butter in a separate bowl. Stir to mix well.
4. Rub the turkey with the herb mixture on a clean work surface, then brush the turkey with Dijon mixture.
5. Arrange the turkey on the air flow racks.
6. Slide the racks into the air fryer oven. Press the Power Button and cook at 390ºF (199ºC) for 30 minutes.
7. Flip the turkey breast halfway through.
8. When cooking is complete, an instant-read thermometer inserted in the thickest part of the turkey breast should reach at least 165ºF (74ºC).
9. Transfer the cooked turkey breast on a large plate and slice to serve.

Thai Green Beans Drumsticks

Prep time: 5 minutes | Cook time: 25 minutes | Serves 4

8 skin-on chicken drumsticks
1 teaspoon kosher salt, divided
1 pound (454 g) green beans, trimmed
2 garlic cloves, minced
2 tablespoons vegetable oil
$1/_3$ cup Thai sweet chili sauce

1. Salt the drumsticks on all sides with ½ teaspoon of kosher salt. Let sit for a few minutes, then blot dry with a paper towel. Put on a baking pan.
2. Slide the pan into the air fryer oven. Press the Power Button and cook at 375ºF (190ºC) for 25 minutes.
3. While the chicken cooks, place the green beans in a large bowl. Add the remaining kosher salt, the garlic, and oil. Toss to coat.
4. After 15 minutes, remove from the air fryer oven. Brush the drumsticks with the sweet chili sauce. Put the green beans in the pan. Return to the air fryer oven and continue cooking.
5. When cooking is complete, the green beans should be sizzling and browned in spots and the chicken cooked through, reading 165ºF (74ºC) on a meat thermometer. Serve the chicken with the green beans on the side.

China Flavor Turkey

Prep time: 10 minutes | Cook time: 25 minutes | Serves 6

2 pounds (907 g) turkey thighs
1 teaspoon Chinese five-spice powder
¼ teaspoon Sichuan pepper
1 teaspoon pink Himalayan salt
1 tablespoon Chinese rice vinegar
1 tablespoon mustard
1 tablespoon chili sauce
2 tablespoons soy sauce
Cooking spray

1. Spritz the air flow racks with cooking spray.
2. Rub the turkey thighs with five-spice powder, Sichuan pepper, and salt on a clean work surface.
3. Put the turkey thighs on the air flow racks and spritz with cooking spray.

4. Slide the racks into the air fryer oven. Press the Power Button and cook at 360ºF (182ºC) for 22 minutes.
5. Flip the thighs at least three times during the cooking.
6. When cooking is complete, the thighs should be well browned.
7. Meanwhile, heat the remaining ingredients in a saucepan over medium-high heat. Cook for 3 minutes or until the sauce is thickened and reduces to two thirds.
8. Transfer the thighs onto a plate and baste with sauce before serving.

Sweet-and-Sour Gold Nuggets

Prep time: 15 minutes | Cook time: 15 minutes | Serves 4

1 cup cornstarch
Chicken seasoning or rub, to taste
Salt and ground black pepper, to taste
2 eggs
2 (4-ounce/ 113-g)
boneless, skinless chicken breasts, cut into 1-inch pieces
1½ cups sweet-and-sour sauce
Cooking spray

1. Spritz the air flow racks with cooking spray.
2. Combine the cornstarch, chicken seasoning, salt, and pepper in a large bowl. Stir to mix well. Whisk the eggs in a separate bowl.
3. Dredge the chicken pieces in the bowl of cornstarch mixture first, then in the bowl of whisked eggs, and then in the cornstarch mixture again.
4. Arrange the well-coated chicken pieces on the air flow racks. Spritz with cooking spray.
5. Slide the racks into the air fryer oven. Press the Power Button and cook at 360ºF (182ºC) for 15 minutes.
6. Flip the chicken halfway through.
7. When cooking is complete, the chicken should be golden brown and crispy.
8. Transfer the chicken pieces on a large serving plate, then baste with sweet-and-sour sauce before serving.

Creole Cornish Hens

Prep time: 10 minutes | Cook time: 40 minutes | Serves 4

½ tablespoon Creole seasoning
½ tablespoon garlic powder
½ tablespoon onion powder
½ tablespoon freshly ground black pepper
½ tablespoon paprika
2 tablespoons olive oil
2 Cornish hens
Cooking spray

1. Spritz the air flow racks with cooking spray.
2. In a small bowl, mix the Creole seasoning, garlic powder, onion powder, pepper, and paprika.
3. Pat the Cornish hens dry and brush each hen all over with the olive oil. Rub each hen with the seasoning mixture. Put the Cornish hens on the air flow racks.
4. Press the Power Button and cook at 375ºF (190ºC) for 30 minutes.
5. After 15 minutes, remove from the air fryer oven. Flip the hens over and baste it with any drippings collected in the bottom drawer of the air fryer oven. Return to the air fryer oven and continue cooking.
6. When cooking is complete, a thermometer inserted into the thickest part of the hens should reach at least 165ºF (74ºC).
7. Let the hens rest for 10 minutes before carving.

Apricot-Glazed Chicken Drumsticks

Prep time: 15 minutes | Cook time: 30 minutes | Makes 6 drumsticks

For the Glaze:
½ cup apricot preserves
½ teaspoon tamari
¼ teaspoon chili powder
2 teaspoons Dijon mustard
For the Chicken:
6 chicken drumsticks
½ teaspoon seasoning salt
1 teaspoon salt
½ teaspoon ground black pepper
Cooking spray

Make the Glaze:
1. Combine the ingredients for the glaze in a saucepan, then heat over low heat for 10 minutes or until thickened.
2. Turn off the heat and sit until ready to use.

Make the Chicken:
1. Spritz the air flow racks with cooking spray.
2. Combine the seasoning salt, salt, and pepper in a small bowl. Stir to mix well.
3. Put the chicken drumsticks on the air flow racks. Spritz with cooking spray and sprinkle with the salt mixture on both sides.
4. Slide the racks into the air fryer oven. Press the Power Button and cook at 370ºF (188ºC) for 20 minutes.
5. Flip the chicken halfway through.
6. When cooking is complete, the chicken should be well browned.
7. Baste the chicken with the glaze and air fry for 2 more minutes or until the chicken tenderloin is glossy.
8. Serve immediately.

Honey Breasts

Prep time: 5 minutes | Cook time: 10 minutes | Serves 4

4 (4-ounce / 113-g) boneless, skinless chicken breasts
Chicken seasoning or rub, to taste
Salt and ground black pepper, to taste
¼ cup honey
2 tablespoons soy sauce
2 teaspoons grated fresh ginger
2 garlic cloves, minced
Cooking spray

1. Spritz the air flow racks with cooking spray.
2. Rub the chicken breasts with chicken seasoning, salt, and black pepper on a clean work surface.
3. Arrange the chicken breasts on the air flow racks and spritz with cooking spray.
4. Slide the racks into the air fryer oven. Press the Power Button and cook at 400ºF (205ºC) for 10 minutes.
5. Flip the chicken breasts halfway through.
6. When cooking is complete, the internal temperature of the thickest part of the chicken should reach at least 165ºF (74ºC).
7. Meanwhile, combine the honey, soy sauce, ginger, and garlic in a saucepan and heat over medium-high heat for 3 minutes or until thickened. Stir constantly.
8. Remove the chicken from the air fryer oven and serve with the honey glaze.

Pineapple Chicken Bites

Prep time: 1 hour 15 minutes | Cook time: 15 minutes | Serves 4

½ cup pineapple juice
2 tablespoons apple cider vinegar
½ tablespoon minced ginger
½ cup ketchup
2 garlic cloves,
minced
½ cup brown sugar
2 tablespoons sherry
½ cup soy sauce
4 chicken breasts, cubed
Cooking spray

1. Combine the pineapple juice, cider vinegar, ginger, ketchup, garlic, and sugar in a saucepan. Stir to mix well. Heat over low heat for 5 minutes or until thickened. Fold in the sherry and soy sauce.
2. Dunk the chicken cubes in the mixture. Press to submerge. Wrap the bowl in plastic and refrigerate to marinate for at least an hour.
3. Spritz the air flow racks with cooking spray.
4. Remove the chicken cubes from the marinade. Shake the excess off and put on the air flow racks. Spritz with cooking spray.
5. Slide the racks into the air fryer oven. Press the Power Button and cook at 360ºF (182ºC) for 15 minutes.
6. Flip the chicken cubes at least three times during the air frying.
7. When cooking is complete, the chicken cubes should be glazed and well browned.
8. Serve immediately.

Super Roasted Whole Chicken

Prep time: 15 minutes | Cook time: 1 hour | Serves 6

1 teaspoon Italian seasoning
½ teaspoon garlic powder
½ teaspoon paprika
1 teaspoon salt
½ teaspoon freshly ground black pepper
½ teaspoon onion powder
2 tablespoons olive oil
1 (3-pound / 1.4-kg) whole chicken, giblets removed, pat dry
Cooking spray

1. Spritz the air flow racks with cooking spray.
2. In a small bowl, mix the Italian seasoning, garlic powder, paprika, salt, pepper, and onion powder.
3. Brush the chicken with the olive oil and rub it with the seasoning mixture.
4. Tie the chicken legs with butcher's twine. Put the chicken on the air flow racks, breast side down.
5. Slide the racks in the air fryer oven. Press the Power Button and cook at 350ºF (180ºC) for an hour.
6. After 30 minutes, remove from the air fryer oven. Flip the chicken over and baste it with any drippings collected in the bottom drawer of the air fryer oven. Return to the air fryer oven and continue cooking.
7. When cooking is complete, a thermometer inserted into the thickest part of the thigh should reach at least 165ºF (74ºC).
8. Let the chicken rest for 10 minutes before carving and serving.

Pineapple Chicken Breasts

Prep time: 10 minutes | Cook time: 10 minutes | Serves 6

1½ pounds (680 g) boneless, skinless chicken breasts, cut into 1-inch chunks
¾ cup soy sauce
2 tablespoons ketchup
2 tablespoons brown sugar
2 tablespoons rice vinegar
1 red bell pepper, cut into 1-inch chunks
1 green bell pepper, cut into 1-inch chunks
6 scallions, cut into 1-inch pieces
1 cup (¾-inch chunks) fresh pineapple, rinsed and drained
Cooking spray

1. Put the chicken in a large bowl. Add the soy sauce, ketchup, brown sugar, vinegar, red and green peppers, and scallions. Toss to coat.
2. Spritz a baking pan with cooking spray and place the chicken and vegetables on the pan.
3. Slide the pan into the air fryer oven. Press the Power Button and cook at 375ºF (190ºC) for 10 minutes.
4. After 6 minutes, remove from the air fryer oven. Add the pineapple chunks to the pan and stir. Return to the air fryer oven and continue cooking.
5. When cooking is complete, remove from the air fryer oven. Serve with steamed rice, if desired.

Peach Chicken with Dark Cherries

Prep time: 8 minutes | Cook time: 15 minutes | Serves 4

⅓ cup peach preserves
1 teaspoon ground rosemary
½ teaspoon black pepper
½ teaspoon salt
½ teaspoon marjoram
1 teaspoon light olive oil
1 pound (454 g) boneless chicken breasts, cut in 1½-inch chunks
1 (10-ounce / 284-g) package frozen dark cherries, thawed and drained
Cooking spray

1. In a medium bowl, mix peach preserves, rosemary, pepper, salt, marjoram, and olive oil.
2. Stir in chicken chunks and toss to coat well with the preserve mixture.
3. Spritz the air flow racks with cooking spray and lay chicken chunks on the air flow racks.
4. Press the Power Button and cook at 400ºF (205ºC) for 15 minutes.
5. After 7 minutes, remove from the air fryer oven. Flip the chicken chunks. Return to the air fryer oven and continue cooking.
6. When cooking is complete, the chicken should no longer pink and the juices should run clear.
7. Scatter the cherries over and cook for an additional minute to heat cherries.
8. Serve immediately.

Pepper Stuffed Chicken Rolls

Prep time: 10 minutes | Cook time: 12 minutes | Serves 4

2 (4-ounce / 113-g) boneless, skinless chicken breasts, slice in half horizontally
1 tablespoon olive oil
Juice of ½ lime
2 tablespoons taco
seasoning
½ green bell pepper, cut into strips
½ red bell pepper, cut into strips
¼ onion, sliced

1. Unfold the chicken breast slices on a clean work surface. Rub with olive oil, then drizzle with lime juice and sprinkle with taco seasoning.
2. Top the chicken slices with equal amount of bell peppers and onion. Roll them up and secure with toothpicks.

3. Arrange the chicken roll-ups on the air flow racks.
4. Slide the racks into the air fryer oven. Press the Power Button and cook at 400ºF (205ºC) for 12 minutes.
5. Flip the chicken roll-ups halfway through.
6. When cooking is complete, the internal temperature of the chicken should reach at least 165ºF (74ºC).
7. Remove the chicken from the air fryer oven. Discard the toothpicks and serve immediately.

Turkey Stuffed Bell Peppers

Prep time: 20 minutes | Cook time: 15 minutes | Serves 4

½ pound (227 g) lean ground turkey
4 medium bell peppers
1 (15-ounce / 425-g) can black beans, drained and rinsed
1 cup shredded Cheddar cheese
1 cup cooked long-grain brown rice
1 cup mild salsa
1¼ teaspoons chili powder
1 teaspoon salt
½ teaspoon ground cumin
½ teaspoon freshly ground black pepper
Chopped fresh cilantro, for garnish
Cooking spray

1. In a large skillet over medium-high heat, cook the turkey, breaking it up with a spoon, until browned, about 5 minutes. Drain off any excess fat.
2. Cut about ½ inch off the tops of the peppers and then cut in half lengthwise. Remove and discard the seeds and set the peppers aside.
3. In a large bowl, combine the browned turkey, black beans, Cheddar cheese, rice, salsa, chili powder, salt, cumin, and black pepper. Spoon the mixture into the bell peppers.
4. Lightly spray the air flow racks with cooking spray. Arrange the bell peppers on the racks.
5. Slide the racks in the air fryer oven. Press the Power Button and cook at 350ºF (180ºC) for 15 minutes.
6. When cooking is complete, the stuffed peppers should be lightly charred and wilted.
7. Allow to cool for a few minutes and garnish with cilantro before serving.

Scotch Turkey Eggs

Prep time: 15 minutes | Cook time: 12 minutes | Serves 4

1 egg	4 hard-boiled eggs, peeled
1 cup panko bread crumbs	Salt and ground black pepper, to taste
½ teaspoon rosemary	Cooking spray
1 pound (454 g) ground turkey	

1. Spritz the air flow racks with cooking spray.
2. Whisk the egg with salt in a bowl. Combine the bread crumbs with rosemary in a shallow dish.
3. Stir the ground turkey with salt and ground black pepper in a separate large bowl, then divide the ground turkey into four portions.
4. Wrap each hard-boiled egg with a portion of ground turkey. Dredge in the whisked egg, then roll over the bread crumb mixture.
5. Put the wrapped eggs on the air flow racks and spritz with cooking spray.
6. Slide the racks into the air fryer oven. Press the Power Button and cook at 400ºF (205ºC) for 12 minutes.
7. Flip the eggs halfway through.
8. When cooking is complete, the scotch eggs should be golden brown and crunchy.
9. Serve immediately.

Spanish Chicken Baguette

Prep time: 10 minutes | Cook time: 20 minutes | Serves 2

1¼ pounds (567 g) assorted small chicken parts, breasts cut into halves	sweet peppers
	¼ cup light mayonnaise
¼ teaspoon salt	¼ teaspoon smoked paprika
¼ teaspoon ground black pepper	½ clove garlic, crushed
2 teaspoons olive oil	Baguette, for serving
½ pound (227 g) mini	Cooking spray

1. Spritz the air flow racks with cooking spray.
2. Toss the chicken with salt, ground black pepper, and olive oil in a large bowl.
3. Arrange the sweet peppers and chicken on the air flow racks.

4. Slide the racks into the air fryer oven. Press the Power Button and cook at 375ºF (190ºC) for 20 minutes.
5. Flip the chicken and transfer the peppers on a plate halfway through.
6. When cooking is complete, the chicken should be well browned.
7. Meanwhile, combine the mayo, paprika, and garlic in a small bowl. Stir to mix well.
8. Assemble the baguette with chicken and sweet pepper, then spread with mayo mixture and serve.

Tandoori Drumsticks

Prep time: 70 minutes | Cook time: 14 minutes | Serves 4

8 (4- to 5-ounce / 113- to 142-g) skinless bone-in chicken drumsticks	fresh ginger
	2 teaspoons ground cinnamon
½ cup plain full-fat or low-fat yogurt	2 teaspoons ground coriander
¼ cup buttermilk	2 teaspoons mild paprika
2 teaspoons minced garlic	1 teaspoon salt
2 teaspoons minced	1 teaspoon Tabasco hot red pepper sauce

1. In a large bowl, stir together all the ingredients except for chicken drumsticks until well combined. Add the chicken drumsticks to the bowl and toss until well coated. Cover in plastic and set in the refrigerator to marinate for 1 hour, tossing once.
2. Arrange the marinated drumsticks on the air flow racks, leaving enough space between them.
3. Slide the racks into the air fryer oven. Press the Power Button and cook at 375ºF (190ºC) for 14 minutes.
4. Flip the drumsticks once halfway through to ensure even cooking.
5. When cooking is complete, the internal temperature of the chicken drumsticks should reach 160ºF (71ºC) on a meat thermometer.
6. Transfer the drumsticks to plates. Rest for 5 minutes before serving.

Chicken Thighs with Corn and Potatoes

Prep time: 10 minutes | Cook time: 25 minutes | Serves 4

4 bone-in, skin-on chicken thighs
2 teaspoons kosher salt, divided
1 cup Bisquick baking mix
½ cup butter, melted, divided
1 pound (454 g) small red potatoes, quartered
3 ears corn, shucked and cut into rounds 1- to 1½-inches thick
⅓ cup heavy whipping cream
½ teaspoon freshly ground black pepper

1. Sprinkle the chicken on all sides with 1 teaspoon of kosher salt. Put the baking mix in a shallow dish. Brush the thighs on all sides with ¼ cup of butter, then dredge them in the baking mix, coating them all on sides. Put the chicken in the center of a baking pan.
2. Put the potatoes in a large bowl with 2 tablespoons of butter and toss to coat. Put them on one side of the chicken on the pan.
3. Put the corn in a medium bowl and drizzle with the remaining butter. Sprinkle with ¼ teaspoon of kosher salt and toss to coat. Put on the pan on the other side of the chicken.
4. Slide the pan into the air fryer oven. Press the Power Button and cook at 375ºF (190ºC) for 25 minutes.
5. After 20 minutes, remove from the air fryer oven and transfer the potatoes back to the bowl. Return the pan to air fryer oven and continue cooking.
6. As the chicken continues cooking, add the cream, black pepper, and remaining kosher salt to the potatoes. Lightly mash the potatoes with a potato masher.
7. When cooking is complete, the corn should be tender and the chicken cooked through, reading 165ºF (74ºC) on a meat thermometer. Remove the pan from the air fryer oven and serve the chicken with the smashed potatoes and corn on the side.

Herbed Chicken and Potatoes

Prep time: 15 minutes | Cook time: 25 minutes | Serves 2

2 teaspoons minced fresh oregano, divided
2 teaspoons minced fresh thyme, divided
2 teaspoons extra-virgin olive oil, plus extra as needed
1 pound (454 g) fingerling potatoes, unpeeled
2 (12-ounce / 340-g) bone-in split chicken breasts, trimmed
1 garlic clove, minced
¼ cup oil-packed sun-dried tomatoes, patted dry and chopped
1½ tablespoons red wine vinegar
1 tablespoon capers, rinsed and minced
1 small shallot, minced
Salt and ground black pepper, to taste

1. Combine 1 teaspoon of oregano, 1 teaspoon of thyme, ¼ teaspoon of salt, ¼ teaspoon of ground black pepper, 1 teaspoons of olive oil in a large bowl. Add the potatoes and toss to coat well.
2. Combine the chicken with remaining thyme, oregano, and olive oil. Sprinkle with garlic, salt, and pepper. Toss to coat well.
3. Put the potatoes on the air flow racks, then arrange the chicken on top of the potatoes.
4. Slide the racks into the air fryer oven. Press the Power Button and cook at 350ºF (180ºC) for 25 minutes.
5. Flip the chicken and potatoes halfway through.
6. When cooking is complete, the internal temperature of the chicken should reach at least 165ºF (74ºC) and the potatoes should be wilted.
7. Meanwhile, combine the sun-dried tomatoes, vinegar, capers, and shallot in a separate large bowl. Sprinkle with salt and ground black pepper. Toss to mix well.
8. Remove the chicken and potatoes from the air fryer oven and allow to cool for 10 minutes. Serve with the sun-dried tomato mix.

Chicken and Pepper Kebabs

Prep time: 17 minutes | Cook time: 10 minutes | Serves 4

1 pound (454 g) boneless, skinless chicken breast, cut into 1½-inch chunks
1 green bell pepper, deseeded and cut into 1-inch pieces
1 red bell pepper, deseeded and cut into 1-inch pieces
1 large onion, cut into large chunks
2 tablespoons fajita seasoning
3 tablespoons vegetable oil, divided
2 teaspoons kosher salt, divided
2 cups corn, drained
¼ teaspoon granulated garlic
1 teaspoon freshly squeezed lime juice
1 tablespoon mayonnaise
3 tablespoons grated Parmesan cheese

Special Equipment:
12 wooden skewers, soaked in water for at least 30 minutes

1. Put the chicken, bell peppers, and onion in a large bowl. Add the fajita seasoning, 2 tablespoons of vegetable oil, and 1½ teaspoons of kosher salt. Toss to coat evenly.
2. Alternate the chicken and vegetables on the skewers, making about 12 skewers.
3. Put the corn in a medium bowl and add the remaining vegetable oil. Add the remaining kosher salt and the garlic, and toss to coat. Put the corn in an even layer on a baking pan and place the skewers on top.
4. Slide the pan into the air fryer oven. Press the Power Button and cook at 375ºF (190ºC) for 10 minutes.
5. After about 5 minutes, remove from the air fryer oven and turn the skewers. Return to the air fryer oven and continue cooking.
6. When cooking is complete, remove from the air fryer oven. Put the skewers on a platter. Put the corn back to the bowl and combine with the lime juice, mayonnaise, and Parmesan cheese. Stir to mix well. Serve the skewers with the corn.

Chicken Thighs with Pickled Cherry Peppers

Prep time: 10 minutes | Cook time: 27 minutes | Serves 4

4 bone-in, skin-on chicken thighs (about 1½ pounds / 680 g)
1½ teaspoon kosher salt, divided
1 link sweet Italian sausage (about 4 ounces / 113 g), whole
8 ounces (227 g) miniature bell peppers, halved and deseeded
1 small onion, thinly sliced
2 garlic cloves, minced
1 tablespoon olive oil
4 hot pickled cherry peppers, deseeded and quartered, along with 2 tablespoons pickling liquid from the jar
¼ cup chicken stock
Cooking spray

1. Salt the chicken thighs on both sides with 1 teaspoon of kosher salt. Spritz a baking pan with cooking spray and place the thighs skin-side down on the pan. Add the sausage.
2. Slide the pan into the air fryer oven. Press the Power Button and cook at 375ºF (190ºC) for 27 minutes.
3. While the chicken and sausage cook, place the bell peppers, onion, and garlic in a large bowl. Sprinkle with the remaining kosher salt and add the olive oil. Toss to coat.
4. After 10 minutes, remove from the air fryer oven and flip the chicken thighs and sausage. Add the pepper mixture to the pan. Return to the air fryer oven and continue cooking.
5. After another 10 minutes, remove from the air fryer oven and add the pickled peppers, pickling liquid, and stock. Stir the pickled peppers into the peppers and onion. Return to the air fryer oven and continue cooking.
6. When cooking is complete, the peppers and onion should be soft and the chicken should read 165ºF (74ºC) on a meat thermometer. Remove from the air fryer oven. Slice the sausage into thin pieces and stir it into the pepper mixture. Spoon the peppers over four plates. Top with a chicken thigh.

Chapter 10 Wraps and Sandwiches

Chicken Cheese Wraps

Prep time: 30 minutes | Cook time: 5 minutes | Serves 12

2 large-sized chicken breasts, cooked and shredded
2 spring onions, chopped
10 ounces (284 g) Ricotta cheese
1 tablespoon rice vinegar
1 tablespoon molasses
1 teaspoon grated fresh ginger
¼ cup soy sauce
$1/_3$ teaspoon sea salt
¼ teaspoon ground black pepper, or more to taste
48 wonton wrappers
Cooking spray

1. Spritz the air flow racks with cooking spray.
2. Combine all the ingredients, except for the wrappers in a large bowl. Toss to mix well.
3. Unfold the wrappers on a clean work surface, then divide and spoon the mixture in the middle of the wrappers.
4. Dab a little water on the edges of the wrappers, then fold the edge close to you over the filling. Tuck the edge under the filling and roll up to seal.
5. Arrange the wraps on the racks.
6. Slide the racks into the air fryer oven. Press the Power Button and cook at 375ºF (190ºC) for 5 minutes.
7. Flip the wraps halfway through the cooking time.
8. When cooking is complete, the wraps should be lightly browned.
9. Serve immediately.

Cheesy Spinach and Basil Pockets

Prep time: 20 minutes | Cook time: 10 minutes | Makes 8 pockets

2 large eggs, divided
1 tablespoon water
1 cup baby spinach, roughly chopped
¼ cup sun-dried tomatoes, finely chopped
1 cup ricotta cheese
1 cup basil, chopped
¼ teaspoon red pepper flakes
¼ teaspoon kosher salt
2 refrigerated rolled pie crusts
2 tablespoons sesame seeds

1. Spritz the air flow racks with cooking spray.
2. Whisk an egg with water in a small bowl.
3. Combine the spinach, tomatoes, the other egg, ricotta cheese, basil, red pepper flakes, and salt in a large bowl. Whisk to mix well.
4. Unfold the pie crusts on a clean work surface and slice each crust into 4 wedges. Scoop up 3 tablespoons of the spinach mixture on each crust and leave ½ inch space from edges.
5. Fold the crust wedges in half to wrap the filling and press the edges with a fork to seal.
6. Arrange the wraps on the racks and spritz with cooking spray. Sprinkle with sesame seeds.
7. Slide the racks into the air fryer oven. Press the Power Button and cook at 380ºF (193ºC) for 10 minutes.
8. Flip the wraps halfway through the cooking time.
9. When cooked, the wraps will be crispy and golden.
10. Serve immediately.

Eggplant Subs

Prep time: 15 minutes | Cook time: 12 minutes | Makes 3 subs

6 peeled eggplant slices (about ½ inch thick and 3 inches in diameter)
¼ cup jarred pizza sauce
6 tablespoons grated Parmesan cheese
3 Italian sub rolls, split open lengthwise, warmed
Cooking spray

1. Spritz the air flow racks with cooking spray.
2. Arrange the eggplant slices on the racks and spritz with cooking spray.
3. Slide the racks into the air fryer oven. Press the Power Button and cook at 350ºF (180ºC) for 10 minutes.
4. Flip the slices halfway through the cooking time.
5. When cooked, the eggplant slices should be lightly wilted and tender.
6. Divide and spread the pizza sauce and cheese on top of the eggplant slice
7. Slide the racks into the air fryer oven. Press the Power Button and cook at 375ºF (190ºC) for 2 minutes. When cooked, the cheese will be melted.
8. Assemble each sub roll with two slices of eggplant and serve immediately.

Fish Tacos

Prep time: 20 minutes | Cook time: 5 minutes | Serves 4

2 tablespoons milk
1/3 cup mayonnaise
1/4 teaspoon garlic powder
1 teaspoon chili powder
1½ cups panko bread crumbs
½ teaspoon salt
4 teaspoons canola oil
1 pound (454 g) skinless tilapia fillets, cut into 3-inch-long and 1-inch-wide strips
4 small flour tortillas
Lemon wedges, for topping
Cooking spray

1. Spritz the air flow racks with cooking spray.
2. Combine the milk, mayo, garlic powder, and chili powder in a bowl. Stir to mix well. Combine the panko with salt and canola oil in a separate bowl. Stir to mix well.
3. Dredge the tilapia strips in the milk mixture first, then dunk the strips in the panko mixture to coat well. Shake the excess off.
4. Arrange the tilapia strips on the racks.
5. Slide the racks into the air fryer oven. Press the Power Button and cook at 400ºF (205ºC) for 5 minutes.
6. Flip the strips halfway through the cooking time.
7. When cooking is complete, the strips will be opaque on all sides and the panko will be golden brown.
8. Unfold the tortillas on a large plate, then divide the tilapia strips over the tortillas. Squeeze the lemon wedges on top before serving.

Pork Sliders

Prep time: 10 minutes | Cook time: 14 minutes | Makes 6 sliders

1 pound (454 g) ground pork
1 tablespoon Thai curry paste
1½ tablespoons fish sauce
¼ cup thinly sliced scallions, white and green parts
2 tablespoons minced
peeled fresh ginger
1 tablespoon light brown sugar
1 teaspoon ground black pepper
6 slider buns, split open lengthwise, warmed
Cooking spray

1. Spritz the air flow racks with cooking spray.
2. Combine all the ingredients, except for the buns in a large bowl. Stir to mix well.
3. Divide and shape the mixture into six balls, then bash the balls into six 3-inch-diameter patties.
4. Arrange the patties on the racks and spritz with cooking spray.
5. Slide the racks into the air fryer oven. Press the Power Button and cook at 375ºF (190ºC) for 14 minutes.
6. Flip the patties halfway through the cooking time.
7. When cooked, the patties should be well browned.
8. Assemble the buns with patties to make the sliders and serve immediately.

Shrimp and Zucchini Dumplings

Prep time: 35 minutes | Cook time: 5 minutes | Serves 10

½ pound (227 g) peeled and deveined shrimp, finely chopped
1 medium zucchini, coarsely grated
1 tablespoon fish sauce
1 tablespoon green curry paste
2 scallions, thinly sliced
¼ cup basil, chopped
30 round dumpling wrappers
Cooking spray

1. Combine the chopped shrimp, zucchini, fish sauce, curry paste, scallions, and basil in a large bowl. Stir to mix well.
2. Unfold the dumpling wrappers on a clean work surface, dab a little water around the edges of each wrapper, then scoop up 1 teaspoon of filling in the middle of each wrapper.
3. Make the dumplings: Fold the wrappers in half and press the edges to seal.
4. Spritz the air flow racks with cooking spray.
5. Transfer the dumplings to the racks and spritz with cooking spray.
6. Slide the racks into the air fryer oven. Press the Power Button and cook at 350ºF (180ºC) for 5 minutes.
7. Flip the dumplings halfway through the cooking time.
8. When cooking is complete, the dumplings should be crunchy and lightly browned.
9. Serve immediately.

Cream Cheese Wontons

Prep time: 5 minutes | Cook time: 6 minutes | Serves 4

2 ounces (57 g) cream cheese, softened	16 square wonton wrappers
1 tablespoon sugar	Cooking spray

1. Spritz the air flow racks with cooking spray.
2. In a mixing bowl, stir together the cream cheese and sugar until well mixed. Prepare a small bowl of water alongside.
3. On a clean work surface, lay the wonton wrappers. Scoop ¼ teaspoon of cream cheese in the center of each wonton wrapper. Dab the water over the wrapper edges. Fold each wonton wrapper diagonally in half over the filling to form a triangle.
4. Arrange the wontons on the racks. Spritz the wontons with cooking spray.
5. Slide the racks into the air fryer oven. Press the Power Button and cook at 350°F (180°C) for 6 minutes.
6. Flip the wontons halfway through the cooking time.
7. When cooking is complete, the wontons will be golden brown and crispy.
8. Divide the wontons among four plates. Let rest for 5 minutes before serving.

Salsa Cod Tacos

Prep time: 5 minutes | Cook time: 15 minutes | Serves 4

2 eggs	1 pound (454 g) cod fillet, slice into large pieces
1¼ cups Mexican beer	
1½ cups coconut flour	4 toasted corn tortillas
1½ cups almond flour	
½ tablespoon chili powder	4 large lettuce leaves, chopped
1 tablespoon cumin	¼ cup salsa
Salt, to taste	Cooking spray

1. Spritz the air flow racks with cooking spray.
2. Break the eggs in a bowl, then pour in the beer. Whisk to combine well.
3. Combine the coconut flour, almond flour, chili powder, cumin, and salt in a separate bowl. Stir to mix well.
4. Dunk the cod pieces in the egg mixture, then shake the excess off and dredge into the flour mixture to coat well. Arrange the cod on the racks.
5. Slide the racks into the air fryer oven. Press the Power Button and cook at 375°F (190°C) for 15 minutes.
6. Flip the cod halfway through the cooking time.
7. When cooking is complete, the cod should be golden brown.
8. Unwrap the toasted tortillas on a large plate, then divide the cod and lettuce leaves on top. Baste with salsa and wrap to serve.

Chicken and Cabbage Egg Rolls

Prep time: 10 minutes | Cook time: 23 to 24 minutes | Serves 4

1 pound (454 g) ground chicken	2 cups white cabbage, shredded
2 teaspoons olive oil	1 onion, chopped
2 garlic cloves, minced	¼ cup soy sauce
	8 egg roll wrappers
1 teaspoon grated fresh ginger	1 egg, beaten
	Cooking spray

1. Spritz the air flow racks with cooking spray.
2. Heat olive oil in a saucepan over medium heat. Sauté the garlic and ginger in the olive oil for 1 minute, or until fragrant. Add the ground chicken to the saucepan. Sauté for 5 minutes, or until the chicken is cooked through. Add the cabbage, onion and soy sauce and sauté for 5 to 6 minutes, or until the vegetables become soft. Remove the saucepan from the heat.
3. Unfold the egg roll wrappers on a clean work surface. Divide the chicken mixture among the wrappers and brush the edges of the wrappers with the beaten egg. Tightly roll up the egg rolls, enclosing the filling. Arrange the rolls on the racks.
4. Slide the racks into the air fryer oven. Press the Power Button and cook at 370°F (188°C) for 12 minutes.
5. Flip the rolls halfway through the cooking time.
6. When cooked, the rolls will be crispy and golden brown.
7. Transfer to a platter and let cool for 5 minutes before serving.

Lamb Hamburgers

Prep time: 15 minutes | Cook time: 16 minutes | Makes 4 burgers

1½ pounds (680 g) ground lamb
¼ cup crumbled feta
1½ teaspoons tomato paste
1½ teaspoons minced garlic
1 teaspoon ground dried ginger
1 teaspoon ground coriander
¼ teaspoon salt
¼ teaspoon cayenne pepper
4 kaiser rolls or hamburger buns, split open lengthwise, warmed
Cooking spray

1. Spritz the air flow racks with cooking spray.
2. Combine all the ingredients, except for the buns, in a large bowl. Coarsely stir to mix well.
3. Shape the mixture into four balls, then pound the balls into four 5-inch diameter patties.
4. Arrange the patties on the racks and spritz with cooking spray.
5. Slide the racks into the air fryer oven. Press the Power Button and cook at 375°F (190°C) for 16 minutes.
6. Flip the patties halfway through the cooking time.
7. When cooking is complete, the patties should be well browned.
8. Assemble the buns with patties to make the burgers and serve immediately.

Salsa Bacon and Cheese Wraps

Prep time: 15 minutes | Cook time: 10 minutes | Serves 3

3 corn tortillas
3 slices bacon, cut into strips
2 scrambled eggs
3 tablespoons salsa
1 cup grated Pepper Jack cheese
3 tablespoons cream cheese, divided
Cooking spray

1. Spritz the air flow racks with cooking spray.
2. Unfold the tortillas on a clean work surface, divide the bacon and eggs in the middle of the tortillas, then spread with salsa and scatter with cheeses. Fold the tortillas over.
3. Arrange the tortillas on the racks.

4. Slide the racks into the air fryer oven. Press the Power Button and cook at 390°F (199°C) for 10 minutes.
5. Flip the tortillas halfway through the cooking time.
6. When cooking is complete, the cheeses will be melted and the tortillas will be lightly browned.
7. Serve immediately.

Black Bean and Sweet Potato Burritos

Prep time: 15 minutes | Cook time: 30 minutes | Makes 6 burritos

2 sweet potatoes, peeled and cut into a small dice
1 tablespoon vegetable oil
Kosher salt and ground black pepper, to taste
6 large flour tortillas
1 (16-ounce / 454-g) can refried black beans, divided
1½ cups baby spinach, divided
6 eggs, scrambled
¾ cup grated Cheddar cheese, divided
¼ cup salsa
¼ cup sour cream
Cooking spray

1. Put the sweet potatoes in a large bowl, then drizzle with vegetable oil and sprinkle with salt and black pepper. Toss to coat well.
2. Put the potatoes on the air flow racks.
3. Slide the racks into the air fryer oven. Press the Power Button and cook at 400°F (205°C) for 10 minutes.
4. Flip the potatoes halfway through the cooking time.
5. When done, the potatoes should be lightly browned. Remove the potatoes from the air fryer oven.
6. Unfold the tortillas on a clean work surface. Divide the black beans, spinach, air fried sweet potatoes, scrambled eggs, and cheese on top of the tortillas.
7. Fold the long side of the tortillas over the filling, then fold in the shorter side to wrap the filling to make the burritos.
8. Wrap the burritos in the aluminum foil and put on the racks.
9. Slide the racks into the air fryer oven. Press the Power Button and cook at 350°F (180°C) for 20 minutes. Flip the burritos halfway through the cooking time.
10. Remove the burritos from the air fryer oven and spread with sour cream and salsa. Serve immediately.

Salsa Chicken Taquitos

Prep time: 15 minutes | Cook time: 12 minutes | Serves 4

1 cup cooked chicken, shredded	Mozzarella cheese
¼ cup Greek yogurt	Salt and ground black pepper, to taste
¼ cup salsa	4 flour tortillas
1 cup shredded	Cooking spray

1. Spritz the air flow racks with cooking spray.
2. Combine all the ingredients, except for the tortillas, in a large bowl. Stir to mix well.
3. Make the taquitos: Unfold the tortillas on a clean work surface, then scoop up 2 tablespoons of the chicken mixture in the middle of each tortilla. Roll the tortillas up to wrap the filling.
4. Arrange the taquitos on the racks and spritz with cooking spray.
5. Slide the racks into the air fryer oven. Press the Power Button and cook at 380ºF (193ºC) for 12 minutes.
6. Flip the taquitos halfway through the cooking time.
7. When cooked, the taquitos should be golden brown and the cheese should be melted.
8. Serve immediately.

Potato Taquitos

Prep time: 5 minutes | Cook time: 6 minutes | Makes 12 taquitos

2 cups mashed potatoes	Mexican cheese
½ cup shredded	12 corn tortillas
	Cooking spray

1. Line a baking pan with parchment paper.
2. In a bowl, combine the potatoes and cheese until well mixed. Microwave the tortillas on high heat for 30 seconds, or until softened. Add some water to another bowl and set alongside.
3. On a clean work surface, lay the tortillas. Scoop 3 tablespoons of the potato mixture in the center of each tortilla. Roll up tightly and secure with toothpicks if necessary.
4. Arrange the filled tortillas, seam side down, in the prepared baking pan. Spritz the tortillas with cooking spray.

5. Slide the pan into the air fryer oven. Press the Power Button and cook at 400ºF (205ºC) for 6 minutes.
6. Flip the tortillas halfway through the cooking time.
7. When cooked, the tortillas should be crispy and golden brown.
8. Serve hot.

Philly Cheesesteaks

Prep time: 20 minutes | Cook time: 20 minutes | Serves 2

12 ounces (340 g) boneless rib-eye steak, sliced thinly	½ small onion, halved and thinly sliced
½ teaspoon Worcestershire sauce	1 tablespoon vegetable oil
½ teaspoon soy sauce	2 soft hoagie rolls, split three-fourths of the way through
Kosher salt and ground black pepper, to taste	1 tablespoon butter, softened
½ green bell pepper, stemmed, deseeded, and thinly sliced	2 slices provolone cheese, halved

1. Combine the steak, Worcestershire sauce, soy sauce, salt, and ground black pepper in a large bowl. Toss to coat well. Set aside.
2. Combine the bell pepper, onion, salt, ground black pepper, and vegetable oil in a separate bowl. Toss to coat the vegetables well.
3. Pour the steak and vegetables on the air flow racks.
4. Slide the racks into the air fryer oven. Press the Power Button and cook at 400ºF (205ºC) for 15 minutes.
5. When cooked, the steak will be browned and vegetables will be tender. Transfer them on a plate. Set aside.
6. Brush the hoagie rolls with butter and place on the racks.
7. Slide the racks in the air fryer oven and toast for 3 minutes. When done, the rolls should be lightly browned.
8. Transfer the rolls to a clean work surface and divide the steak and vegetable mix in between the rolls. Spread with cheese. Put the stuffed rolls back on the racks.
9. Cook for 2 minutes. Return the racks to the air fryer oven. When done, the cheese should be melted.
10. Serve immediately.

Montreal Beef Burgers

Prep time: 15 minutes | Cook time: 10 minutes | Serves 4

1 teaspoon cumin seeds
1 teaspoon mustard seeds
1 teaspoon coriander seeds
1 teaspoon dried minced garlic
1 teaspoon dried red pepper flakes
1 teaspoon kosher salt
2 teaspoons ground black pepper
1 pound (454 g) 85% lean ground beef
2 tablespoons Worcestershire sauce
4 hamburger buns
Mayonnaise, for serving
Cooking spray

1. Spritz the air flow racks with cooking spray.
2. Put the seeds, garlic, red pepper flakes, salt, and ground black pepper in a food processor. Pulse to coarsely ground the mixture.
3. Put the ground beef in a large bowl. Pour in the seed mixture and drizzle with Worcestershire sauce. Stir to mix well.
4. Divide the mixture into four parts and shape each part into a ball, then bash each ball into a patty. Arrange the patties on the racks.
5. Slide the racks into the air fryer oven. Press the Power Button and cook at 350ºF (180ºC) for 10 minutes.
6. Flip the patties with tongs halfway through the cooking time.
7. When cooked, the patties will be well browned.
8. Assemble the buns with the patties, then drizzle the mayo over the patties to make the burgers. Serve immediately.

Pork and Cabbage Gyoza

Prep time: 10 minutes | Cook time: 10 minutes | Makes 48 gyozas

1 pound (454 g) ground pork
1 head Napa cabbage (about 1 pound / 454 g), sliced thinly and minced
½ cup minced scallions
1 teaspoon minced fresh chives
1 teaspoon soy sauce
1 teaspoon minced fresh ginger
1 tablespoon minced garlic
1 teaspoon granulated sugar
2 teaspoons kosher salt
48 to 50 wonton or dumpling wrappers
Cooking spray

1. Spritz the air flow racks with cooking spray. Set aside.
2. Make the filling: Combine all the ingredients, except for the wrappers in a large bowl. Stir to mix well.
3. Unfold a wrapper on a clean work surface, then dab the edges with a little water. Scoop up 2 teaspoons of the filling mixture in the center.
4. Make the gyoza: Fold the wrapper over to filling and press the edges to seal. Pleat the edges if desired. Repeat with remaining wrappers and fillings.
5. Arrange the gyozas on the racks and spritz with cooking spray.
6. Slide the racks into the air fryer oven. Press the Power Button and cook at 360ºF (182ºC) for 10 minutes.
7. Flip the gyozas halfway through the cooking time.
8. When cooked, the gyozas will be golden brown.
9. Serve immediately.

Pork and Carrot Momos

Prep time: 20 minutes | Cook time: 20 minutes | Serves 4

2 tablespoons olive oil
1 pound (454 g) ground pork
1 shredded carrot
1 onion, chopped
1 teaspoon soy sauce
16 wonton wrappers
Salt and ground black pepper, to taste
Cooking spray

1. Heat the olive oil in a nonstick skillet over medium heat until shimmering.
2. Add the ground pork, carrot, onion, soy sauce, salt, and ground black pepper and sauté for 10 minutes or until the pork is well browned and carrots are tender.
3. Unfold the wrappers on a clean work surface, then divide the cooked pork and vegetables on the wrappers. Fold the edges around the filling to form momos. Nip the top to seal the momos.
4. Arrange the momos on the air flow racks and spritz with cooking spray.
5. Slide the racks into the air fryer oven. Press the Power Button and cook at 320ºF (160ºC) for 10 minutes.
6. When cooking is complete, the wrappers will be lightly browned.
7. Serve immediately.

Turkey Sliders

Prep time: 10 minutes | Cook time: 15 minutes | Serves 6

12 burger buns	Cooking spray
Turkey Sliders:	
¾ pound (340 g) turkey, minced	chopped scallions
1 tablespoon oyster sauce	1 tablespoon chopped fresh cilantro
¼ cup pickled jalapeno, chopped	1 to 2 cloves garlic, minced
2 tablespoons	Sea salt and ground black pepper, to taste
Chive Mayo:	
1 tablespoon chives	Zest of 1 lime
1 cup mayonnaise	1 teaspoon salt

1. Spritz the air flow racks with cooking spray.
2. Combine the ingredients for the turkey sliders in a large bowl. Stir to mix well. Shape the mixture into 6 balls, then bash the balls into patties.
3. Arrange the patties on the racks and spritz with cooking spray.
4. Slide the racks into the air fryer oven. Press the Power Button and cook at 365ºF (185ºC) for 15 minutes.
5. Flip the patties halfway through the cooking time.
6. Meanwhile, combine the ingredients for the chive mayo in a small bowl. Stir to mix well.
7. When cooked, the patties will be well browned.
8. Smear the patties with chive mayo, then assemble the patties between two buns to make the sliders. Serve immediately.

Turkey and Leek Hamburger

Prep time: 10 minutes | Cook time: 20 minutes | Serves 4

1 cup leftover turkey, cut into bite-sized chunks	½ cup sour cream
1 leek, sliced	1 heaping tablespoon fresh cilantro, chopped
1 Serrano pepper, deveined and chopped	1 teaspoon hot paprika
2 bell peppers, deveined and chopped	¾ teaspoon kosher salt
2 tablespoons Tabasco sauce	½ teaspoon ground black pepper
	4 hamburger buns
	Cooking spray

1. Spritz a baking pan with cooking spray.
2. Mix all the ingredients, except for the buns, in a large bowl. Toss to combine well.
3. Pour the mixture in the baking pan.
4. Slide the pan into the air fryer oven. Press the Power Button and cook at 385ºF (196ºC) for 20 minutes.
5. When done, the turkey will be well browned and the leek will be tender.
6. Assemble the hamburger buns with the turkey mixture and serve immediately.

Korean Beef Tacos

Prep time: 1 hour 15 minutes | Cook time: 12 minutes | Serves 6

2 tablespoons gochujang	salt
1 tablespoon soy sauce	1½ pounds (680 g) thinly sliced beef chuck
2 tablespoons sesame seeds	1 medium red onion, sliced
2 teaspoons minced fresh ginger	6 corn tortillas, warmed
2 cloves garlic, minced	¼ cup chopped fresh cilantro
2 tablespoons toasted sesame oil	½ cup kimchi
2 teaspoons sugar	½ cup chopped green onions
½ teaspoon kosher	

1. Combine the gochujang, soy sauce, sesame seeds, ginger, garlic, sesame oil, sugar, and salt in a large bowl. Stir to mix well.
2. Dunk the beef chunk in the large bowl. Press to submerge, then wrap the bowl in plastic and refrigerate to marinate for at least 1 hour.
3. Remove the beef chunk from the marinade and transfer to the air flow racks. Add the onion to the racks.
4. Slide the racks into the air fryer oven. Press the Power Button and cook at 400ºF (205ºC) for 12 minutes.
5. Stir the mixture halfway through the cooking time.
6. When cooked, the beef will be well browned.
7. Unfold the tortillas on a clean work surface, then divide the fried beef and onion on the tortillas. Spread the cilantro, kimchi, and green onions on top.
8. Serve immediately.

Green Bean, Mushroom, and Chickpea Wraps

Prep time: 15 minutes | Cook time: 9 minutes | Serves 4

8 ounces (227 g) green beans
2 portobello mushroom caps, sliced
1 large red pepper, sliced
2 tablespoons olive oil, divided
¼ teaspoon salt
1 (15-ounce / 425-g) can chickpeas, drained
3 tablespoons lemon juice
¼ teaspoon ground black pepper
4 (6-inch) whole-grain wraps
4 ounces (113 g) fresh herb or garlic goat cheese, crumbled
1 lemon, cut into wedges

1. Add the green beans, mushrooms, red pepper to a large bowl. Drizzle with 1 tablespoon olive oil and season with salt. Toss until well coated.
2. Transfer the vegetable mixture to a baking pan.
3. Slide the pan into the air fryer oven. Press the Power Button and cook at 400ºF (205ºC) for 9 minutes.
4. Stir the vegetable mixture three times during cooking.
5. When cooked, the vegetables should be tender.
6. Meanwhile, mash the chickpeas with lemon juice, pepper and the remaining 1 tablespoon oil until well blended
7. Unfold the wraps on a clean work surface. Spoon the chickpea mash on the wraps and spread all over.
8. Divide the cooked veggies among wraps. Sprinkle 1 ounce crumbled goat cheese on top of each wrap. Fold to wrap. Squeeze the lemon wedges on top and serve.

Vermicelli and Veg Spring Rolls

Prep time: 10 minutes | Cook time: 18 minutes | Serves 4

4 spring roll wrappers
½ cup cooked vermicelli noodles
1 teaspoon sesame oil
1 tablespoon freshly minced ginger
1 tablespoon soy sauce
1 clove garlic, minced
½ red bell pepper, deseeded and chopped
½ cup chopped carrot
½ cup chopped mushrooms
¼ cup chopped scallions
Cooking spray

1. Spritz the air flow racks with cooking spray and set aside.
2. Heat the sesame oil in a saucepan on medium heat. Sauté the ginger and garlic in the sesame oil for 1 minute, or until fragrant. Add soy sauce, red bell pepper, carrot, mushrooms and scallions. Sauté for 5 minutes or until the vegetables become tender. Mix in vermicelli noodles. Turn off the heat and remove them from the saucepan. Allow to cool for 10 minutes.
3. Lay out one spring roll wrapper with a corner pointed toward you. Scoop the noodle mixture on spring roll wrapper and fold corner up over the mixture. Fold left and right corners toward the center and continue to roll to make firmly sealed rolls.
4. Arrange the spring rolls on the racks and spritz with cooking spray.
5. Slide the racks into the air fryer oven. Press the Power Button and cook at 340ºF (171ºC) for 12 minutes.
6. Flip the spring rolls halfway through the cooking time.
7. When done, the spring rolls will be golden brown and crispy.
8. Serve warm.

Chapter 11 pizza

Pizza with Pineapple and Ham

Prep time: 10 minutes | Cook time: 25 minutes | Makes 2 (12- to 14-inch) pizzas

Extra-virgin olive oil, for brushing
4 slices center-cut bacon
Simple Pizza Dough or Pro Dough
1 cup Garlic Tomato Pizza Sauce
1 cup grated

Mozzarella cheese
¼ pound (113 g) smoked ham, cut into ½-inch dice
1 cup diced fresh pineapple
2 tablespoons grated Parmesan cheese

1. Brush two baking sheets with olive oil.
2. In a medium skillet over medium heat, cook the bacon until crisp, 2 to 3 minutes per side. Transfer to a paper towel–lined plate to cool. Cut into bits.
3. Roll out one of the dough balls to the desired size and place it on the prepared baking sheet.
4. Leaving a 1-inch border, spread half of the sauce evenly onto the dough. Sprinkle on half of the Mozzarella, followed by half of the ham, chopped bacon, pineapple, and grated Parmesan cheese.
5. Slide the baking sheet into the air fryer oven. Press the Power Button and cook at 400ºF (205ºC) for 10 minutes, until the crust is golden and the cheese has melted.
6. Remove the pizza from the air fryer oven and transfer it to a cutting board. Let it rest for 5 minutes, then slice and serve.
7. Repeat with the remaining dough ball and toppings.

Fig and Prosciutto Pizza

Prep time: 10 minutes | Cook time: 20 minutes | Makes 2 (12- to 14-inch) pizzas

2 tablespoons extra-virgin olive oil, plus more for brushing
Simple Pizza Dough or Pro Dough
¼ cup fig jam
½ cup shredded Mozzarella cheese
½ cup crumbled goat cheese

8 slices prosciutto
8 figs, stemmed and quartered
4 fresh thyme sprigs, stemmed
¼ teaspoon fine sea salt
⅛ teaspoon freshly ground black pepper

1. Brush two baking sheets with olive oil.
2. Roll out one of the dough balls to the desired size, and place it on the prepared baking sheet.
3. Leaving a 1-inch border, spoon half of the fig jam evenly onto the dough. Top with half of the Mozzarella, goat cheese, and prosciutto. Arrange half of the figs on the pizza, sprinkle on half of the thyme, and season with half of the salt and pepper.
4. Slide the baking sheet into the air fryer oven. Press the Power Button and cook at 400ºF (205ºC) for 10 minutes, until the crust is golden and the cheese has melted.
5. Remove the pizza from the air fryer oven and transfer it to a cutting board. Let it rest for 5 minutes, then drizzle with half of the olive oil. Slice and serve.
6. Repeat with the remaining dough ball and toppings.

Pear Pizza

Prep time: 15 minutes | Cook time: 25 minutes | Makes 1 (12- to 14-inch) pizza

½ recipe Simple Pizza Dough
4 Bosc pears
½ lemon
Zest of 1 orange
1 tablespoon chopped fresh basil leaves

1 teaspoon chopped fresh rosemary leaves
2 tablespoons sugar
⅛ teaspoon freshly ground black pepper
2 tablespoons extra-virgin olive oil

1. On a baking sheet, roll out the pizza dough to form a 12- to 14-inch disc.
2. Peel, halve, and cut away the core of the pears. Slice each pear half into thin wedges. Squeeze lemon juice over the pears.
3. Arrange the pears, starting at the outer edge of the crust (leaving no border), in a spiral toward the center. Sprinkle the orange zest, basil, rosemary, sugar, and pepper over the pears. Drizzle with the olive oil.
4. Slide the baking sheet into the air fryer oven. Press the Power Button and cook at 400ºF (205ºC) for 25 minutes, until the pizza appears golden and crisp.
5. Remove the pizza from the air fryer oven and let sit for 5 minutes. Slice and serve warm or at room temperature.

Turkish Pizza

Prep time: 20 minutes | Cook time: 10 minutes | Serves 4

4 (6-inch) flour tortillas
For the Meat Topping:

4 ounces (113 g) ground lamb or 85% lean ground beef	paste
	¼ teaspoon sweet paprika
¼ cup finely chopped green bell pepper	¼ teaspoon ground cumin
¼ cup chopped fresh parsley	⅛ to ¼ teaspoon red pepper flakes
1 small plum tomato, deseeded and chopped	⅛ teaspoon ground allspice
2 tablespoons chopped yellow onion	⅛ teaspoon kosher salt
1 garlic clove, minced	⅛ teaspoon black pepper
2 teaspoons tomato	

For Serving:

¼ cup chopped fresh mint	virgin olive oil
1 teaspoon extra-	1 lemon, cut into wedges

1. Combine all the ingredients for the meat topping in a medium bowl until well mixed.
2. Lay the tortillas on a clean work surface. Spoon the meat mixture on the tortillas and spread all over.
3. Put the tortillas on the air flow racks.
4. Slide the racks into the air fryer oven. Press the Power Button and cook at 400ºF (205ºC) for 10 minutes.
5. When cooking is complete, the edge of the tortilla should be golden and the meat should be lightly browned.
6. Transfer them to a serving dish. Top with chopped fresh mint and drizzle with olive oil. Squeeze the lemon wedges on top and serve.

Hazelnut Spread and Strawberry Pizza

Prep time: 10 minutes | Cook time: 10 minutes | Serves 4

2 tablespoons all-purpose flour, plus more as needed	oil
	1 cup sliced fresh strawberries
½ store-bought pizza dough (about 8 ounces / 227 g)	1 tablespoon sugar
	½ cup chocolate-hazelnut spread
1 tablespoon canola	

1. Dust a clean work surface with the flour. Place the dough on the floured surface, and roll it out to a 9-inch round of even thickness. Dust your rolling pin and work surface with additional flour, as needed, to ensure the dough does not stick.
2. Brush the surface of the rolled-out dough evenly with half the oil. Flip the dough over, and brush with the remaining oil. Poke the dough with a fork 5 or 6 times across its surface to prevent air pockets from forming during cooking.
3. Place the dough on a greased baking sheet. Slide the baking sheet into the air fryer oven. Press the Power Button and cook at 400ºF (205ºC) for 10 minutes.
4. After 5 minutes, flip the dough. Continue cooking for the remaining 5 minutes.
5. Meanwhile, in a medium mixing bowl, combine the strawberries and sugar.
6. Transfer the pizza to a cutting board and let cool. Top with the chocolate-hazelnut spread and strawberries. Cut into pieces and serve.

Mozzarella and Pepperoni Pizza

Prep time: 5 minutes | Cook time: 20 minutes | Makes 2 (12-inch) pizzas

Extra-virgin olive oil, for brushing	1 cup grated Mozzarella cheese
Simple Pizza Dough	6 ounces (170 g) pepperoni, sliced thin
1 cup Garlic Tomato Pizza Sauce	¼ teaspoon salt

1. Brush two baking sheets with olive oil.
2. Roll out one of the dough balls and place it on the prepared baking sheet.
3. Leaving a 1-inch border, spread half of the sauce evenly over the dough. Top with half the Mozzarella and then half the pepperoni. Sprinkle with half the salt.
4. Slide the baking sheet into the air fryer oven. Press the Power Button and cook at 400ºF (205ºC) for 10 minutes, until the crust is golden and the cheese has melted,.
5. Remove the pizza from the air fryer oven and transfer it to a cutting board. Let it rest for 5 minutes, then slice and serve.
6. Repeat with the remaining dough ball and toppings.

Chicken and Pepperoni Pizza

Prep time: 15 minutes | Cook time: 15 minutes | Serves 6

2 cups cooked chicken, cubed
1 cup pizza sauce
20 slices pepperoni
¼ cup grated Parmesan cheese
1 cup shredded Mozzarella cheese
Cooking spray

1. Spritz a baking pan with cooking spray.
2. Arrange the chicken cubes in the prepared baking pan, then top the cubes with pizza sauce and pepperoni. Stir to coat the cubes and pepperoni with sauce. Scatter the cheeses on top.
3. Slide the pan into the air fryer oven. Press the Power Button and cook at 375ºF (190ºC) for 15 minutes.
4. When cooking is complete, the pizza should be frothy and the cheeses should be melted.
5. Serve immediately.

Tomato and Basil Pizza

Prep time: 15 minutes | Cook time: 20 minutes | Makes 2 (12- to 14-inch) pizzas

Extra-virgin olive oil, for brushing
Simple Pizza Dough
1 cup Garlic Tomato Pizza Sauce
¾ cup grated Mozzarella
¾ cup grated fontina cheese
2 plum tomatoes, sliced thin
1/3 cup crumbled goat cheese
½ cup Parmesan cheese
8 fresh basil leaves, torn or roughly chopped
1 tablespoon chopped fresh parsley
¼ teaspoon salt
⅛ teaspoon freshly ground black pepper

1. Brush two baking sheets with olive oil.
2. Roll out one of the dough balls to the desired size, and place it on the prepared baking sheet.
3. Leaving a 1-inch border, spread half of the sauce evenly over the dough. Sprinkle on half of the Mozzarella and fontina. Arrange half of the tomato slices on top, and finish with half of the goat cheese and Parmesan.

4. Slide the baking sheet into the air fryer oven. Press the Power Button and cook at 400ºF (205ºC) for 10 minutes, until the crust is golden and the cheese has melted.
5. Remove the pizza from the air fryer oven and transfer it to a cutting board. Let it rest for 5 minutes, then top with half of the basil and parsley and season with half of the salt and pepper. Slice and serve.
6. Repeat with the remaining dough ball and toppings.

Zucchini-Onion Pizza

Prep time: 10 minutes | Cook time: 10 minutes | Serves 2

2 tablespoons all-purpose flour, plus more as needed
½ store-bought pizza dough (about 8 ounces / 227 g)
1 tablespoon canola oil, divided
½ cup pizza sauce
1 cup shredded Mozzarella cheese
½ zucchini, thinly sliced
½ red onion, sliced
½ red bell pepper, seeded and thinly sliced

1. Dust a clean work surface with the flour.
2. Place the dough on the floured surface and roll it into a 9-inch round of even thickness. Dust your rolling pin and work surface with additional flour, as needed, to ensure the dough does not stick.
3. Evenly brush the surface of the rolled-out dough with ½ tablespoon of oil. Flip the dough over and brush the other side with the remaining ½ tablespoon of oil. Poke the dough with a fork 5 or 6 times across its surface to prevent air pockets from forming while it cooks.
4. Place the dough on a greased baking sheet. Slide the baking sheet into the air fryer oven. Press the Power Button and cook at 400ºF (205ºC) for 10 minutes.
5. After 5 minutes, flip the dough, then spread the pizza sauce evenly over it. Sprinkle with the cheese, and top with the zucchini, onion, and pepper.
6. Continue cooking for the remaining 5 minutes until the cheese is melted and the veggie slices begin to crisp.
7. When cooking is complete, let cool slightly before slicing.

Zucchini and Pistachio Pizza

Prep time: 15 minutes | Cook time: 30 minutes | Makes 2 (12- to 14-inch) pizzas

2 tablespoons extra-virgin olive oil, plus more for brushing
1 medium green zucchini, halved lengthwise and cut thinly into half-moons
1 medium yellow summer squash, halved lengthwise and cut thinly into half-moons

¼ teaspoon salt
Simple Pizza Dough
1 medium red onion, sliced thin
1 teaspoon fresh thyme leaves
¼ teaspoon red pepper flakes
1 teaspoon freshly squeezed lemon juice
¼ cup shelled pistachios, toasted

1. Brush two baking sheets with olive oil.
2. In a large strainer set over a large bowl, toss the zucchini and summer squash well with the salt, and let it sit for about 5 minutes. Use a kitchen towel to press and squeeze the liquid from the squash mixture, removing as much moisture as possible.
3. Roll out one of the dough balls to the desired size, and place it on the prepared baking sheet.
4. In a large mixing bowl, toss together the drained squash mixture, onion, thyme, red pepper flakes, olive oil, and lemon juice. Arrange half of the vegetables on the dough.
5. Slide the baking sheet into the air fryer oven. Press the Power Button and cook at 400ºF (205ºC) for 10 minutes, until the crust is golden and the cheese has melted.
6. Remove the pizza from the air fryer oven and transfer it to a cutting board. Let it rest for 5 minutes, then garnish with half of the toasted pistachios. Slice and serve.
7. Repeat with the remaining dough ball and toppings.

Spring Pea Pizza

Prep time: 10 minutes | Cook time: 25 minutes | Makes 2 (12- to 14-inch) pizzas

2 tablespoons extra-virgin olive oil, plus more for brushing
½ cup shelled fresh English peas (or frozen and thawed peas)
10 ramps

¼ teaspoon fine sea salt
Simple Pizza Dough or Pro Dough
¾ cup ricotta cheese
2 tablespoons chopped fresh mint

1. Brush two baking sheets with olive oil.
2. If using fresh peas, bring a large pot of salted water to a boil. Fill a large bowl with ice water. Blanch the peas for 1 minute then, using a slotted spoon, transfer them to the ice water. Drain and set aside.
3. Spread the ramps on a baking sheet, drizzle with the olive oil, and sprinkle with the salt. Press the Power Button and cook at 400ºF (205ºC) for 5 minutes to wilt. Transfer to a cutting board and cut into thirds.
4. Roll out one of the dough balls to the desired size, and place it on the prepared baking sheet.
5. Spoon half of the ricotta in dollops all over the dough. Scatter on half of the peas, ramps, and mint.
6. Slide the baking sheet into the air fryer oven. Press the Power Button and cook at 400ºF (205ºC) for 10 minutes, until the crust is golden.
7. Remove the pizza from the air fryer oven, transfer it to a cutting board, and let it sit for 5 minutes. Slice and serve.
8. Repeat with the remaining dough ball and toppings.

Brussels Sprout Pizza

Prep time: 10 minutes | Cook time: 30 minutes | Makes 2 (12- to 14-inch) pizzas

2 tablespoons extra-virgin olive oil, plus more for brushing and drizzling
1 red onion, sliced
½ teaspoon fine sea salt, divided
⅛ teaspoon freshly ground black pepper
Simple Pizza Dough or Pro Dough
6 ounces (170 g) fresh Mozzarella cheese, shredded
12 Brussels sprouts, shredded or finely sliced
8 sage leaves, rolled and sliced thin
¼ cup grated Parmesan cheese
2 pinches red pepper flakes

1. Brush two baking sheets with olive oil.
2. Spread the onion on a sheet tray, drizzle with the olive oil, and toss to coat. Season with ¼ teaspoon of salt, and the pepper. Transfer the baking sheet to the air fryer oven and Press the Power Button and cook at 400ºF (205ºC) for 12 minutes, or until the onions are caramelized. Remove from the air fryer oven and set aside.
3. Roll out one of the dough balls to the desired size, and place it on the prepared baking sheet.
4. Top the dough with half of the Mozzarella, Brussels sprouts, and cooked red onion. Sprinkle on the remaining ¼ teaspoon of salt, half of the sage, and half of the Parmesan, followed by a drizzle of olive oil and a pinch of red pepper flakes.
5. Slide the baking sheet into the air fryer oven. Press the Power Button and cook at 400ºF (205ºC) for 10 minutes, until the crust is golden and the cheese has melted.
6. Remove the pizza from the air fryer oven and transfer it to a cutting board. Let it rest for 5 minutes. Slice and serve.
7. Repeat with the remaining dough ball and toppings.

Arugula Prosciutto Pizza

Prep time: 10 minutes | Cook time: 20 minutes | Makes 2 (12- to 14-inch) pizzas

2 tablespoons extra-virgin olive oil, plus more for brushing
Simple Pizza Dough or Pro Dough
1 cup Garlic Tomato Pizza Sauce
8 slices prosciutto
6 ounces (170 g) fresh Mozzarella cheese, sliced or shredded
3 cups arugula
¼ teaspoon salt
⅛ teaspoon freshly ground black pepper
3 ounces (85 g) Parmesan cheese, shaved with a vegetable peeler

1. Brush two baking sheets with olive oil.
2. Roll out one of the dough balls to the desired size, and place it on the prepared baking sheet.
3. Leaving a 1-inch border, spread half of the sauce evenly onto the dough. Lay half of the prosciutto slices on top, then finish with half of the Mozzarella.
4. Slide the baking sheet into the air fryer oven. Press the Power Button and cook at 400ºF (205ºC) for 10 minutes, until the crust is golden and the cheese has melted.
5. Remove the pizza from the air fryer oven and transfer it to a cutting board. Let it rest for 5 minutes, then top with half of the arugula, olive oil, salt, pepper, and Parmesan. Slice and serve.
6. Repeat with the remaining dough ball and toppings.

Ricotta Margherita Pizza with Fresh Basil

Prep time: 10 minutes | Cook time: 20 minutes | Makes 2 (12- to 14-inch) pizzas

1 tablespoon extra-virgin olive oil, plus more for brushing
Simple Pizza Dough or Pro Dough
1 cup Garlic Tomato Pizza Sauce
1 teaspoon dried oregano
½ cup fresh ricotta cheese
6 ounces (170 g) fresh Mozzarella cheese, sliced thin
¼ teaspoon fine sea salt
⅛ teaspoon freshly ground black pepper
8 fresh basil leaves, torn

1. Brush two baking sheets with olive oil.
2. Roll out one of the dough balls to the desired size, and place it on the prepared baking sheet.
3. Leaving a 1-inch border, spoon half of the sauce onto the dough, spreading it evenly. Sprinkle on half of the oregano.
4. Spoon half of the ricotta cheese in small dollops all over the pizza, then arrange half of the Mozzarella slices on top. Season with half of the salt and pepper, and scatter on half of the torn basil leaves.
5. Slide the baking sheet into the air fryer oven. Press the Power Button and cook at 400ºF (205ºC) for 10 minutes, until the crust is golden and the cheese has melted.
6. Remove the pizza from the air fryer oven and transfer it to a cutting board. Let it rest for 5 minutes. Slice and serve.
7. Repeat with the remaining dough ball and toppings.

Chorizo and Pepper Pizza

Prep time: 15 minutes | Cook time: 30 minutes | Makes 2 (12- to 14-inch) pizzas

2 tablespoons extra-virgin olive oil, plus extra for brushing
3 fresh chorizo sausage links
Simple Pizza Dough
1 cup Garlic Tomato Pizza Sauce
1 cup grated Mozzarella cheese
4 smoked piquillo peppers, drained and sliced lengthwise
4 slices prosciutto, torn into small pieces
¼ cup halved black olives
¼ cup chopped fresh flat-leaf parsley
½ cup grated manchego cheese
⅛ teaspoon freshly ground black pepper

1. Brush two baking sheets with olive oil.
2. In a medium skillet over medium heat, heat the oil until hot but not smoking. Add the sausages and cook for 7 to 10 minutes, turning occasionally, until they are browned on all sides. Remove the skillet from the heat and set it aside to cool. When the chorizo is cool enough to handle, cut it into thin slices.
3. Roll out one of the dough balls to the desired size, and place it on the prepared baking sheet.
4. Leaving a 1-inch border, spoon the sauce evenly onto the pizza. Top with half of the Mozzarella cheese, followed by half of the piquillo peppers. Scatter half of the chorizo and prosciutto over the pizza, followed by half of the olives and parsley.
5. Slide the baking sheet into the air fryer oven. Press the Power Button and cook at 400ºF (205ºC) for 10 minutes, until the crust is golden and the cheese has melted.
6. Remove the pizza from the air fryer oven, transfer it to a cutting board, and let it rest for 5 minutes. Top with half of the manchego and pepper, slice, and serve.
7. Repeat with the remaining dough ball and toppings.

Chapter 12 Desserts

Chocolate Bread Pudding

Prep time: 10 minutes | Cook time: 10 minutes | Serves 8

1 egg	2 tablespoons cocoa
1 egg yolk	powder
¾ cup chocolate milk	1 teaspoon vanilla
3 tablespoons brown	5 slices firm white
sugar	bread, cubed
3 tablespoons peanut	Nonstick cooking
butter	spray

1. Spritz a baking pan with nonstick cooking spray.
2. Whisk together the egg, egg yolk, chocolate milk, brown sugar, peanut butter, cocoa powder, and vanilla until well combined.
3. Fold in the bread cubes and stir to mix well. Allow the bread soak for 10 minutes.
4. When ready, transfer the egg mixture to the prepared baking pan.
5. Slide the pan into the air fryer oven. Press the Power Button and cook at 330°F (166°C) for 10 minutes.
6. When done, the pudding should be just firm to the touch.
7. Serve at room temperature.

Walnuts Tart

Prep time: 5 minutes | Cook time: 13 minutes | Serves 6

1 cup coconut milk	1 teaspoon vanilla
½ cup walnuts,	essence
ground	¼ teaspoon ground
½ cup Swerve	cardamom
½ cup almond flour	¼ teaspoon ground
½ stick butter, at	cloves
room temperature	Cooking spray
2 eggs	

1. Coat a baking pan with cooking spray.
2. Combine all the ingredients except the oil in a large bowl and stir until well blended. Spoon the batter mixture into the baking pan.
3. Slide the pan into the air fryer oven. Press the Power Button and cook at 360°F (182°C) for 13 minutes.
4. When cooking is complete, a toothpick inserted into the center of the tart should come out clean.
5. Remove from the air fryer oven and place on a wire rack to cool. Serve immediately.

Lemon Ricotta Cake

Prep time: 5 minutes | Cook time: 25 minutes | Serves 6

17.5 ounces (496 g)	3 tablespoons flour
ricotta cheese	1 lemon, juiced and
5.4 ounces (153 g)	zested
sugar	2 teaspoons vanilla
3 eggs, beaten	extract

1. In a large mixing bowl, stir together all the ingredients until the mixture reaches a creamy consistency.
2. Pour the mixture into a baking pan and place in the air fryer oven.
3. Slide the pan into the air fryer oven. Press the Power Button and cook at 320°F (160°C) for 25 minutes.
4. When cooking is complete, a toothpick inserted in the center should come out clean.
5. Allow to cool for 10 minutes on a wire rack before serving.

Chocolate Brownies

Prep time: 10 minutes | Cook time: 20 minutes | Makes 1 dozen brownies

1 egg	⅓ cup all-purpose
¼ cup brown sugar	flour
2 tablespoons white	¼ cup cocoa powder
sugar	¼ cup white chocolate
2 tablespoons	chips
safflower oil	Nonstick cooking
1 teaspoon vanilla	spray

1. Spritz a baking pan with nonstick cooking spray.
2. Whisk together the egg, brown sugar, and white sugar in a medium bowl. Mix in the safflower oil and vanilla and stir to combine.
3. Add the flour and cocoa powder and stir just until incorporated. Fold in the white chocolate chips.
4. Scrape the batter into the prepared baking pan.
5. Slide the pan into the air fryer oven. Press the Power Button and cook at 340°F (171°C) for 20 minutes.
6. When done, the brownie should spring back when touched lightly with your fingers.
7. Transfer to a wire rack and let cool for 30 minutes before slicing to serve.

Coconut Fudge Pie

Prep time: 15 minutes | Cook time: 26 minutes | Serves 8

1½ cups sugar
½ cup self-rising flour
$\frac{1}{3}$ cup unsweetened cocoa powder
3 large eggs, beaten
12 tablespoons (1½ sticks) butter, melted
1½ teaspoons vanilla extract
1 (9-inch) unbaked pie crust
¼ cup confectioners' sugar (optional)

1. Thoroughly combine the sugar, flour, and cocoa powder in a medium bowl. Add the beaten eggs and butter and whisk to combine. Stir in the vanilla.
2. Pour the prepared filling into the pie crust and transfer to the air flow racks.
3. Slide the racks into the air fryer oven. Press the Power Button and cook at 350ºF (180ºC) for 26 minutes.
4. When cooking is complete, the pie should be set.
5. Allow the pie to cool for 5 minutes. Sprinkle with the confectioners' sugar, if desired. Serve warm.

Brown Sugar Peaches with Blueberries

Prep time: 10 minutes | Cook time: 10 minutes | Serves 6

3 peaches, peeled, halved, and pitted
2 tablespoons packed brown sugar
1 cup plain Greek yogurt
¼ teaspoon ground
cinnamon
1 teaspoon pure vanilla extract
1 cup fresh blueberries

1. Arrange the peaches on the air flow racks, cut-side up. Top with a generous sprinkle of brown sugar.
2. Slide the racks into the air fryer oven. Press the Power Button and cook at 380ºF (193ºC) for 10 minutes.
3. Meanwhile, whisk together the yogurt, cinnamon, and vanilla in a small bowl until smooth.
4. When cooking is complete, the peaches should be lightly browned and caramelized.
5. Remove the peaches from the air fryer oven to a plate. Serve topped with the yogurt mixture and fresh blueberries.

Crunchy Bananas with Chocolate Sauce

Prep time: 10 minutes | Cook time: 7 minutes | Serves 6

¼ cup cornstarch
¼ cup plain bread crumbs
1 large egg, beaten
3 bananas, halved
crosswise
Cooking spray
Chocolate sauce, for serving

1. Put the cornstarch, bread crumbs, and egg in three separate bowls.
2. Roll the bananas in the cornstarch, then in the beaten egg, and finally in the bread crumbs to coat well.
3. Spritz the air flow racks with cooking spray.
4. Arrange the banana halves on the air flow racks and mist them with cooking spray.
5. Slide the racks into the air fryer oven. Press the Power Button and cook at 350ºF (180ºC) for 7 minutes.
6. After about 5 minutes, flip the bananas and continue to air fry for another 2 minutes.
7. When cooking is complete, remove the bananas from the air fryer oven to a serving plate. Serve with the chocolate sauce drizzled over the top.

Brown Sugar Cinnamon Baked Apples

Prep time: 15 minutes | Cook time: 12 minutes | Serves 4

1 cup packed light brown sugar
2 teaspoons ground cinnamon
2 medium Granny Smith apples, peeled and diced

1. Thoroughly combine the brown sugar and cinnamon in a medium bowl.
2. Add the apples to the bowl and stir until well coated. Transfer the apples to a baking pan.
3. Slide the pan into the air fryer oven. Press the Power Button and cook at 350ºF (180ºC) for 12 minutes.
4. After about 9 minutes, stir the apples and cook for an additional 3 minutes. When cooking is complete, the apples should be softened.
5. Serve warm.

Chocolate Coconut Cake

Prep time: 5 minutes | Cook time: 15 minutes | Serves 6

½ cup unsweetened chocolate, chopped
½ stick butter, at room temperature
1 tablespoon liquid stevia

1½ cups coconut flour
2 eggs, whisked
½ teaspoon vanilla extract
Pinch of fine sea salt
Cooking spray

1. Put the chocolate, butter, and stevia in a microwave-safe bowl. Microwave for about 30 seconds until melted.
2. Let the chocolate mixture cool for 5 to 10 minutes.
3. Add the remaining ingredients to the bowl of chocolate mixture and whisk to incorporate.
4. Lightly spray a baking pan with cooking spray.
5. Scrape the chocolate mixture into the prepared baking pan.
6. Slide the pan into the air fryer oven. Press the Power Button and cook at 330ºF (166ºC) for 15 minutes.
7. When cooking is complete, the top should spring back lightly when gently pressed with your fingers.
8. Let the cake cool for 5 minutes and serve.

S'mores

Prep time: 5 minutes | Cook time: 3 minutes | Makes 12 S'mores

12 whole cinnamon graham crackers, halved
2 (1.55-ounce / 44-

g) chocolate bars, cut into 12 pieces
12 marshmallows

1. Arrange 12 graham cracker squares on the air flow racks.
2. Top each square with a piece of chocolate.
3. Slide the racks into the air fryer oven. Press the Power Button and cook at 350ºF (180ºC) for 2 minutes.
4. Remove the racks and place a marshmallow on each piece of melted chocolate. Cook for another 1 minute.
5. Remove from the air fryer oven to a serving plate.
6. Serve topped with the remaining graham cracker squares

Coconut Pineapple Sticks

Prep time: 10 minutes | Cook time: 10 minutes | Serves 4

½ fresh pineapple, cut into sticks
¼ cup desiccated coconut

1. Put the desiccated coconut on a plate and roll the pineapple sticks in the coconut until well coated.
2. Lay the pineapple sticks on the air flow racks.
3. Slide the racks into the air fryer oven. Press the Power Button and cook at 400ºF (205ºC) for 10 minutes.
4. When cooking is complete, the pineapple sticks should be crisp-tender.
5. Serve warm.

Mixed Berry Crumble

Prep time: 5 minutes | Cook time: 35 minutes | Serves 6

2 ounces (57 g) unsweetened mixed berries
½ cup granulated Swerve
2 tablespoons golden flaxseed meal

1 teaspoon xanthan gum
½ teaspoon ground cinnamon
¼ teaspoon ground star anise

Topping:

½ stick butter, cut into small pieces
1 cup powdered Swerve
⅔ cup almond flour
⅓ cup unsweetened

coconut, finely shredded
½ teaspoon baking powder
Cooking spray

1. Coat 6 ramekins with cooking spray.
2. In a mixing dish, stir together the mixed berries, granulated Swerve, flaxseed meal, xanthan gum, cinnamon, star anise. Divide the berry mixture evenly among the prepared ramekins.
3. Combine the remaining ingredients in a separate mixing dish and stir well. Scatter the topping over the berry mixture.
4. Slide the ramekins into the air fryer oven. Press the Power Button and cook at 330ºF (166ºC) for 35 minutes.
5. When done, the topping should be golden brown.
6. Serve warm.

Peach and Apple Crisp

Prep time: 10 minutes | Cook time: 10 to 12 minutes | Serves 4

2 peaches, peeled, pitted, and chopped
1 apple, peeled and chopped
2 tablespoons honey
3 tablespoons packed brown sugar
2 tablespoons
unsalted butter, at room temperature
½ cup quick-cooking oatmeal
⅓ cup whole-wheat pastry flour
½ teaspoon ground cinnamon

1. Put the peaches, apple, and honey in a baking pan and toss until thoroughly combined.
2. Mix the brown sugar, butter, oatmeal, pastry flour, and cinnamon in a medium bowl and stir until crumbly. Sprinkle this mixture generously on top of the peaches and apples.
3. Slide the pan into the air fryer oven. Press the Power Button and cook at 380ºF (193ºC) for 10 minutes.
4. Cook until the fruit is bubbling and the topping is golden brown.
5. Once cooking is complete, remove from the air fryer oven and allow to cool for 5 minutes before serving.

Chia Pudding

Prep time: 5 minutes | Cook time: 4 minutes | Serves 2

1 cup chia seeds
1 cup unsweetened coconut milk
1 teaspoon liquid stevia
1 tablespoon coconut oil
1 teaspoon butter, melted

1. Mix the chia seeds, coconut milk, and stevia in a large bowl. Add the coconut oil and melted butter and stir until well blended.
2. Divide the mixture evenly between the ramekins, filling only about ⅔ of the way.
3. Slide the ramekins into the air fryer oven. Press the Power Button and cook at 360ºF (182ºC) for 4 minutes.
4. When cooking is complete, allow to cool for 5 minutes and serve warm.

Mixed Berries with Pecan Streusel

Prep time: 5 minutes | Cook time: 17 minutes | Serves 3

½ cup mixed berries
Topping:
1 egg, beaten
3 tablespoons almonds, slivered
3 tablespoons chopped pecans
2 tablespoons chopped walnuts
Cooking spray

3 tablespoons granulated Swerve
2 tablespoons cold salted butter, cut into pieces
½ teaspoon ground cinnamon

1. Lightly spray a baking dish with cooking spray.
2. Make the topping: In a medium bowl, stir together the beaten egg, nuts, Swerve, butter, and cinnamon until well blended.
3. Put the mixed berries in the bottom of the baking dish and spread the topping over the top.
4. Slide the baking dish into the air fryer oven. Press the Power Button and cook at 340ºF (171ºC) for 17 minutes.
5. When cooking is complete, the fruit should be bubbly and topping should be golden brown.
6. Allow to cool for 5 to 10 minutes before serving.

Mixed Berry Crisp with Coconut Chips

Prep time: 5 minutes | Cook time: 20 minutes | Serves 6

1 tablespoon butter, melted
12 ounces (340 g) mixed berries
⅓ cup granulated Swerve
1 teaspoon pure vanilla extract
½ teaspoon ground cinnamon
¼ teaspoon ground cloves
¼ teaspoon grated nutmeg
½ cup coconut chips, for garnish

1. Coat a baking pan with melted butter.
2. Put the remaining ingredients except the coconut chips in the prepared baking pan.
3. Slide the pan into the air fryer oven. Press the Power Button and cook at 330ºF (166ºC) for 20 minutes.
4. When cooking is complete, remove from the air fryer oven. Serve garnished with the coconut chips.

Chocolate Mascarpone Cheesecake

Prep time: 5 minutes | Cook time: 18 minutes | Serves 6

Crust:

½ cup butter, melted	2 tablespoons stevia
½ cup coconut flour	Cooking spray

Topping:

4 ounces (113 g) unsweetened chocolate	temperature
	1 teaspoon vanilla extract
1 cup mascarpone cheese, at room	2 drops peppermint extract

1. Lightly coat a baking pan with cooking spray.
2. In a mixing bowl, whisk together the butter, flour, and stevia until well combined. Transfer the mixture to the prepared baking pan.
3. Slide the pan into the air fryer oven. Press the Power Button and cook at 350ºF (180ºC) for 18 minutes.
4. When done, a toothpick inserted in the center should come out clean.
5. Remove the crust from the air fryer oven to a wire rack to cool.
6. Once cooled completely, place it in the freezer for 20 minutes.
7. When ready, combine all the ingredients for the topping in a small bowl and stir to incorporate.
8. Spread this topping over the crust and let it sit for another 15 minutes in the freezer.
9. Serve chilled.

Orange and Hazelnut Cake

Prep time: 5 minutes | Cook time: 20 minutes | Serves 6

1 stick butter, at room temperature	unbleached almond flour
5 tablespoons liquid monk fruit	1 teaspoon baking soda
2 eggs plus 1 egg yolk, beaten	½ teaspoon baking powder
⅓ cup hazelnuts, roughly chopped	½ teaspoon ground cinnamon
3 tablespoons sugar-free orange marmalade	½ teaspoon ground allspice
6 ounces (170 g)	½ ground anise seed
	Cooking spray

1. Lightly spritz a baking pan with cooking spray.
2. In a mixing bowl, whisk the butter and liquid monk fruit until the mixture is pale and smooth. Mix in the beaten eggs, hazelnuts, and marmalade and whisk again until well incorporated.
3. Add the almond flour, baking soda, baking powder, cinnamon, allspice, anise seed and stir to mix well.
4. Scrape the batter into the prepared baking pan.
5. Slide the pan into the air fryer oven. Press the Power Button and cook at 310ºF (154ºC) for 20 minutes.
6. When cooking is complete, the top of the cake should spring back when gently pressed with your fingers.
7. Transfer to a wire rack and let the cake cool to room temperature. Serve immediately.

Chocolate Pecan Pie

Prep time: 20 minutes | Cook time: 25 minutes | Serves 8

1 (9-inch) unbaked pie crust

Filling:

2 large eggs	chips
⅓ cup butter, melted	1½ cups coarsely chopped pecans
1 cup sugar	
½ cup all-purpose flour	2 tablespoons bourbon
1 cup milk chocolate	

1. Whisk the eggs and melted butter in a large bowl until creamy.
2. Add the sugar and flour and stir to incorporate. Mix in the milk chocolate chips, pecans, and bourbon and stir until well combined.
3. Use a fork to prick holes in the bottom and sides of the pie crust. Pour the prepared filling into the pie crust. Place the pie crust on the air flow racks.
4. Slide the racks into the air fryer oven. Press the Power Button and cook at 350ºF (180ºC) for 25 minutes.
5. When cooking is complete, a toothpick inserted in the center should come out clean.
6. Allow the pie cool for 10 minutes on the racks before serving.

Fudge Cocoa Brownies

Prep time: 5 minutes | Cook time: 21 minutes | Serves 8

1 stick butter, melted
1 cup Swerve
2 eggs
1 cup coconut flour
½ cup unsweetened cocoa powder
2 tablespoons flaxseed meal
1 teaspoon baking powder
1 teaspoon vanilla essence
Pinch of salt
Pinch of ground cardamom
Cooking spray

1. Spray a baking pan with cooking spray.
2. Beat together the melted butter and Swerve in a large mixing dish until fluffy. Whisk in the eggs.
3. Add the coconut flour, cocoa powder, flaxseed meal, baking powder, vanilla essence, salt, and cardamom and stir with a spatula until well incorporated. Spread the mixture evenly into the prepared baking pan.
4. Slide the pan into the air fryer oven. Press the Power Button and cook at 350ºF (180ºC) for 21 minutes.
5. When cooking is complete, a toothpick inserted in the center should come out clean.
6. Remove from the air fryer oven and place on a wire rack to cool completely. Cut into squares and serve immediately.

White Chocolate Cookies

Prep time: 5 minutes | Cook time: 11 minutes | Serves 10

8 ounces (227 g) unsweetened white chocolate
2 eggs, well beaten
¾ cup butter, at room temperature
1⅔ cups almond flour
½ cup coconut flour
¾ cup granulated Swerve
2 tablespoons coconut oil
1/3 teaspoon grated nutmeg
1/3 teaspoon ground allspice
1/3 teaspoon ground anise star
¼ teaspoon fine sea salt

1. Line a baking sheet with parchment paper.
2. Combine all the ingredients in a mixing bowl and knead for about 3 to 4 minutes, or until a soft dough forms. Transfer to the refrigerator to chill for 20 minutes.

3. Make the cookies: Roll the dough into 1-inch balls and transfer to the parchment-lined baking sheet, spacing 2 inches apart. Flatten each with the back of a spoon.
4. Slide the baking sheet into the air fryer oven. Press the Power Button and cook at 350ºF (180ºC) for 11 minutes.
5. When cooking is complete, the cookies should be golden and firm to the touch.
6. Transfer to a wire rack and let the cookies cool completely. Serve immediately.

Coconut Pecan Cookies

Prep time: 10 minutes | Cook time: 25 minutes | Serves 10

1½ cups coconut flour
1½ cups extra-fine almond flour
½ teaspoon baking powder
1/3 teaspoon baking soda
3 eggs plus an egg yolk, beaten
¾ cup coconut oil, at room temperature
1 cup unsalted pecan nuts, roughly chopped
¾ cup monk fruit
¼ teaspoon freshly grated nutmeg
1/3 teaspoon ground cloves
½ teaspoon pure vanilla extract
½ teaspoon pure coconut extract
⅛ teaspoon fine sea salt

1. Line the air flow racks with parchment paper.
2. Mix the coconut flour, almond flour, baking powder, and baking soda in a large mixing bowl.
3. In another mixing bowl, stir together the eggs and coconut oil. Add the wet mixture to the dry mixture.
4. Mix in the remaining ingredients and stir until a soft dough forms.
5. Drop about 2 tablespoons of dough on the parchment paper for each cookie and flatten each biscuit until it's 1 inch thick.
6. Slide the racks into the air fryer oven. Press the Power Button and cook at 370ºF (188ºC) for 25 minutes.
7. When cooking is complete, the cookies should be golden and firm to the touch.
8. Remove from the air fryer oven to a plate. Let the cookies cool to room temperature and serve.

Peach and Blackberry Cobbler

Prep time: 10 minutes | Cook time: 20 minutes | Serves 4

Filling:

1 (6-ounce / 170-g) package blackberries	arrowroot or cornstarch
1½ cups chopped peaches, cut into ½-inch thick slices	2 tablespoons coconut sugar
2 teaspoons	1 teaspoon lemon juice

Topping:

2 tablespoons sunflower oil	½ cup rolled oats
1 tablespoon maple syrup	⅓ cup whole-wheat pastry flour
1 teaspoon vanilla	1 teaspoon cinnamon
3 tablespoons coconut sugar	¼ teaspoon nutmeg
	⅛ teaspoon sea salt

Make the Filling:
1. Combine the blackberries, peaches, arrowroot, coconut sugar, and lemon juice in a baking pan.
2. Using a rubber spatula, stir until well incorporated. Set aside.

Make the Topping:
1. Combine the oil, maple syrup, and vanilla in a mixing bowl and stir well. Whisk in the remaining ingredients. Spread this mixture evenly over the filling.
2. Slide the pan into the air fryer oven. Press the Power Button and cook at 320°F (160°C) for 20 minutes.
3. When cooked, the topping should be crispy and golden brown. Serve warm

Raspberry Muffins

Prep time: 5 minutes | Cook time: 15 minutes | Serves 6

2 cups almond flour	½ teaspoon grated lemon zest
¾ cup Swerve	¼ teaspoon salt
1¼ teaspoons baking powder	2 eggs
⅓ teaspoon ground allspice	1 cup sour cream
⅓ teaspoon ground anise star	½ cup coconut oil
	½ cup raspberries

1. Line a muffin pan with 6 paper liners.
2. In a mixing bowl, mix the almond flour, Swerve, baking powder, allspice, anise, lemon zest, and salt.

3. In another mixing bowl, beat the eggs, sour cream, and coconut oil until well mixed. Add the egg mixture to the flour mixture and stir to combine. Mix in the raspberries.
4. Scrape the batter into the prepared muffin cups, filling each about three-quarters full.
5. Slide the pan into the air fryer oven. Press the Power Button and cook at 345°F (174°C) for 15 minutes.
6. When cooking is complete, the tops should be golden and a toothpick inserted in the middle should come out clean.
7. Allow the muffins to cool for 10 minutes in the muffin pan before removing and serving.

Pumpkin Pudding with Vanilla Wafers

Prep time: 10 minutes | Cook time: 15 minutes | Serves 4

1 cup canned pumpkin purée	1 tablespoon unsalted butter, melted
¼ cup brown sugar	1 teaspoon pure vanilla extract
3 tablespoons all-purpose flour	4 low-fat vanilla wafers, crumbled
1 egg, whisked	Cooking spray
2 tablespoons milk	

1. Coat a baking pan with cooking spray. Set aside.
2. Mix the pumpkin purée, brown sugar, flour, whisked egg, milk, melted butter, and vanilla in a medium bowl and whisk to combine. Transfer the mixture to the baking pan.
3. Slide the pan into the air fryer oven. Press the Power Button and cook at 350°F (180°C) for 15 minutes.
4. When cooking is complete, the pudding should be set.
5. Remove the pudding from the air fryer oven to a wire rack to cool.
6. Divide the pudding into four bowls and serve with the vanilla wafers sprinkled on top.

Coconut Chocolate Cake

Prep time: 5 minutes | Cook time: 15 minutes | Serves 10

1¼ cups unsweetened chocolate
1 stick butter
1 teaspoon liquid stevia
¹/₃ cup shredded coconut
2 tablespoons coconut milk
2 eggs, beaten
Cooking spray

1. Lightly spritz a baking pan with cooking spray.
2. Put the chocolate, butter, and stevia in a microwave-safe bowl. Microwave for about 30 seconds until melted. Let the chocolate mixture cool to room temperature.
3. Add the remaining ingredients to the chocolate mixture and stir until well incorporated. Pour the batter into the prepared baking pan.
4. Slide the pan into the air fryer oven. Press the Power Button and cook at 330ºF (166ºC) for 15 minutes.
5. When cooking is complete, a toothpick inserted in the center should come out clean.
6. Remove from the air fryer oven and allow to cool for about 10 minutes before serving.

Sumptuous Caramelized Fruit Skewers

Prep time: 10 minutes | Cook time: 4 minutes | Serves 4

2 peaches, peeled, pitted, and thickly sliced
3 plums, halved and pitted
3 nectarines, halved and pitted
1 tablespoon honey
½ teaspoon ground cinnamon
¼ teaspoon ground allspice
Pinch cayenne pepper

Special Equipment:
8 metal skewers

1. Thread, alternating peaches, plums, and nectarines onto the metal skewers that fit into the air fryer oven.
2. Thoroughly combine the honey, cinnamon, allspice, and cayenne in a small bowl. Brush generously the glaze over the fruit skewers.
3. Transfer the fruit skewers to the air flow racks.
4. Slide the racks into the air fryer oven. Press the Power Button and cook at 400ºF (205ºC) for 4 minutes.
5. When cooking is complete, the fruit should be caramelized.
6. Remove the fruit skewers from the air fryer oven and let rest for 5 minutes before serving.

Oatmeal Chocolate Chip Cookies

Prep time: 10 minutes | Cook time: 20 minutes | Makes 4 dozen (1-by-1½-inch) bars

1 cup unsalted butter, at room temperature
1 cup dark brown sugar
½ cup granulated sugar
2 large eggs
1 tablespoon vanilla extract
Pinch salt
2 cups old-fashioned rolled oats
1½ cups all-purpose flour
1 teaspoon baking powder
1 teaspoon baking soda
2 cups chocolate chips

1. Stir together the butter, brown sugar, and granulated sugar in a large mixing bowl until smooth and light in color.
2. Crack the eggs into the bowl, one at a time, mixing after each addition. Stir in the vanilla and salt.
3. Mix the oats, flour, baking powder, and baking soda in a separate bowl. Add the mixture to the butter mixture and stir until mixed. Stir in the chocolate chips.
4. Spread the dough into a sheet pan.
5. Slide the pan into the air fryer oven. Press the Power Button and cook at 350ºF (180ºC) for 20 minutes.
6. After 15 minutes, check the cookie, rotating the pan if the crust is not browning evenly. Continue cooking for 18 to 20 minutes or until golden brown.
7. When cooking is complete, remove from the air fryer oven and allow to cool completely before slicing and serving.

Pineapple Rings

Prep time: 5 minutes | Cook time: 7 minutes | Serves 6

1 cup rice milk
2/3 cup flour
½ cup water
¼ cup unsweetened flaked coconut
4 tablespoons sugar
½ teaspoon baking soda
½ teaspoon baking powder

½ teaspoon vanilla essence
½ teaspoon ground cinnamon
¼ teaspoon ground anise star
Pinch of kosher salt
1 medium pineapple, peeled and sliced

1. In a large bowl, stir together all the ingredients except the pineapple.
2. Dip each pineapple slice into the batter until evenly coated.
3. Arrange the pineapple slices on the air flow racks.
4. Slide the racks into the air fryer oven. Press the Power Button and cook at 380ºF (193ºC) for 7 minutes.
5. When cooking is complete, the pineapple rings should be golden brown.
6. Remove from the air fryer oven to a plate and cool for 5 minutes before serving.

Pound Cake

Prep time: 5 minutes | Cook time: 30 minutes | Serves 8

1 stick butter, at room temperature
1 cup Swerve
4 eggs
1½ cups coconut flour
½ cup buttermilk
½ teaspoon baking soda
½ teaspoon baking

powder
¼ teaspoon salt
1 teaspoon vanilla essence
Pinch of ground star anise
Pinch of freshly grated nutmeg
Cooking spray

1. Spray a baking pan with cooking spray.
2. With an electric mixer or hand mixer, beat the butter and Swerve until creamy. One at a time, mix in the eggs and whisk until fluffy. Add the remaining ingredients and stir to combine.
3. Transfer the batter to the prepared baking pan.
4. Slide the pan into the air fryer oven. Press the Power Button and cook at 320ºF (160ºC) for 30 minutes.

5. Rotate the pan halfway through the cooking time.
6. When cooking is complete, the center of the cake should be springy.
7. Allow the cake to cool in the pan for 10 minutes before removing and serving.

Triple Berry Crisp

Prep time: 10 minutes | Cook time: 12 minutes | Serves 4

½ cup fresh blueberries
½ cup chopped fresh strawberries
1/3 cup frozen raspberries, thawed
1 tablespoon honey
1 tablespoon freshly

squeezed lemon juice
2/3 cup whole-wheat pastry flour
3 tablespoons packed brown sugar
2 tablespoons unsalted butter, melted

1. Put the blueberries, strawberries, and raspberries in a baking pan and drizzle the honey and lemon juice over the top.
2. Combine the pastry flour and brown sugar in a small mixing bowl.
3. Add the butter and whisk until the mixture is crumbly. Scatter the flour mixture on top of the fruit.
4. Slide the pan into the air fryer oven. Press the Power Button and cook at 380ºF (193ºC) for 12 minutes.
5. When cooking is complete, the fruit should be bubbly and the topping should be golden brown.
6. Remove from the air fryer oven and serve on a plate.

Rhubarb and Strawberry Crumble

Prep time: 10 minutes | Cook time: 12 to 17 minutes | Serves 6

1½ cups sliced fresh strawberries
⅓ cup sugar
¾ cup sliced rhubarb
⅔ cup quick-cooking oatmeal
¼ cup packed brown sugar
½ cup whole-wheat pastry flour
½ teaspoon ground cinnamon
3 tablespoons unsalted butter, melted

1. Put the strawberries, sugar, and rhubarb in a baking pan and toss to coat.
2. Combine the oatmeal, brown sugar, pastry flour, and cinnamon in a medium bowl.
3. Add the melted butter to the oatmeal mixture and stir until crumbly. Sprinkle this generously on top of the strawberries and rhubarb.
4. Slide the pan into the air fryer oven. Press the Power Button and cook at 370°F (188°C) for 12 minutes.
5. Cook until the fruit is bubbly and the topping is golden brown. Continue cooking for an additional 2 to 5 minutes if needed.
6. When cooking is complete, remove from the air fryer oven and serve warm.

Orange Cake

Prep time: 5 minutes | Cook time: 17 minutes | Serves 6

1 stick butter, melted
¾ cup granulated Swerve
2 eggs, beaten
¾ cup coconut flour
¼ teaspoon salt
⅓ teaspoon grated nutmeg
⅓ cup coconut milk
1¼ cups almond flour
½ teaspoon baking powder
2 tablespoons unsweetened orange jam
Cooking spray

1. Coat a baking pan with cooking spray. Set aside.
2. In a large mixing bowl, whisk together the melted butter and granulated Swerve until fluffy.
3. Mix in the beaten eggs and whisk again until smooth. Stir in the coconut flour, salt, and nutmeg and gradually pour in the coconut milk. Add the remaining ingredients and stir until well incorporated.
4. Scrape the batter into the baking pan.

5. Slide the pan into the air fryer oven. Press the Power Button and cook at 355°F (179°C) for 17 minutes.
6. When cooking is complete, the top of the cake should spring back when gently pressed with your fingers.
7. Remove from the air fryer oven to a wire rack to cool. Serve chilled.

Blackberry Chocolate Cake

Prep time: 10 minutes | Cook time: 22 minutes | Serves 8

½ cup butter, at room temperature
2 ounces (57 g) Swerve
4 eggs
1 cup almond flour
1 teaspoon baking soda
⅓ teaspoon baking powder
½ cup cocoa powder
1 teaspoon orange zest
⅓ cup fresh blackberries

1. With an electric mixer or hand mixer, beat the butter and Swerve until creamy.
2. One at a time, mix in the eggs and beat again until fluffy.
3. Add the almond flour, baking soda, baking powder, cocoa powder, orange zest and mix well. Add the butter mixture to the almond flour mixture and stir until well blended. Fold in the blackberries.
4. Scrape the batter into a baking pan.
5. Slide the pan into the air fryer oven. Press the Power Button and cook at 335°F (168°C) for 22 minutes.
6. When cooking is complete, a toothpick inserted into the center of the cake should come out clean.
7. Allow the cake cool on a wire rack to room temperature. Serve immediately.

Chapter 13 Dehydrate

Candied Bacon

Prep time: 10 minutes | Cook time: 4 hours | Makes 6 slices

6 slices bacon
3 tablespoons light brown sugar
2 tablespoons rice vinegar
2 tablespoons chilli paste
1 tablespoon soy sauce

1. Mix brown sugar, rice vinegar, chilli paste, and soy sauce in a bowl.
2. Add bacon slices and mix until the slices are evenly coated.
3. Marinate for up to 3 hours or until ready to dehydrate.
4. Discard the marinade, then place the bacon onto the air flow racks.
5. Slide the racks into the air fryer oven. Press the Power Button and cook at 170ºF (77ºC) for 4 hours.
6. Remove from the air fryer oven when done and let the bacon cool down for 5 minutes, then serve.

Smoked Venison Jerky

Prep time: 30 minutes | Cook time: 4 hours | Makes 1 to 2 pounds

3 to 5 pounds (1.4 to 2.3 kg) deer roast
Hi-Mountain cure and jerky mix or another brand
3 to 5 teaspoons liquid smoke

1. Start by slicing your roast into thin strips, and removing any silver skin on each piece of the meat.
2. Lay it all out flat, and then mix up your seasoning per the box. Sprinkle on both sides of the meat, massaging it in.
3. Then transfer the meat into a bag and add in the liquid smoke. Massage bag.
4. Store in the fridge for 24 hours to let it marinade and cure.
5. Lay the jerky out on the air flow racks, don't let the pieces touch.
6. Slide the racks into the air fryer oven. Press the Power Button and cook at 160ºF (71ºC) for 3 to 4 hours.
7. Make sure to flip and randomly check, and remove the meat when it is cooked to your texture liking.

Oven-Dried Mushrooms

Prep time: 30 minutes | Cook time: 4 hours | Makes 2½ quarts

4 to 5 pounds (1.8 to 2.3 kg) fresh mushrooms, washed, rinsed and drained well.

1. Rinse whole mushrooms well under cold running water. Gently scrub any visible dirt away with out damaging the mushroom. Pat dry with paper towels if needed.
2. Break the stem off of each mushroom and slice into ¼ to ½ inch thick slices with a sharp knife.
3. Place the sliced mushrooms on the parchment-lined air flow racks.
4. Slide the racks into the air fryer oven. Press the Power Button and cook at 170ºF (77ºC) for 4 hours.
5. Check the mushrooms after 1 hour and flip them over for even drying. Check the mushroom slices every hour.
6. As the mushroom slices dry, remove them from the air fryer oven and allow to cool on the racks or a paper towel.
7. Store dried mushroom slices in an airtight glass container.

Peach Fruit Leather

Prep time: 15 minutes | Cook time: 6 hours 15 minutes | Serves 4

4 peaches, pitted and each peach cut into 6 pieces

1. Line three air flow racks with parchment paper. Place peach slices on parchment.
2. Slide the racks into the air fryer oven. Press the Power Button and cook at 400ºF (205ºC) for 15 minutes.
3. Transfer the cooked peaches to a blender or food processor and blend until smooth.
4. Line a baking sheet with parchment paper and pour peach purée onto paper, spreading as necessary with a spatula into an even layer.
5. Slide the sheet into the air fryer oven. Press the Power Button and cook at 130ºF (54ºC) for 6 hours or until leather is desired consistency.

Dehydrated Cinnamon Pineapple

Prep time: 10 minutes | Cook time: 12 hours | Serves 6

1 pineapple, peeled, cored and sliced ¼ inch thick
1 tablespoon coconut palm sugar

2 teaspoons ground cinnamon
½ teaspoon ground ginger
½ teaspoon Himalayan pink salt

1. Toss the pineapple slices with the sugar, cinnamon, ginger and salt.
2. Place the pineapple slices in a single layer on three air flow racks. Place the racks on the bottom, middle, and top shelves of the air fryer oven.
3. Press the Power Button and cook at 120ºF (49ºC) for 12 hours.

Chewy Kiwi Chips

Prep time: 15 minutes | Cook time: 6 to 12 hours | Makes 10 to 12 slices

2 kiwis

1. Peel the kiwis, using a paring knife to slice the skin off or a vegetable peeler.
2. Slice the peeled kiwis into ¼ inch slices.
3. Place the kiwi slices on the air flow racks. Slide the racks into the air fryer oven. Press the Power Button and cook at 135ºF (57ºC) for 6 to 12 hours.
4. These should be slightly chewy when done.

Tasty Salmon Jerky

Prep time: 20 minutes | Cook time: 3 hours | Serves 10

1¾ pounds (794 g) filet wild Alaskan salmon, skin on, bones removed
½ cup low sodium soy sauce
1 tablespoon lemon juice
1 tablespoon brown sugar
2 teaspoons mixed whole peppercorns

1 teaspoon lemon zest
½ teaspoon liquid smoke
½ teaspoon celery seeds
½ teaspoon onion powder
½ teaspoon garlic powder
¼ teaspoon kosher salt

1. Freeze salmon for 1 hour.
2. In the meantime, in a large bowl, combine the soy sauce, lemon juice, sugar, peppercorns, lemon zest, liquid smoke, celery seeds, onion and garlic powders, and salt.
3. Remove the salmon from the freezer and cut it into thin strips (about ½ inch), then place in the marinade. Cover and marinate for 1 to 3 hours in the fridge.
4. Remove strips and place on a plate, patting dry with a paper towel.
5. Place the salmon strips on three air flow racks in a single layer. Slide the racks into the air fryer oven. Press the Power Button and cook at 170ºF (77ºC) for 3 hours, flipping over halfway through. Salmon is done when dried all the way through, but slightly chewy.
6. Store in a cool dry place in a sealed container.

Dehydrated Strawberries

Prep time: 10 minutes | Cook time: 2 hours | Serves 4

1 pound (454 g) fresh strawberries

1. Line three air flow racks with parchment paper.
2. Wash strawberries and cut off stem ends. Cut strawberries into slices, about ⅛ inch thick.
3. Place sliced strawberries on the air flow racks. Space them so the pieces are not touching.
4. Slide the racks into the air fryer oven. Press the Power Button and cook at 170ºF (77ºC) for 30 minutes. Use tongs to turn the berries. Cook for another 30 minutes. Repeat this until strawberry slices are leathery.
5. Allow the slices to cool completely. Transfer dried strawberry slices to an airtight container. They will keep up to 5 days.

Cinnamon Oranges

Prep time: 10 minutes | Cook time: 6 hours | Serves 3

2 large oranges, cut into ⅛-inch-thick slices
½ teaspoon ground star anise
½ teaspoon ground cinnamon

1 tablespoon chocolate hazelnut spread (optional)

1. Sprinkle spices on the orange slices.
2. Place orange slices on the air flow racks. Slide the racks into the air fryer oven. Press the Power Button and cook at 140ºF (60ºC) for 6 hours.
3. Remove when done, and if desired serve with chocolate hazelnut spread.

Homemade Beef Jerky

Prep time: 10 minutes | Cook time: 3 to 4 hours | Serves 8

12 ounces (340 g) top sirloin beef
1 garlic clove, minced
1 inch piece fresh gingerroot, peeled and grated
2 tablespoons reduced sodium soy sauce

1 tablespoon turbinado sugar
1 tablespoon chili paste (such as Sambal Oelek)
1 tablespoon rice vinegar

1. Using a sharp knife, thinly slice beef and place in a resealable bag.
2. In a bowl, combine garlic, ginger, soy sauce, sugar chili paste and rice vinegar; whisk well.
3. Pour marinade into bag, seal and place in the refrigerator for at least 4 or up to 24 hours.
4. When ready to cook, remove pieces of beef from a marinade and pat dry with a paper towel.
5. Place the beef on three air flow racks. Slide the racks into the air fryer oven. Press the Power Button and cook at 160ºF (71ºC) for 3 to 4 hours.
6. Checking the jerky periodically for desired doneness. Allow to cool completely and then store in an airtight container.

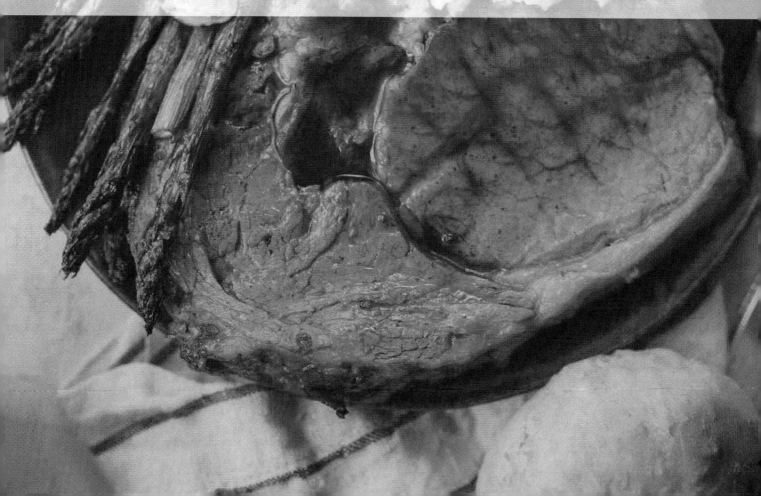

Chapter 14 Rotisserie

Brown Sugar-Brined Chicken

Prep time: 5 minutes | Cook time: 1 hour | Serves 4

1 (4-pound / 1.8-kg) chicken
Brine:

2 quarts cold water	crushed
½ cup table salt (or 1 cup kosher salt)	3 bay leaves, crumbled
¼ cup brown sugar	1 tablespoon
½ head of garlic (6 to 8 cloves), skin on,	peppercorns, crushed or coarsely ground

1. Combine the brine ingredients in large container, and stir until the salt and sugar dissolve. Submerge the chicken in the brine. Store in the refrigerator for at least one hour, preferably four hours, no longer than eight hours.
2. Remove the chicken from the brine and pat dry with paper towels, picking off any pieces of bay leaves or garlic that stick to the chicken. Fold the wingtips underneath the wings, then truss the chicken. Skewer the chicken on the rotisserie shaft, securing it with the rotisserie forks. Let the chicken rest at room temperature.
3. Put the shaft in the air fryer oven with a drip tray underneath. Press the Power Button and cook at 400°F (205°C) for 1 hour until the chicken reaches 160°F (71°C) in the thickest part of the breast.
4. Remove the chicken from the rotisserie shaft and remove the twine trussing the chicken. Be careful - the shaft and forks are blazing hot. Let the chicken rest for 15 minutes, then carve and serve.

Carrot and Apple Stuffed Turkey

Prep time: 30 minutes | Cook time: 3 hours | Serves 12 to 14

1 (12-pound/5.4-kg) turkey, giblet removed, rinsed and pat dry
For the Seasoning:

¼ cup lemon pepper	2 cloves garlic, minced
2 tablespoons chopped fresh parsley	2 teaspoons ground black pepper
1 tablespoon celery salt	1 teaspoon sage

For the Stuffing:

1 medium onion, cut into 8 equal parts	1 apple, cored and cut into 8 thick slices
1 carrot, sliced	

1. Mix together the seasoning in a small bowl. Rub over the surface and inside of the turkey.
2. Stuff the turkey with the onions, carrots, and apples. Using the rotisserie shaft, push through the turkey and attach the rotisserie forks.
3. If desired, place aluminum foil onto the drip tray.
4. Place the prepared turkey with rotisserie shaft in the air fryer oven. Press the Power Button and cook at 350°F (180°C) for 3 hours.
5. When cooking is complete, the internal temperature should read at least 180°F (82°C). Remove the turkey using the rotisserie fetch tool and, using gloves, carefully remove the turkey from the shaft.
6. Server hot.

Maple-Mustard Glazed Ham

Prep time: 10 minutes | Cook time: 3 hours | Serves 12

1 (8-pound / 3.6-kg) bone in ham (shank or butt end)
Glaze:

½ cup maple syrup (preferably Grade B maple syrup)	½ cup brown sugar
	¼ cup Dijon mustard

1. One hour before cooking, remove the ham from its wrapper and pat dry with paper towels. Cut the rind of the ham in a 1 inch diamond pattern, cutting about ¼ inch deep. Skewer the ham on the rotisserie shaft, securing it with the rotisserie forks. Let the ham rest at room temperature until it is time to cook.
2. Whisk the glaze ingredients in a small bowl until the brown sugar dissolves.
3. Put the shaft in the air fryer oven and set a drip tray underneath. Press the Power Button and cook at 325°F (163°C) for about 3 hours, until it reaches 135°F (57°C) in its thickest part. During the last half hour of cooking, brush the roast with glaze every ten minutes.
4. Remove the ham from the rotisserie shaft. Be careful - the shaft and forks are blazing hot. Let the ham rest for 15 minutes, then slice and serve.

Tapenade-Stuffed Leg of Lamb

Prep time: 10 minutes | Cook time: 45 minutes | Serves 3

1 (2½-pound / 1.1-kg) boneless leg of lamb
1 tablespoon kosher salt
Tapenade:

1 clove garlic, peeled	ground black pepper
2 basil leaves	1 anchovy fillet,
1 cup pitted Kalamata	rinsed (optional)
olives, rinsed	2 tablespoons
1 teaspoon capers	grapeseed oil or
Juice of ½ lemon	vegetable oil
½ teaspoon fresh	

1. Season the leg of lamb with the salt, then refrigerate for at least two hours, preferably overnight.
2. Drop the garlic clove into a running food processor and process until completely minced. Turn the processor off, add the basil, and process with one second pulses until finely minced. Add the olives, capers, lemon juice, pepper, and anchovy. Process with one second pulses until finely minced, scraping down the sides of the bowl if necessary. Turn the processor on and slowly pour the oil through the feed tube into the running processor. Once all the oil is added the tapenade should be a thick paste. Use immediately, or store in the refrigerator for up to a week.
3. One hour before cooking, remove the lamb from the refrigerator. Right before heating the air fryer oven, spread the tapenade over the cut side of the lamb, fold the roast back into its original shape, and truss it. (You're going to lose a little of the tapenade as you truss the roast; that's OK.) Skewer the lamb on the rotisserie shaft, securing it with the rotisserie forks. Let the lamb rest at room temperature until the air fryer oven is ready.
4. Put the shaft in the air fryer oven with a drip tray underneath. Press the Power Button and cook at 400ºF (205ºC) for 45 minutes the lamb until it reaches 130ºF (54ºC) in its thickest part for medium. (Cook to 115ºF (46ºC) for rare, 120ºF (49ºC) for medium-rare.)
5. Remove the lamb from the rotisserie shaft and remove the twine trussing the roast. Be careful - the shaft and forks are blazing hot. Let the lamb rest for 15 minutes, then carve and serve.

Honey Sriracha Pork Tenderloin

Prep time: 20 minutes | Cook time: 25 minutes | Serves 2 to 3

1 pound (454 g) pork	2 tablespoons honey
tenderloin	1½ teaspoons kosher
2 tablespoons	salt
Sriracha hot sauce	

1. Stir together the Sriracha hot sauce, honey and salt in a bowl. Rub the sauce all over the pork tenderloin.
2. Using the rotisserie shaft, push through the pork tenderloin and attach the rotisserie forks.
3. If desired, place aluminum foil onto the drip tray.
4. Place the prepared pork tenderloin with rotisserie shaft in the air fryer oven. Press the Power Button and cook at 350ºF (180ºC) for 20 minutes.
5. When cooking is complete, remove the pork tenderloin using the rotisserie fetch tool and, using gloves, carefully remove the pork from the shaft.
6. Let rest for 5 minutes and serve.

Rotisserie Beef Roast

Prep time: 5 minutes | Cook time: 38 minutes | Serves 6

2.5 pound (1.1 kg)	1 tablespoon Poultry
beef roast	seasoning
1 tablespoon olive oil	

1. Tie the beef roast and rub the olive oil all over the roast. Sprinkle with the seasoning.
2. Using the rotisserie shaft, push through the beef roast and attach the rotisserie forks.
3. If desired, place aluminum foil onto the drip tray.
4. Place the prepared beef with rotisserie shaft in the air fryer oven. Press the Power Button and cook at 360ºF (182ºC) for 38 minutes for medium rare beef.
5. When cooking is complete, remove the beef roast using the rotisserie fetch tool and, using gloves, carefully remove the beef roast from the shaft.
6. Let cool for 5 minutes before serving.

Garlic Beef Rib Roast

Prep time: 10 minutes | Cook time: 1 hour | Serves 6 to 8

1 (5-pound / 2.3-kg) bone-in beef rib roast (a two bone roast)
Rub:
8 cloves garlic, minced or pressed through a garlic press

1½ tablespoons kosher salt

2 tablespoons mixed peppercorns, crushed

1. Season the rib roast with the salt. Refrigerate for at least two hours, preferably overnight.
2. One hour before cooking, remove the rib roast from the refrigerator. Rub the garlic and crushed pepper all over the rib roast. Truss the roast, then skewer it on the rotisserie shaft, securing it with the rotisserie forks. Let the beef rest at room temperature until the air fryer oven is ready.
3. Put the shaft in the air fryer oven and set a drip tray underneath. Press the Power Button and cook at 400°F (205°C) for about 1 hour, until it reaches 120°F (49°C) in its thickest part for medium-rare. (Cook to 115°F (46°C) for rare, 130°F (54°C) for medium.)
4. Remove the rib roast from the rotisserie shaft and remove the twine trussing the roast. Be careful - the shaft and forks are blazing hot. Let the roast rest for 15 minutes. Cut the bones off of the roast, slice the roast, and serve.

Rotisserie Honey-Glazed Ham

Prep time: 20 minutes | Cook time: 3 hours | Serves 6

1 (5-pound/2.3-kg) cooked boneless ham, pat dry
For the Glaze:
½ cup honey
2 teaspoons lemon juice
1 teaspoon ground

cloves
1 teaspoon cinnamon
½ cup brown sugar

1. Using the rotisserie shaft, push through the ham and attach the rotisserie forks.
2. If desired, place aluminum foil onto the drip tray.

3. Place the prepared ham with rotisserie shaft in the air fryer oven. Press the Power Button and cook at 250°F (121°C) for 3 hours.
4. Place the prepared ham with rotisserie shaft into the air fryer oven.
5. Meanwhile, combine the ingredients for the glaze in a small bowl. Stir to mix well.
6. When the ham has reached 145°F (63°C), brush the glaze mixture over all surfaces of the ham.
7. When cooking is complete, remove the ham using the rotisserie fetch tool and, using gloves, carefully remove the ham from the shaft.
8. Let it rest for 10 minutes covered loosely with foil and then carve and serve.

Spice Rubbed Turkey Breast

Prep time: 15 minutes | Cook time: 1½ hours | Serves 10 to 12

1 (7-pound / 3.2-kg) turkey breast
Spice Rub:
2 tablespoons kosher salt
1 tablespoon coarse ground black pepper
1 tablespoon coarse ground coriander

seed
1 teaspoon brown sugar
4 cloves garlic, minced or pressed through a garlic press

1. Mix the spice rub ingredients in a small bowl. Rub the turkey breast with the spice rub, inside and out. Gently work your fingers under the skin on the breast, then rub some of the spice rub directly onto the breast meat. Refrigerate overnight.
2. Two hours before cooking, remove the turkey breast from the refrigerator. Skewer the breast on the rotisserie shaft, securing it with the rotisserie forks. Let the turkey rest at room temperature until it is time to cook.
3. Put the shaft in the air fryer oven and set a drip tray underneath. Press the Power Button and cook at 350°F (180°C) for about 1½ hours, until the turkey reaches 150°F (66°C) in the thickest part of the breast.
4. Remove the turkey breast from the rotisserie shaft. Be very careful - the shaft and forks are blazing hot. Let the turkey rest for 15 to 30 minutes, then carve and serve.

Whole Rotisserie Chicken

Prep time: 10 minutes | Cook time: 45 minutes | Serves 4

3 pounds (1.4 kg) tied whole chicken
3 cloves garlic, halved
1 whole lemon, quartered
2 sprigs fresh rosemary whole
2 tablespoons olive oil

Chicken Rub:

½ teaspoon fresh ground pepper
½ teaspoon salt
1 teaspoon garlic powder
1 teaspoon dried oregano
1 teaspoon paprika
1 sprig rosemary (leaves only)

1. Mix together the rub ingredients in a small bowl. Set aside.
2. Place the chicken on a clean cutting board. Ensure the cavity of the chicken is clean. Stuff the chicken cavity with the garlic, lemon, and rosemary.
3. Tie your chicken with twine if needed. Pat the chicken dry.
4. Drizzle the olive oil all over and coat the entire chicken with a brush.
5. Shake the rub on the chicken and rub in until the chicken is covered.
6. Using the rotisserie shaft, push through the chicken and attach the rotisserie forks.
7. If desired, place aluminum foil onto the drip tray.
8. Place the prepared chicken with rotisserie shaft in the air fryer oven. Press the Power Button and cook at 375ºF (190ºC) for 40 minutes. Check the temperature in 5 minute increments after the 40 minutes.
9. At 40 minutes, check the temperature every 5 minutes until the chicken reaches 165ºF (74ºC) in the breast, or 185ºF (85ºC) in the thigh.
10. Once cooking is complete, remove the chicken using the rotisserie fetch tool and, using gloves, carefully remove the chicken from the shaft.
11. Let the chicken sit, covered, for 5 to 10 minutes.
12. Slice and serve.

Garlic Prime Rib Roast

Prep time: 5 minutes | Cook time: 2 hours | Serves 8 to 10

1 (4-bone) prime rib roast (8 to 10 pounds / 3.6 to 4.5 kg)

Rub:

3½ tablespoons kosher salt
3 or 4 cloves garlic, minced
1½ tablespoons olive oil
1 tablespoon coarsely ground black pepper

1. Trim off any straggling pieces of meat or fat from the roast. If the fat cap is too thick, cut it down to between ¼ to ½ inch in thickness depending on how you like your prime rib. Run a long sword skewer through the center of the roast lengthwise to create a pilot hole. Run the rotisserie shaft through the hole and secure with the forks. Balance as necessary. This is a large roast and it is important that it be well balanced.
2. To make the rub: Combine the rub ingredients in a small bowl and apply evenly to the roast. Concentrate the rub on the rounded end and not the cut sides, though it should still get some. The rub will then be on the edges of the slices once the roast has been carved.
3. Place the roast in the air fryer oven and set a drip tray underneath. Press the Power Button and cook at 400ºF (205ºC) for 2 hours until it is near the desired doneness: 125ºF (52ºC) for rare, 135ºF (57ºC) for medium rare, 145ºF (63ºC) for medium, 155ºF (68ºC) for medium well, or 165ºF (74ºC) for well done. The roast will shrink during cooking, so adjust the forks when appropriate.
4. Carefully remove the rotisserie forks and slide the shaft out, and then place the roast on a large cutting board. Tent the roast with aluminum foil and let the meat rest for 15 to 20 minutes. The roast temperature will continue to rise an additional 5ºF during the rest phase. Cut away the bones first by passing a knife against the bones and cutting through (save the bones for later). Cut the meat into slices ⅓ to ½ inch thick.

Brazilian Rotisserie Pineapple

Prep time: 5 minutes | Cook time: 45 minutes | Serves 2

1 pineapple, trimmed and peeled
¼ cup sugar

¼ teaspoon cinnamon

1. Poke a guide hole through the core of the pineapple with a thin, long-bladed knife. Skewer the pineapple on the shaft, securing it with a shaft fork. Mix the sugar and cinnamon in a small bowl.
2. Put the shaft in the air fryer oven and set a drip tray underneath. Press the Power Button and cook at 400ºF (205ºC) for about 45 minutes, until the pineapple is softened and starting to brown. During the last 15 minutes of cooking, sprinkle the pineapple with cinnamon sugar every five minutes.
3. Remove the pineapple from the rotisserie shaft. Be careful - the shaft and forks are blazing hot. Let the pineapple rest for 10 minutes, then slice and serve.

Dijon Mustard Chicken

Prep time: 5 minutes | Cook time: 1 hour | Serves 4

1 (4-pound / 1.8-kg) chicken
Mustard Paste:
¼ cup Dijon mustard

1 tablespoon kosher salt
1 tablespoon Herbes de Provence
1 teaspoon freshly ground black pepper

1. Mix the mustard paste ingredients in a small bowl. Rub the chicken with the mustard paste, inside and out. Gently work your fingers under the skin on the breast, then rub some of the paste directly onto the breast meat. Refrigerate for at least two hours, preferably overnight.
2. One hour before cooking, remove the chicken from the refrigerator. Fold the wingtips under the wings and truss the chicken. Skewer the chicken on the rotisserie shaft, securing it with the rotisserie forks. Let the chicken rest at room temperature.
3. Put the shaft in the air fryer oven with a drip tray underneath. Press the Power Button and cook at 400ºF (205ºC) for 1 hour until the chicken reaches 160ºF (71ºC) in the thickest part of the breast.
4. Remove the chicken from the rotisserie shaft and remove the twine trussing the chicken. Be careful - the shaft and forks are blazing hot. Let the chicken rest for 15 minutes, then carve and serve.

Chapter 15 Holiday Specials

Pigs in a Blanket

Prep time: 10 minutes | Cook time: 8 minutes | Makes 16 rolls

1 can refrigerated crescent roll dough
1 small package mini smoked sausages, patted dry
2 tablespoons melted butter
2 teaspoons sesame seeds
1 teaspoon onion powder

1. Put the crescent roll dough on a clean work surface and separate into 8 pieces. Cut each piece in half and you will have 16 triangles.
2. Make the pigs in the blanket: Arrange each sausage on each dough triangle, then roll the sausages up.
3. Brush the pigs with melted butter and place of the pigs in the blanket on the air flow racks. Sprinkle with sesame seeds and onion powder.
4. Slide the racks into the air fryer oven. Press the Power Button and cook at 330ºF (166ºC) for 8 minutes.
5. Flip the pigs halfway through the cooking time.
6. When cooking is complete, the pigs should be fluffy and golden brown.
7. Serve immediately.

Pão de Queijo

Prep time: 37 minutes | Cook time: 12 minutes | Makes 12 balls

2 tablespoons butter, plus more for greasing
½ cup milk
1½ cups tapioca flour
½ teaspoon salt
1 large egg
⅔ cup finely grated aged Asiago cheese

1. Put the butter in a saucepan and pour in the milk, heat over medium heat until the liquid boils. Keep stirring.
2. Turn off the heat and mix in the tapioca flour and salt to form a soft dough. Transfer the dough in a large bowl, then wrap the bowl in plastic and let sit for 15 minutes.
3. Break the egg in the bowl of dough and whisk with a hand mixer for 2 minutes or until a sanity dough forms. Fold the cheese in the dough. Cover the bowl in plastic again and let sit for 10 more minutes.
4. Grease a baking pan with butter.

5. Scoop 2 tablespoons of the dough into the baking pan. Repeat with the remaining dough to make dough 12 balls. Keep a little distance between each two balls.
6. Slide the pan into the air fryer oven. Press the Power Button and cook at 375ºF (190ºC) for 12 minutes.
7. Flip the balls halfway through the cooking time.
8. When cooking is complete, the balls should be golden brown and fluffy.
9. Remove the balls from the air fryer oven and allow to cool for 5 minutes before serving.

Sriracha Shrimp

Prep time: 15 minutes | Cook time: 10 minutes | Serves 4

1 tablespoon Sriracha sauce
1 teaspoon Worcestershire sauce
2 tablespoons sweet chili sauce
¾ cup mayonnaise
1 egg, beaten
1 cup panko bread crumbs
1 pound (454 g) raw shrimp, shelled and deveined, rinsed and drained
Lime wedges, for serving
Cooking spray

1. Spritz the air flow racks with cooking spray.
2. Combine the Sriracha sauce, Worcestershire sauce, chili sauce, and mayo in a bowl. Stir to mix well. Reserve ⅓ cup of the mixture as the dipping sauce.
3. Combine the remaining sauce mixture with the beaten egg. Stir to mix well. Put the panko in a separate bowl.
4. Dredge the shrimp in the sauce mixture first, then into the panko. Roll the shrimp to coat well. Shake the excess off.
5. Put the shrimp on the air flow racks, then spritz with cooking spray.
6. Slide the racks into the air fryer oven. Press the Power Button and cook at 360ºF (182ºC) for 10 minutes.
7. Flip the shrimp halfway through the cooking time.
8. When cooking is complete, the shrimp should be opaque.
9. Remove the shrimp from the air fryer oven and serve with reserve sauce mixture and squeeze the lime wedges over.

Teriyaki Shrimp Skewers

Prep time: 10 minutes | Cook time: 6 minutes | Makes 12 skewered shrimp

1½ tablespoons mirin
1½ teaspoons ginger juice
1½ tablespoons soy sauce
12 large shrimp (about 20 shrimps

per pound), peeled and deveined
1 large egg
¾ cup panko bread crumbs
Cooking spray

Special Equipment:
12 wooden skewers, soaked in water for at least 30 minutes

1. Combine the mirin, ginger juice, and soy sauce in a large bowl. Stir to mix well.
2. Dunk the shrimp in the bowl of mirin mixture, then wrap the bowl in plastic and refrigerate for 1 hour to marinate.
3. Spritz the air flow racks with cooking spray.
4. Run 12 skewers through each shrimp.
5. Whisk the egg in the bowl of marinade to combine well. Pour the bread crumbs on a plate.
6. Dredge the shrimp skewers in the egg mixture, then shake the excess off and roll over the bread crumbs to coat well.
7. Arrange the shrimp skewers on the air flow racks and spritz with cooking spray.
8. Slide the racks into the air fryer oven. Press the Power Button and cook at 400°F (205°C) for 6 minutes.
9. Flip the shrimp skewers halfway through the cooking time.
10. When done, the shrimp will be opaque and firm.
11. Serve immediately.

Cheese Blintzes

Prep time: 5 minutes | Cook time: 10 minutes | Makes 8 blintzes

2 (7½-ounce / 213-g) packages farmer cheese, mashed
¼ cup cream cheese
¼ teaspoon vanilla extract

¼ cup granulated white sugar
8 egg roll wrappers
4 tablespoons butter, melted

1. Combine the farmer cheese, cream cheese, vanilla extract, and sugar in a bowl. Stir to mix well.

2. Unfold the egg roll wrappers on a clean work surface, spread ¼ cup of the filling at the edge of each wrapper and leave a ½-inch edge uncovering.
3. Wet the edges of the wrappers with water and fold the uncovered edge over the filling. Fold the left and right sides in the center, then tuck the edge under the filling and fold to wrap the filling.
4. Brush the wrappers with melted butter, then arrange the wrappers in a single layer on the air flow racks, seam side down. Leave a little space between each two wrappers.
5. Slide the racks into the air fryer oven. Press the Power Button and cook at 375°F (190°C) for 10 minutes.
6. When cooking is complete, the wrappers will be golden brown.
7. Serve immediately.

Chocolate Buttermilk Cake

Prep time: 20 minutes | Cook time: 20 minutes | Serves 8

1 cup all-purpose flour
2/3 cup granulated white sugar
¼ cup unsweetened cocoa powder
¾ teaspoon baking soda

¼ teaspoon salt
2/3 cup buttermilk
2 tablespoons plus 2 teaspoons vegetable oil
1 teaspoon vanilla extract
Cooking spray

1. Spritz a baking pan with cooking spray.
2. Combine the flour, cocoa powder, baking soda, sugar, and salt in a large bowl. Stir to mix well.
3. Mix in the buttermilk, vanilla, and vegetable oil. Keep stirring until it forms a grainy and thick dough.
4. Scrape the chocolate batter from the bowl and transfer to the pan, level the batter in an even layer with a spatula.
5. Slide the pan into the air fryer oven. Press the Power Button and cook at 325°F (163°C) for 20 minutes.
6. After 15 minutes, remove from the air fryer oven. Check the doneness. Return to the air fryer oven and continue cooking.
7. When done, a toothpick inserted in the center should come out clean.
8. Invert the cake on a cooling rack and allow to cool for 15 minutes before slicing to serve.

Balsamic Tomatoes

Prep time: 5 minutes | Cook time: 10 minutes | Serves 4 to 6

2 pounds (907 g) cherry tomatoes
2 tablespoons olive oil
2 teaspoons balsamic vinegar
½ teaspoon salt
½ teaspoon ground black pepper

1. Toss the cherry tomatoes with olive oil in a large bowl to coat well. Pour the tomatoes in a baking pan.
2. Slide the pan into the air fryer oven. Press the Power Button and cook at 400ºF (205ºC) for 10 minutes.
3. Stir the tomatoes halfway through the cooking time.
4. When cooking is complete, the tomatoes will be blistered and lightly wilted.
5. Transfer the blistered tomatoes to a large bowl and toss with balsamic vinegar, salt, and black pepper before serving.

Homemade Churros

Prep time: 35 minutes | Cook time: 10 minutes | Makes 12 churros

4 tablespoons butter
¼ teaspoon salt
½ cup water
½ cup all-purpose flour
2 large eggs
2 teaspoons ground cinnamon
¼ cup granulated white sugar
Cooking spray

1. Put the butter, salt, and water in a saucepan. Bring to a boil until the butter is melted on high heat. Keep stirring.
2. Reduce the heat to medium and fold in the flour to form a dough. Keep cooking and stirring until the dough is dried out and coat the pan with a crust.
3. Turn off the heat and scrape the dough in a large bowl. Allow to cool for 15 minutes.
4. Break and whisk the eggs into the dough with a hand mixer until the dough is sanity and firm enough to shape.
5. Scoop up 1 tablespoon of the dough and roll it into a ½-inch-diameter and 2-inch-long cylinder. Repeat with remaining dough to make 12 cylinders in total.
6. Combine the cinnamon and sugar in a large bowl and dunk the cylinders into the cinnamon mix to coat.
7. Arrange the cylinders on a plate and refrigerate for 20 minutes.
8. Spritz the air flow racks with cooking spray. Put the cylinders on the air flow racks and spritz with cooking spray.
9. Slide the racks into the air fryer oven. Press the Power Button and cook at 375ºF (190ºC) for 10 minutes.
10. Flip the cylinders halfway through the cooking time.
11. When cooked, the cylinders should be golden brown and fluffy.
12. Serve immediately.

Chocolate Coconut Macaroons

Prep time: 10 minutes | Cook time: 8 minutes |Makes 24 macaroons

3 large egg whites, at room temperature
¼ teaspoon salt
¾ cup granulated white sugar
4½ tablespoons unsweetened cocoa powder
2¼ cups unsweetened shredded coconut

1. Line the air flow racks with parchment paper.
2. Whisk the egg whites with salt in a large bowl with a hand mixer on high speed until stiff peaks form.
3. Whisk in the sugar with the hand mixer on high speed until the mixture is thick. Mix in the cocoa powder and coconut.
4. Scoop 2 tablespoons of the mixture and shape the mixture in a ball. Repeat with remaining mixture to make 24 balls in total.
5. Arrange the balls in a single layer on the air flow racks and leave a little space between each two balls.
6. Slide the racks into the air fryer oven. Press the Power Button and cook at 375ºF (190ºC) for 8 minutes.
7. When cooking is complete, the balls should be golden brown.
8. Serve immediately.

Arancini

Prep time: 5 minutes | Cook time: 30 minutes | Makes 10 arancini

⅔ cup raw white Arborio rice
2 teaspoons butter
½ teaspoon salt
1⅓ cups water
2 large eggs, well beaten

1¼ cups seasoned Italian-style dried bread crumbs
10 ¾-inch semi-firm Mozzarella cubes
Cooking spray

1. Pour the rice, butter, salt, and water in a pot. Stir to mix well and bring a boil over medium-high heat. Keep stirring.
2. Reduce the heat to low and cover the pot. Simmer for 20 minutes or until the rice is tender.
3. Turn off the heat and let sit, covered, for 10 minutes, then open the lid and fluffy the rice with a fork. Allow to cool for 10 more minutes.
4. Pour the beaten eggs in a bowl, then pour the bread crumbs in a separate bowl.
5. Scoop 2 tablespoons of the cooked rice up and form it into a ball, then press the Mozzarella into the ball and wrap.
6. Dredge the ball in the eggs first, then shake the excess off the dunk the ball in the bread crumbs. Roll to coat evenly. Repeat to make 10 balls in total with remaining rice.
7. Transfer the balls on the air flow racks and spritz with cooking spray.
8. Slide the racks into the air fryer oven. Press the Power Button and cook at 375ºF (190ºC) for 10 minutes.
9. When cooking is complete, the balls should be lightly browned and crispy.
10. Remove the balls from the air fryer oven and allow to cool before serving.

Banana Cake

Prep time: 25 minutes | Cook time: 20 minutes | Serves 8

1 cup plus 1 tablespoon all-purpose flour
¼ teaspoon baking soda
¾ teaspoon baking powder
¼ teaspoon salt
9½ tablespoons granulated white sugar

5 tablespoons butter, at room temperature
2½ small ripe bananas, peeled
2 large eggs
5 tablespoons buttermilk
1 teaspoon vanilla extract
Cooking spray

1. Spritz a baking pan with cooking spray.
2. Combine the flour, baking soda, baking powder, and salt in a large bowl. Stir to mix well.
3. Beat the sugar and butter in a separate bowl with a hand mixer on medium speed for 3 minutes.
4. Beat in the bananas, eggs, buttermilk, and vanilla extract into the sugar and butter mix with a hand mixer.
5. Pour in the flour mixture and whip with hand mixer until sanity and smooth.
6. Scrape the batter into the pan and level the batter with a spatula.
7. Slide the pan into the air fryer oven. Press the Power Button and cook at 325ºF (163ºC) for 20 minutes.
8. After 15 minutes, remove from the air fryer oven. Check the doneness. Return to the air fryer oven and continue cooking.
9. When done, a toothpick inserted in the center should come out clean.
10. Invert the cake on a cooling rack and allow to cool for 15 minutes before slicing to serve.

Simple Nuggets

Prep time: 15 minutes | Cook time: 4 minutes | Makes 20 nuggets

1 cup all-purpose flour, plus more for dusting
1 teaspoon baking powder
½ teaspoon butter, at room temperature, plus more for brushing
¼ teaspoon salt
¼ cup water
⅛ teaspoon onion powder
¼ teaspoon garlic powder
⅛ teaspoon seasoning salt
Cooking spray

1. Line the air flow racks with parchment paper.
2. Mix the flour, baking powder, butter, and salt in a large bowl. Stir to mix well. Gradually whisk in the water until a sanity dough forms.
3. Put the dough on a lightly floured work surface, then roll it out into a ½-inch thick rectangle with a rolling pin.
4. Cut the dough into about twenty 1- or 2-inch squares, then arrange the squares in a single layer on the air flow racks. Spritz with cooking spray.
5. Combine onion powder, garlic powder, and seasoning salt in a small bowl. Stir to mix well, then sprinkle the squares with the powder mixture.
6. Slide the racks into the air fryer oven. Press the Power Button and cook at 370ºF (188ºC) for 4 minutes.
7. Flip the squares halfway through the cooking time.
8. When cooked, the dough squares should be golden brown.
9. Remove the golden nuggets from the air fryer oven and brush with more butter immediately. Serve warm.

Cinnamon Rolls with Cream Glaze

Prep time: 2 hours 15 minutes | Cook time: 5 minutes | Serves 8

1 pound (454 g) frozen bread dough, thawed
2 tablespoons melted butter
1½ tablespoons cinnamon
¾ cup brown sugar
Cooking spray

Cream Glaze:
4 ounces (113 g) softened cream cheese
½ teaspoon vanilla extract
2 tablespoons melted butter
1¼ cups powdered erythritol

1. Put the bread dough on a clean work surface, then roll the dough out into a rectangle with a rolling pin.
2. Brush the top of the dough with melted butter and leave 1-inch edges uncovered.
3. Combine the cinnamon and sugar in a small bowl, then sprinkle the dough with the cinnamon mixture.
4. Roll the dough over tightly, then cut the dough log into 8 portions. Wrap the portions in plastic, better separately, and let sit to rise for 1 or 2 hours.
5. Meanwhile, combine the ingredients for the glaze in a separate small bowl. Stir to mix well.
6. Spritz the air flow racks with cooking spray. Transfer the risen rolls to the air flow racks.
7. Slide the racks into the air fryer oven. Press the Power Button and cook at 350ºF (180ºC) for 5 minutes.
8. Flip the rolls halfway through the cooking time.
9. When cooking is complete, the rolls will be golden brown.
10. Serve the rolls with the glaze.

Chapter 16 Staples

Asian Dipping Sauce

Prep time: 15 minutes | Cook time: 0 minutes | Makes about 1 cup

¼ cup rice vinegar
¼ cup hoisin sauce
¼ cup low-sodium chicken or vegetable stock
3 tablespoons soy sauce

1 tablespoon minced or grated ginger
1 tablespoon minced or pressed garlic
1 teaspoon chili-garlic sauce or sriracha (or more to taste)

1. Stir together all the ingredients in a small bowl, or place in a jar with a tight-fitting lid and shake until well mixed.
2. Use immediately.

Ancho Chile Sauce

Prep time: 15 minutes | Cook time: 0 minutes | Makes 2 cups

3 large ancho chiles, stems and seeds removed, torn into pieces
1½ cups hot water
2 garlic cloves, peeled and lightly smashed
2 tablespoons wine

vinegar
1½ teaspoons sugar
½ teaspoon dried oregano
½ teaspoon ground cumin
2 teaspoons kosher salt

1. Mix together the chile pieces and hot water in a bowl and let stand for 10 to 15 minutes.
2. Pour the chiles and water into a blender jar. Fold in the garlic, vinegar, sugar, oregano, cumin, and salt and blend until smooth.

Homemade Caesar Dressing

Prep time: 5 minutes | Cook time: 0 minutes | Makes about ²/₃ cup

½ cup extra-virgin olive oil
2 tablespoons freshly squeezed lemon juice
1 teaspoon anchovy paste

¼ teaspoon kosher salt or ⅛ teaspoon fine salt
¼ teaspoon minced or pressed garlic
1 egg, beaten

1. Add all the ingredients to a tall, narrow container.
2. Purée the mixture with an immersion blender until smooth.
3. Use immediately.

Creamy Polenta

Prep time: 3 minutes | Cook time: 1 hour 5 minutes | Makes about 4 cups

1 cup polenta
2 cups chicken or vegetable stock
2 cups milk
2 tablespoons

unsalted butter, cut into 4 pieces
1 teaspoon kosher salt

1. Add the grits to a baking pan. Stir in the stock, milk, butter, and salt.
2. Press the Power Button and cook at 325ºF (163ºC) for 1 hour and 5 minutes.
3. After 15 minutes, remove from the air fryer oven and stir the polenta. Return to the air fryer oven and continue cooking.
4. After 30 minutes, remove the pan again and stir the polenta again. Return to the air fryer oven and continue cooking for 15 to 20 minutes, or until the polenta is soft and creamy and the liquid is absorbed.
5. When done, remove from the air fryer oven.
6. Serve immediately.

Baked Rice

Prep time: 3 minutes | Cook time: 35 minutes | Makes about 4 cups

1 cup long-grain white rice, rinsed and drained
1 tablespoon unsalted butter, melted, or 1 tablespoon extra-

virgin olive oil
2 cups water
1 teaspoon kosher salt or ½ teaspoon fine salt

1. Add the butter and rice to a baking pan and stir to coat. Pour in the water and sprinkle with the salt. Stir until the salt is dissolved.
2. Press the Power Button and cook at 325ºF (163ºC) for 35 minutes.
3. After 20 minutes, remove from the air fryer oven. Stir the rice. Transfer the pan back to the air fryer oven and continue cooking for 10 to 15 minutes, or until the rice is mostly cooked through and the water is absorbed.
4. When done, remove from the air fryer oven and cover with aluminum foil. Let stand for 10 minutes. Using a fork, gently fluff the rice.
5. Serve immediately.

Classic Marinara Sauce

Prep time: 15 minutes | Cook time: 30 minutes | Makes about 3 cups

¼ cup extra-virgin olive oil
3 garlic cloves, minced
1 small onion, chopped (about ½ cup)
2 tablespoons minced or puréed sun-dried tomatoes (optional)
1 (28-ounce / 794-g) can crushed tomatoes

½ teaspoon dried basil
½ teaspoon dried oregano
¼ teaspoon red pepper flakes
1 teaspoon kosher salt or ½ teaspoon fine salt, plus more as needed

1. Heat the oil in a medium saucepan over medium heat.
2. Add the garlic and onion and sauté for 2 to 3 minutes, or until the onion is softened. Add the sun-dried tomatoes (if desired) and cook for 1 minute until fragrant. Stir in the crushed tomatoes, scraping any brown bits from the bottom of the pot. Fold in the basil, oregano, red pepper flakes, and salt. Stir well.
3. Bring to a simmer. Cook covered for about 30 minutes, stirring occasionally.
4. Turn off the heat and allow the sauce to cool for about 10 minutes.
5. Taste and adjust the seasoning, adding more salt if needed.
6. Use immediately.

Spicy Southwest Seasoning

Prep time: 5 minutes | Cook time: 0 minutes | Makes about ¾ cups

3 tablespoons ancho chile powder
3 tablespoons paprika
2 tablespoons dried oregano
2 tablespoons freshly ground black pepper

2 teaspoons cayenne
2 teaspoons cumin
1 tablespoon granulated onion
1 tablespoon granulated garlic

1. Stir together all the ingredients in a small bowl.
2. Use immediately or place in an airtight container in the pantry.

Roasted Button Mushrooms

Prep time: 8 minutes | Cook time: 30 minutes | Makes about 1½ cups

1 pound (454 g) button mushrooms, washed, stems trimmed, and cut into quarters or thick slices
¼ cup water

1 teaspoon kosher salt or ½ teaspoon fine salt
3 tablespoons unsalted butter, cut into pieces, or extra-virgin olive oil

1. Put a large piece of aluminum foil on a sheet pan. Put the mushroom pieces in the middle of the foil. Spread them out into an even layer. Pour the water over them, season with the salt, and add the butter. Wrap the mushrooms in the foil.
2. Press the Power Button and cook at 325ºF (163ºC) for 15 minutes.
3. After 15 minutes, remove from the air fryer oven. Transfer the foil packet to a cutting board and carefully unwrap it. Pour the mushrooms and cooking liquid from the foil onto the sheet pan.
4. Return the pan to the air fryer oven. Press the Power Button and cook at 350ºF (180ºC) for 15 minutes.
5. After about 10 minutes, remove from the air fryer oven and stir the mushrooms. Return to the air fryer oven and continue cooking for anywhere from 5 to 15 more minutes, or until the liquid is mostly gone and the mushrooms start to brown.
6. Serve immediately.

Pro Dough

Prep time: 40 minutes | Cook time: 0 minutes | Makes 2 (12- to 14-inch) pizzas

¼ teaspoon active dry yeast
1½ cups warm water
4 cups "00" flour or all-purpose flour, plus

more for dusting
2 teaspoons salt
Extra-virgin olive oil, for greasing

1. In a medium bowl, add the yeast to the warm water and let it stand for 10 minutes. While the yeast is blooming, rinse the bowl of a standing mixer with hot water and dry thoroughly. It should be warm to the touch. In the warm mixing bowl, combine the flour and salt. Add the yeast mixture and mix on low speed with a dough hook for 2 minutes. Raise the speed to medium-low and continue to mix for about 10 minutes, until the dough is cohesive and smooth and has pulled away from the sides of the bowl.
2. Knead again on medium-low speed for an additional 10 minutes, or until the dough is soft and warm to the touch.
3. Transfer the dough to a large, lightly oiled bowl, rolling the dough to coat it on all sides. Cover with plastic wrap and refrigerate overnight.
4. The next day, transfer the dough to a lightly floured board and punch it down. Cut it into 2 or 4 equal pieces and shape into smooth balls. Lightly flour the balls, place them on a baking tray, and cover with a damp kitchen towel. Let the dough rise again in the refrigerator for at least 4 hours or overnight.
5. Remove the dough from the refrigerator, place on a lightly floured baking sheet, and cover with a damp kitchen towel. Let it rise for 1½ to 2 hours, until it is doubled in size.
6. Proceed with the desired recipe.

Garlic Tomato Pizza Sauce

Prep time: 10 minutes | Cook time: 25 minutes | Makes 1 quart

2 tablespoons extra-virgin olive oil
1 small yellow onion, chopped (½ cup)
3 garlic cloves, smashed
1 (28-ounce / 794-g) can whole peeled San

Marzano tomatoes, undrained
1 teaspoon fine sea salt
⅛ teaspoon freshly ground black pepper
1 to 2 tablespoons sugar

1. In a large saucepan over medium-high heat, heat the olive oil until it shimmers. Reduce the heat to medium and add the chopped onion. Cook, stirring occasionally, for 5 minutes. Add the garlic and continue to cook for 2 to 3 minutes more, until the onion is translucent and the garlic is aromatic.
2. Add the tomatoes and their juice, and bring to a simmer, stirring occasionally with a wooden spoon to break them apart. Simmer for 10 to 15 minutes, until the sauce has thickened.
3. Using an immersion blender or food processor, pulse until the sauce is smooth. Season with the salt, pepper, and sugar.

Simple Pizza Dough

Prep time: 15 minutes | Cook time: 0 minutes | Makes 2 (12- to 14-inch) pizzas

1 package active dry yeast
1½ cups warm water (about 110°F)
2 tablespoons extra-virgin olive oil

4 cups all-purpose flour, plus more for dusting
1½ teaspoons salt

1. In a medium bowl, add the yeast to the warm water and let bloom for about 10 minutes. Add the olive oil.
2. In a food processor or standing mixer fitted with a paddle attachment, pulse to blend the flour and salt. With the machine running, add the yeast mixture in a slow, steady stream, mixing just until the dough comes together. Turn the dough out onto a well-floured board, and with lightly floured hands, knead the dough using the heels of your hands, pushing the dough and then folding it over. Shape it into a ball, then cut it into 2 or 4 equal pieces.
3. Place the balls of dough on a lightly floured baking sheet and cover with a clean dishtowel. Let them rise in a warm, draft-free spot until they are doubled in size, about 45 minutes.
4. Proceed with the desired recipe.

Teriyaki Sauce

Prep time: 5 minutes | Cook time: 0 minutes | Makes ¾ cup

½ cup soy sauce
3 tablespoons honey
1 tablespoon rice wine or dry sherry

1 tablespoon rice vinegar
2 teaspoons minced fresh ginger
2 garlic cloves, smashed

1. Beat together all the ingredients in a small bowl.
2. Use immediately.

Shawarma Spice Blend

Prep time: 5 minutes | Cook time: 0 minutes | Makes about 1 tablespoon

1 teaspoon smoked paprika
1 teaspoon cumin
¼ teaspoon turmeric
¼ teaspoon kosher salt

¼ teaspoon cinnamon
¼ teaspoon allspice
¼ teaspoon red pepper flakes
¼ teaspoon freshly ground black pepper

1. Stir together all the ingredients in a small bowl.
2. Use immediately or place in an airtight container in the pantry.

Appendix 1 Measurement Conversion Chart

VOLUME EQUIVALENTS(DRY)

US STANDARD	METRIC (APPROXIMATE)
1/8 teaspoon	0.5 mL
1/4 teaspoon	1 mL
1/2 teaspoon	2 mL
3/4 teaspoon	4 mL
1 teaspoon	5 mL
1 tablespoon	15 mL
1/4 cup	59 mL
1/2 cup	118 mL
3/4 cup	177 mL
1 cup	235 mL
2 cups	475 mL
3 cups	700 mL
4 cups	1 L

VOLUME EQUIVALENTS(LIQUID)

US STANDARD	US STANDARD (OUNCES)	METRIC (APPROXIMATE)
2 tablespoons	1 fl.oz.	30 mL
1/4 cup	2 fl.oz.	60 mL
1/2 cup	4 fl.oz.	120 mL
1 cup	8 fl.oz.	240 mL
1 1/2 cup	12 fl.oz.	355 mL
2 cups or 1 pint	16 fl.oz.	475 mL
4 cups or 1 quart	32 fl.oz.	1 L
1 gallon	128 fl.oz.	4 L

TEMPERATURES EQUIVALENTS

FAHRENHEIT(F)	CELSIUS(C) (APPROXIMATE)
225 °F	107 °C
250 °F	120 °C
275 °F	135 °C
300 °F	150 °C
325 °F	160 °C
350 °F	180 °C
375 °F	190 °C
400 °F	205 °C
425 °F	220 °C
450 °F	235 °C
475 °F	245 °C
500 °F	260 °C

WEIGHT EQUIVALENTS

US STANDARD	METRIC (APPROXIMATE)
1 ounce	28 g
2 ounces	57 g
5 ounces	142 g
10 ounces	284 g
15 ounces	425 g
16 ounces (1 pound)	455 g
1.5 pounds	680 g
2 pounds	907 g

Appendix 2: Air Fryer Cooking Chart

Beef

Item	Temp (°F)	Time (mins)	Item	Temp (°F)	Time (mins)
Beef Eye Round Roast (4 lbs.)	400 °F	45 to 55	Meatballs (1-inch)	370 °F	7
Burger Patty (4 oz.)	370 °F	16 to 20	Meatballs (3-inch)	380 °F	10
Filet Mignon (8 oz.)	400 °F	18	Ribeye, bone-in (1-inch, 8 oz)	400 °F	10 to 15
Flank Steak (1.5 lbs.)	400 °F	12	Sirloin steaks (1-inch, 12 oz)	400 °F	9 to 14
Flank Steak (2 lbs.)	400 °F	20 to 28			

Chicken

Item	Temp (°F)	Time (mins)	Item	Temp (°F)	Time (mins)
Breasts, bone in (1 ¼ lb.)	370 °F	25	Legs, bone-in (1 ¾ lb.)	380 °F	30
Breasts, boneless (4 oz)	380 °F	12	Thighs, boneless (1 ½ lb.)	380 °F	18 to 20
Drumsticks (2 ½ lb.)	370 °F	20	Wings (2 lb.)	400 °F	12
Game Hen (halved 2 lb.)	390 °F	20	Whole Chicken	360 °F	75
Thighs, bone-in (2 lb.)	380 °F	22	Tenders	360 °F	8 to 10

Pork & Lamb

Item	Temp (°F)	Time (mins)	Item	Temp (°F)	Time (mins)
Bacon (regular)	400 °F	5 to 7	Pork Tenderloin	370 °F	15
Bacon (thick cut)	400 °F	6 to 10	Sausages	380 °F	15
Pork Loin (2 lb.)	360 °F	55	Lamb Loin Chops (1-inch thick)	400 °F	8 to 12
Pork Chops, bone in (1-inch, 6.5 oz)	400 °F	12	Rack of Lamb (1.5 – 2 lb.)	380 °F	22

Fish & Seafood

Item	Temp (°F)	Time (mins)	Item	Temp (°F)	Time (mins)
Calamari (8 oz)	400 °F	4	Tuna Steak	400 °F	7 to 10
Fish Fillet (1-inch, 8 oz)	400 °F	10	Scallops	400 °F	5 to 7
Salmon, fillet (6 oz)	380 °F	12	Shrimp	400 °F	5
Swordfish steak	400 °F	10			

Vegetables

INGREDIENT	AMOUNT	PREPARATION	OIL	TEMP	COOK TIME
Asparagus	2 bunches	Cut in half, trim stems	2 Tbsp	420°F	12-15 mins
Beets	1½ lbs	Peel, cut in ½-inch cubes	1Tbsp	390°F	28-30 mins
Bell peppers (for roasting)	4 peppers	Cut in quarters, remove seeds	1Tbsp	400°F	15-20 mins
Broccoli	1 large head	Cut in 1-2-inch florets	1Tbsp	400°F	15-20 mins
Brussels sprouts	1lb	Cut in half, remove stems	1Tbsp	425°F	15-20 mins
Carrots	1lb	Peel, cut in ¼-inch rounds	1 Tbsp	425°F	10-15 mins
Cauliflower	1 head	Cut in 1-2-inch florets	2 Tbsp	400°F	20-22 mins
Corn on the cob	7 ears	Whole ears, remove husks	1 Tbps	400°F	14-17 mins
Green beans	1 bag (12 oz)	Trim	1 Tbps	420°F	18-20 mins
Kale (for chips)	4 oz	Tear into pieces,remove stems	None	325°F	5-8 mins
Mushrooms	16 oz	Rinse, slice thinly	1 Tbps	390°F	25-30 mins
Potatoes, russet	1½ lbs	Cut in 1-inch wedges	1 Tbps	390°F	25-30 mins
Potatoes, russet	1lb	Hand-cut fries, soak 30 mins in cold water, then pat dry	½ -3 Tbps	400°F	25-28 mins
Potatoes, sweet	1lb	Hand-cut fries, soak 30 mins in cold water, then pat dry	1 Tbps	400°F	25-28 mins
Zucchini	1lb	Cut in eighths lengthwise, then cut in half	1 Tbps	400°F	15-20 mins

Appendix 3: Recipe Index

Made in the USA
Columbia, SC
17 July 2024

38828639R00100